My SON: An Addict

Finding Hope for Him and Peace for Me

NextStepChristianRecovery.com

NextStepChristianRecovery.com is a division of Quarry Press • Dallas, Texas

Quarry Press • P.O. Box 181736 • Dallas, Texas 75218

Email: quarrypress@msn.com

My SON: An Addict

Finding Hope for Him and Peace for Me

By Janet P. Barnes

Editors

Janie Bogus

Christie Chrane-Miller

Timothy S. Miller

Kyle Murphy

Don Umphrey

Printed in the United States of America

Cover and interior design by Martell Speigner

Published by Quarry Press

P.O. Box 181736

Dallas, TX 75218

e-mail quarrypress@msn.com

website: NextStepChristianRecovery.com

ISBN 978-1-937766-03-0

Dedication

*Dedicated to those who are willing
to share their experience, strength and hope
after having found peace and serenity
in the midst of a loved one's addiction.*

Foreword

I was about seven years old when I found an old picture in the attic of a relatively young-looking man with a strange-looking hair style. I showed it to mom and asked, "Who is this, Frankenstein?" My reference to the monster was probably prompted by a fellow second-grader chanting something like this to me: "Donald is a friend of mine. He resembles Frankenstein."

She looked at the picture and said, "No, that's my father," and then she started crying. I felt badly for prompting this response and told her truthfully, "I don't even know who Frankenstein is."

But mom kept crying anyway.

We lived in Detroit, Michigan, and my mother had grown up in Bear Creek, a small town in northwest Alabama. We visited with grandma in Bear Creek each summer, but I never saw grandpa there.

I may have been age four or five the only time that I can recall meeting him face-to-face. With my mom and other family members, we drove a couple hours from Bear Creek and walked up the stairs of a big, brick building. Sitting in a wicker-bottomed chair in a room by himself was my white-headed grandfather. He and I hit it off pretty well for a few minutes, playing a game where he put his hand down and then I put my hand down over his and this continued. Then I was ushered out of the room so the adults could talk with him.

Years later, I learned that the big, brick building was Bryce Hospital in Tuscaloosa, Alabama. When it first opened in 1861, it was known as the Alabama State Hospital for the Insane. When mom and I talked about it years later, she said that grandpa told her that he was sorry that I saw him in a place like that. But I'm glad to have the memory of meeting him, and at the time I didn't know I was in a hospital.

At one point before he died, grandpa told mom that he had ruined his life.

Who would have guessed that I would also find myself in a mental hospital some 22 years after my visit with grandpa?

Mom's family had been the wealthiest in Bear Creek due to the business acumen of her grandfather, John R. Phillips. During the Civil War he had served as a sergeant in the Union's First Alabama Cavalry. That's right—Union. After that he was the owner of Phillips Mercantile, a general store that served the region and was also involved in many other business endeavors, including a cotton gin and extensive land holdings.

After her grandfather died in 1925, his family donated the land and helped raise the money to build a new school to replace one that had earlier burned to the ground. It is still called Phillips High School. Among those instrumental in fundraising for the school was my grandfather, O.W. Phillips. He worked at his father's store starting around the turn of the 20th Century and then managed it when his father got older.

Perhaps my grandfather yawned one day as he talked to a salesman, known then as a "drummer," who had called on him at the store, and this may have started a conversation about his problems sleeping at night. This man told him that a few nips of whiskey at bedtime would alleviate such a problem. Grandpa took that advice. Then as the months turned to years, he turned to it in increasingly larger quantities and not just as a proverbial night-cap.

In happier days when my mother was a little girl, her father would take her to the store, put her up on the counter, and she would sing and dance for his customers. Mom was the only child left at home by the time she reached mid-adolescence, and the family fortune was long gone. She had to cope with her father's alcoholism along with her mother.

One day they found grandpa lying on the ground out behind the barn—dead drunk. She and her mother dragged him into the house and managed to get him into bed. Over the years mom told me this same story three times, the last time she was in her early nineties. Each time she cried.

Her father's drunkenness also had a great effect on mom's life. It seems to have impacted her view of herself as being "less than" and also her perception of other people. Undoubtedly, it also affected her marriage to my father, particularly in the area of communication between them.

The topic of addictions and the impact of it on families was never breached at the church where my mother took my sister and me every Sunday morning and Sunday night.

Rarely if ever discussed among family members was my grandfather's mental illness. Doctors at the hospital all those decades ago said that it was due to hardening of the arteries. That is doubtful. An older cousin has used the word "psychosis" in relationship to our grandfather. There may be some truth to that toward the end of his life, but no one talked about his mind being affected by long-term alcohol abuse. Even today, decades after his death, there are family members who deny such a link.

It was only after I succumbed to alcoholism myself that my mom and I discussed her father's problems differently.

I started drinking after football season my senior year of high school. Alcohol seemed to place me on the fast-track to popularity. I went away to college thinking that alcohol could do for me what I could not do for myself. In other words it was the idol I worshipped, my false god.

Ten years after I started drinking—on November 6, 1973—I admitted myself to a mental hospital in such a state of mental misery that suicide seemed like it might be the only way out.

Proverbs 23:29-35 (p. 508) describes my plight. (My story of alcoholism and recovery in relationship to biblical principles is also told in two books that I have written, *Deliver Us I: Recognizing the Influence of Evil on the Road to Redemption* and *Deliver Us II: Discovering Your Idols on the Path to the Promised Land.*)

Gratefully and through the grace of God, the last time I had a drink containing alcohol was in the parking lot of the mental hospital just before admitting myself. While I was there, a fellow patient told me about an organization that encourages problem drinkers to seek God in their lives. I left the hospital after two weeks and heeded his advice. Until I started attending the meetings he told me about, I assumed that I was mentally ill; it had never occurred to me that alcohol was the problem, not the solution.

That is called denial, and it occurs when people lie to themselves.

I first shared my story about my mental hospital experience and alcoholism with a church group around 1980. It became very apparent that God could use the worst parts of my life to His glory as in the Lord's admonition to Paul, "...power is perfected in weakness" (2 Corinthians 12:9, p. 257) leading Paul to conclude, "...for when I am weak, then I am strong" (2 Corinthians 12:10, p. 257).

In the years since, I've shared my story with thousands of people in churches, Bible classes, schools, prisons and jails. To add to this outreach, my wife, Kim, and I founded Quarry Press, Dallas, Texas, in 2001 and have published and marketed several books dealing with addiction recovery.

Being so open about my past, you might suspect that many people would seek me out to talk about their addictive behaviors. This has not been the case. Husbands, wives, mothers, fathers and grandparents take me aside and talk to me quietly about their loved ones who are addicted to alcohol, drugs and sex in one form or another, including pornography.

These well-intentioned loved ones suffer greatly. They are so full of grief that they sometimes wear out my ears by talking and talking and talking. They don't have a clue about what to do about the problems they are encountering but feel a need to keep them hush-hush from others. They want me to tell them how to change the behavior of another person, even though that other person may not want to change.

Of course, a lot of this reminds me of what had gone on in my mother's family.

For nearly a decade I sought someone to write a book I could publish that offers biblical solutions to these people with addicted loved ones. That author turned out to be Janet P. Barnes. She contacted me after we each had attended the 2013 National Prison Ministry Workshop in Florence, Alabama. She was eager to serve the Lord by sharing her story with others.

As a result of having an addicted son, Janet suffered spiritually, mentally and physically. She describes these problems in this volume. More importantly, however, is that she shares the spiritual solutions that not only brought her peace of mind and body but also turned out to be the key to helping her son and also improving her marriage.

What Janet initially lacked in writing experience, she made up for with her enthusiasm, desire and tenacity. I've had the pleasure of working with her and watching her story blossom both in content and writing style. I expect that thousands of people will be helped as a result of her dedication to this project.

With Janet's story within a few months of completion, we decided that we could further help the loved ones of addicted people by adding a workbook section to the end of 14 of her 16 chapters. This, we thought, would enable readers to follow the same spiritual path that Janet discovered. Toward that end, we adapted sections from *12 Steps to a Closer Walk with God: The Workbook, 2nd Edition.* We've sold thousands of copies of that workbook since its first printing in 2003. Working with me on the workbook sections included here were editors Kyle Murphy, Tim Miller and his wife, Christie Chrane-Miller. Then each workbook section received Janet's approval.

It is our hope that this book/workbook will be a blessing to those who suffer because of an addicted loved one.

Don Umphrey, Ph.D., Publisher
June, 2017

Acknowledgements

First of all I give glory to my Heavenly Father who brought it all together and who, "causes all things to work together for good to those who love God…" (Romans 8:28, pp. 223-224).

I am grateful to all my family for their love and support. I have probably learned more from my children and grandchildren than they have learned from me. I am especially grateful to Flynn and Kyle for allowing me to use our story to challenge and encourage others who are struggling with the frustrating effects of addiction in the family.

I would like to thank the late Dr. Dorothy Hardy who volunteered her retirement years at the Florence (Alabama) Library helping aspiring writers, including me, to improve their writing skills.

I am grateful for members of my Al-Anon group who have loved, supported, uplifted, encouraged me, and shared with me the things that I am sharing with you.

Special recognition goes to the ladies class of the Jackson Heights Church of Christ for participating as a pilot class with the first draft of this manuscript, which was originally written for use in Bible classes. I appreciate their support and encouragement in allowing me to improve and practice my writing and teaching skills.

My Christian sister and friend, Mary Peck, has also been helpful in using her expertise to edit my writing through the years and has been an inspiration to me in our work together in jail ministry.

The original copy of this manuscript had been rejected by other publishers, so I was still seeking a publisher. I prayed before attending a jail ministry workshop that someone there could point me in the right direction. It was through that workshop that I crossed paths with professional writer and publisher, Don Umphrey, who expressed interest in my manuscript.

However, rather than the Bible class book that I had in mind originally, he wanted to market it to those who were suffering because they had addicted loved ones. This required a great deal of re-writing and sharing more of my personal experience. Thanks to his continued patience, relentless probing, mentoring and critique (that made me want to give up time and again!) here it is! It has truly been a joint endeavor. His books and workbook have also been a huge boost to my progress in recovery.

I hope you gain spiritually from what I have shared with you here. In the meantime I will be working on another book.

Janet P. Barnes,
June, 2017

Table of Contents

Throughout this volume you will find page numbers following each biblical citation from the New Testament, Psalms and Proverbs. These page numbers will direct you to the cited passages when using *Journey to Recovery Through Christ: CASA's 12-Step Study Bible.*

My Son: An Addict?

I smiled, hugged him and kept the tears in check until exiting the facility, but then the floodgates opened before we reached the car. This was the nightmare from which I hoped to wake up at any minute. Never in my wildest dreams would I have imagined that our son, Kyle, age 16, would be admitted to a drug rehabilitation center.

Could this be the same boy who had excelled at sports and was voted "most popular" his freshman year of high school? The same one who regularly went to church with his family?

Though his drug of choice was "only" marijuana, I was surprised that the counselors still considered him a full-fledged addict. It had been a blur from the first time we knew he was using it to the point of having no choice but to admit him. Emotionally speaking, I just couldn't keep up with it.

Kyle is the third of our four sons. When he arrived, his brothers, Brad and Brian, were in second grade and kindergarten, respectively. Our youngest, Casey, is five years younger than Kyle.

Since our two older boys were in school, there were several years when Kyle was sort of like an only child. He was healthy except for some stomach issues which included constant "spitting up" and projectile vomiting which eased up when he was about a year old but could even be triggered by an odor.

When he started school, nausea and vomiting became a daily occurrence. Though he finally became comfortable with school, these problems plagued him anytime he was in a stressful situation. He was never able to spend the night away from home without calling me to come and get him.

Aside from that, Kyle seemed happy and spent his time involved in sports, playing ball and riding bikes with the neighborhood kids. I had little cause for concern until his friends started getting their drivers licenses. When cars replaced bicycles, I worried about their whereabouts and what they might be doing. I had already raised two boys and though I lived a sheltered life as a teenager, I was not always where my parents thought I was.

The first indication of a problem with Kyle was on New Year's Eve when he was 15. My husband, Flynn, and I were invited to a party at the home of some friends from church, and some of the teens from church were getting together at another location. There weren't many youth activities at our church, and except for Sundays, Kyle seldom associated with the church kids.

He begged to go out with his usual friends. Since the expectations of New Year's Eve parties are well known, I was leery and tried to insist on him going with the church group. As usual, he wore me down while assuring me he would never try drugs or alcohol.

Around 10 p.m. we got a call at our party from the police department. Kyle and some friends had been picked up outside a motel with a bottle of liquor, which they had not yet consumed. He was in custody for "minor in possession of alcohol." We lectured Kyle, grounded him for two weeks and assumed all would be okay after that.

That's the way it had been earlier when Brad had an experience with alcohol. He was grounded, and the next time it was available at a party he called us to come and get him. Then there was Brian. He was our most outspoken, rebellious and emotional son. These traits may have played a part in him getting into a fight and having to perform community service, but to my knowledge he never experimented with alcohol or drugs.

Kyle had been such a happy, compliant child, we least expected any trouble from him. We assumed his arrest would be the end of it, an assumption that turned out to be short-lived.

Problems Escalate

The first or second night he was allowed to go out after being grounded, we received a call that Kyle had been arrested again. This time, he and some friends were in possession of a bag of marijuana. They were driving up a mountain and panicked when they spotted a roadblock ahead. An officer saw them throw something out the car window, prompting the police to search until they found it.

I was shocked. Kyle obviously had not learned from his earlier arrest involving alcohol. This was even more serious, but I continued to delude myself that Kyle would get the message.

The basketball coach at school had gotten wind of Kyle's brushes with the law and was considering dropping him from the team. Kyle had loved sports, and basketball was number one with him. I had been amazed at his ability to dribble and steal a ball by age seven. He was often the game's high-scorer. There was no doubt in my mind he was one of the best players for his age in our hometown of Sheffield, Alabama, and would be eligible for a university scholarship, maybe even the pros.

At the suggestion of school officials, we called the local drug treatment center for advice. They urged us to take in Kyle for evaluation. That really didn't seem necessary to us based on only two incidents, but we wanted to do whatever we could to keep Kyle in school and on the team.

They questioned Kyle and me separately. I'm not sure what Kyle told them, but I confessed that the main cause of his problems may have been the marital discord between Flynn and me. I speculated that if we worked on our marriage and implemented more discipline, we could solve Kyle's problem. The counselors disagreed. Their determination was that he needed inpatient treatment in a facility that was about 60 miles away. This would cause him to miss school.

I was blindsided by this advice and initially wondered if maybe they knew more than I did. Then the thought occurred to me, "This is how they make their money. Of course they would like to admit him." I agreed to a second option that was offered for him to begin night-time sessions of outpatient treatment at a local facility that would allow him to stay in school.

With his basketball career in jeopardy, Kyle knew he was in deep trouble. This convinced me that regardless of whether or not he received treatment, he would steer clear of drugs and alcohol as he had promised. Several of his friends were also in trouble, and their parents were wising up. So it seemed that together, we could all get the problem under control.

After beginning outpatient rehab and being grounded for two more weeks, he was allowed to go out again. What Flynn and I still failed to comprehend is that if he left the house and told us he was going somewhere that sounded innocent enough, he would end up with his drug-using friends.

We were dumbfounded to receive yet another call from the police. They had been called to a house where there was a large gathering of teenagers who were smoking marijuana and drinking. All of them were hauled to the police station.

The police informed us privately that no charges were being filed, but they advised us not to let Kyle know what they had said. We allowed him to think that with charges of "minor in possession of alcohol" and "possession of marijuana" already pending, he had yet another charge to face in court.

I had been naïve and foolish in overruling the counselor and insisting on outpatient rather than inpatient treatment. By this time, even Kyle realized he might be actually headed to jail, so he didn't object when we informed him he was going to be admitted for inpatient treatment. This would be at the earlier-mentioned facility where he would stay for three weeks, detox, and go through counseling, group sessions and 12-step work.

We would be required to attend weekend family sessions. We discussed it with the school officials, and they agreed to send his school work and allow him to make it up.

Despite my embarrassment at having a son in rehab, I was relieved to know that while there, he couldn't accumulate any more charges to face in court and that he would get the help he obviously needed. We were concerned about the cost which amounted to more than $9,000 but were resolved to do whatever it took to save him. We were relieved to learn our insurance would pay most of it.

One Step Forward...

Kyle completed his treatment program successfully which helped play a part in him receiving probation on the alcohol and marijuana charges. He continued to attend outpatient sessions at night at a local facility. While Kyle was there, Flynn and I attended family sessions two nights a week and confronted some of our own issues, a blessing in disguise.

Some nights we met with a group of other family members of addicts where we took turns sharing about our situation or feelings. On other nights Flynn, Kyle and I met with the counselor and one other family and their son or daughter.

In one of these sessions, the counselor asked each of us to describe our home life in one word. Without hesitation Kyle answered "rollercoaster!" I was shocked that he could give such an accurate description so quickly. Sure, there were happy times, but this could change at any moment as Flynn and I would not speak to each other for days on end.

With the outpatient sessions completed, I was again convinced Kyle had learned his lesson and probably would convince the rest of the kids to get clean and sober. He attended church with us and went on family outings. For the next three months he passed mandatory drug tests, resumed playing basketball and seemed headed back to normal. We bought him a car so he could help with getting himself and Casey to school and other functions. Flynn did not think this was a good idea, but I was hoping to save myself some trouble since I was tied down tending to my ailing mother.

I was hoping for the best, yet it concerned me that he still refused the attempts of kids at school and church who reached out to him to get involved in other activities. He still preferred to look like his "hoodlum" friends, wearing long hair, oversized baggy pants and heavy metal jewelry.

Two Steps Back

About three months later he drifted back with the old crowd, explaining to me that after they realized what he had been through, they had all stopped using drugs as well. Though quite skeptical, I wanted to believe him, because most of them were kids he had grown up with and whose parents we had known personally for years.

Before long, his problems resumed with failing to attend school, being held in detention hall quite often, and rebelling against rules at home. Becoming deeply infatuated with a girl seemed to compound the problems. Between his age and his drug use, I knew that Kyle was not capable of having a healthy adolescent relationship with her.

The boy who once couldn't spend the night away from home because of his anxiety preferred to distance himself from the family as much as possible. His stomach problems appeared to have been miraculously cured! When he escaped the house, we never knew when he would reappear.

The car we never should have purchased was totaled within a few months. The wreck would probably not have been ruled his fault if one boy in the car hadn't jumped out and ran, which was suspicious to the police. Kyle was suspended from our insurance policy.

His one positive endeavor was continuing as a star player on the basketball team. We hoped his love for the game would eventually help him kick the addiction. However, one night after a game at a neighboring school, he and a friend were pulled over for a traffic stop and arrested again for possession of marijuana.

Questioned by police, Kyle reported that he bought the marijuana at the basketball game that night from a boy at the other school. This was a lie to avoid implicating the friend who had sold it to him, but it was a huge mistake. In addition to another charge to face in court, he was kicked off the basketball team for the remainder of his junior year since it supposedly occurred at a school function. This was especially devastating to us. He was losing everything that seemingly should have been important to him.

Kyle also was required to attend an "alternative school" for delinquent and troubled students in a neighboring city for six weeks. It was more structured, with rigid rules which if not followed would result in a longer stay there, before he could return to regular school. When he faced the newest possession of marijuana charge in court, he was sentenced to community service, which involved picking up roadside trash every Saturday for three months. With his driving privileges suspended, this meant more chauffeuring for me, when I was already overwhelmed because of my mother's chronic illness, Casey's extracurricular activities, and a new granddaughter with whom I wanted to spend time.

I read countless books and articles about addiction and had an arsenal of information ready every time there was a good opportunity to reason with Kyle. My attempts at logic were met with some of his own. He insisted that marijuana had actually helped rather than harmed him. His stomach problems were gone, and he could play basketball better while "high."

His reasoning: If only it was legal, he wouldn't have these problems.

Trying to reason with him often turned into a shouting match that left us both crying in frustration. He often urged us to try smoking "weed" and it might solve some of our problems. (I sometimes wondered if he could be right!)

It appeared that our amazing, smart, usually compliant son had disappeared and an alien invader inhabited his body. It would do no good to print out "missing" posters or send out search parties. The real Kyle had somehow disintegrated into the universe.

I had no idea how to get him back.

Drowning in Despair

"Where did I lose sight of him?" I wondered in panic, realizing that worry and obsession had once again made me completely oblivious to my surroundings.

Our car had been stalling. So I followed Flynn in our pick-up truck as he drove the ailing auto toward the repair shop. I realized suddenly that he was no longer in front of me. Had he driven off and left me or was he somewhere behind me?

Not seeing him in the distance ahead, I turned back and drove until I saw him standing beside the stalled car on the side of the road. I was so caught up in my own thoughts that I had become unaware of my surroundings and driven right past him as he tried to flag me down. Flynn was angry and justifiably so.

Losing focus was becoming an alarming habit. Several times I had intended to go one place but found myself on another side of town. A few days earlier, I had promised a boy's mother that I would give her son a ride home after basketball practice. It was only when I saw the boy standing outside the school the following morning that I realized I had forgotten and left him stranded at school.

Was I losing my mind?

I was obsessed with trying to figure out a way to rescue Kyle from a self-destructive lifestyle as a drug addict. I blamed Flynn for this problem. I was desperate for him to confront what I perceived as his "anger issues," which I was certain would help improve the situation with Kyle.

While growing up, my painful shyness limited my forming the friendships I craved. At age 15 I first met Flynn at a park through some mutual friends. He was 18. I was flattered when he seemed interested in me. Our first evening together was spent acting like kids, playing on the swings and riding a merry-go-round.

During our three-year courtship we dined out, had fun and planned our future. He lavished attention on me and bought me gifts. His outgoing nature was a huge attraction, because it seemed to complement my shyness. I had trouble conversing with people. But with him around, I didn't have to worry about doing the talking.

Flynn began to attend church regularly and was eventually baptized. He had grown up in a church with different beliefs than mine but had not attended services for years. My family and I were pleased when he became actively involved in our church.

There had been a lot of positives during the first three years of our marriage, but I often found myself brooding about what I perceived as a lack of communication between us. I wanted us to talk more, but he seemed more interested in relaxing in front of the television when he came home from work. One time I left home for several hours and didn't return to fix our evening meal, hoping he would think I had left him for good and take my concerns more seriously. He paid a little more attention to me for a while after that.

Why couldn't he see things my way?

Children Arrive, Tensions Grow

We had more serious disagreements with the arrival of children. The first incident I remember was when our oldest son, Brad, was about 18 months old. We were on vacation and walking along a beach when Brad became tired of walking and cried for me to carry him. Flynn thought he was a little spoiled and should continue walking. We argued for a moment. Then I picked up Brad and walked on ahead of Flynn back to the motel. Angry, Flynn got in the car and sped off, saying he was going home without us. An hour later he returned and apologized. I pretended to accept his apology, but gave him the cold shoulder the next four days of the trip.

With the arrival of our other three sons, many of our disagreements involved disciplinary issues. Sometimes he wanted to ground the kids for what I saw as a minor infraction.

Boys tend to get loud, act silly, wrestle and discover many other ways of being rambunctious. These things would sometimes get on Flynn's nerves, and he would ground them for a few days. This meant I would be stuck in the house with them, which made me furious. I preferred to discipline by taking away a privilege such as television, but this infringed on Flynn's relaxation time.

We could seldom come to any agreement, resulting in discipline that was very inconsistent.

Though we camped, picnicked, dined out and had many happy occasions, he would sometimes get stressed over what I perceived as a trivial issue. Once I asked him to put the stroller in the car so I would not have to hold the baby for hours at a picnic we had planned for the Little League Baseball team he coached.

I didn't realize that the trunk was already full with items he had packed for the picnic. He started to throw things back out of the trunk, so I grabbed the stroller and told him, "Forget it. I just won't go!" I then skipped the picnic and went somewhere else with the baby. Then I sulked for days.

After an episode like this, one of us would finally tire of the tension and pretend all was normal. When he did apologize and express remorse, I continued to nurse a grudge. I seldom apologized for anything because I always considered him to be the one in the wrong. At the time it never dawned on me that he was not 100% responsible for our problems.

Sometimes we would talk about our issues of disagreement, and I would be optimistic that we'd finally left these things behind us. Eventually, though, I would find myself lying in bed at night thinking, "Here we go again!" knowing the next few days would be filled with tension, anxiety and sleeplessness.

Mom's Health Issues

Another major problem for me was the fact that I had assumed the role of my mother's primary caregiver after the death of my father 11 years earlier. Like her mother before her, my mom had serious health problems that were complicated by severe anxiety.

As children, we let the phone ring until mama answered it if we thought grandma might be calling. We dreaded having to listen to a long detailed list of health complaints, doctor visits and medications. Now I was the one designated to answer the phone when my mother called.

Though I knew my grandmother's thought processes were somewhat out of the normal range, I didn't recognize some of the same symptoms in my mother until I was a teenager. Many women of that generation didn't drive, including my mother, so that didn't seem unusual.

However, her fear of water seemed a bit extreme. We were on a picnic near a lake when I was a child, and my dad put my sisters and brother and me on a small boat and rowed a few feet from shore. Still on the bank, mama cried out to us hysterically that we would capsize and drown.

Her "snake phobia" was similar to my grandmother's "dog phobia"—each so extreme they freaked out at hearing the word or seeing a picture of the dreaded creature. As children, we laughed about this. But it was no longer amusing to my sister when her second grade class planned a field trip to Dismals Canyon in nearby Phil Campbell, Alabama. She was the only child not allowed to go because mama feared they might see a snake.

It began to seem strange that my mother never went anywhere without my dad, something I first noticed as a teen. When my sisters and I obtained our drivers licenses, we still didn't go shopping or on outings like most mothers and daughters. Even once when I had to be taken to the emergency room with a severe cut, my 16-year-old sister had to take me.

My mother was also constantly ill and in pain, in spite of the fact there was seldom a definite diagnosis. I tried to convince my mother to seek professional help for what seemed to be hypochondria and severe anxiety. She felt the solution was for someone to be with her at all times and to be careful not to upset her.

It was not an easy task getting others to comply with this. Being left alone triggered her panic attacks, and I received heavy doses of guilt for not putting her needs ahead of those of my family.

Facing daily decisions about which doctor or treatment to consider for her numerous symptoms (without addressing the underlying cause) drove me to the brink of insanity. I remember coming home one evening and falling to my knees and pleading with God, "Please let her feel good for just one day!"

The next day she said something that was foreign to her vocabulary: "I don't understand why, but I don't have any pain today." It proved to me that God does hear our desperate pleas.

The Apple Falls Close to the Tree

I wasn't actually the picture of physical and mental health myself, being plagued with bouts of undiagnosed chronic pain. It usually started with an injury of some sort that would not heal and the pain increased with time.

My mother would never attempt to exercise, so in my determination not to imitate this particular character trait, I exercised religiously. I tried to appear strong and independent by suppressing my thoughts and fears, yet I was terrified of drifting into the same state of mind as my mother. I obsessed continually about whatever pain I was experiencing at the time.

Once on a family vacation, we boarded a "sky ride" to get to the top of Stone Mountain in Georgia. The small enclosure was packed with people. I began to hyperventilate; my heart was pounding, and I felt that I could black out at any moment. I didn't dare tell anyone what was happening. As the cable car started to move faster, a gust of cool, fresh air entered. Though I was still trembling, my breathing evened out. It was a great relief to finally get out at the top.

Not wanting to get back on, I suggested we hike back down the mountain and luckily for me, everyone else agreed.

I recognized my experience on the sky ride as a panic attack, but swore it would not limit me as it had my mother. Yet it happened again unexpectedly on a crowded subway in Atlanta. Later, it happened in a theater when I was sitting in the middle of an aisle, where I would have to climb over several people to get out. From then on, I insisted on an aisle seat.

In public buildings I elected to climb the stairs rather than ride the elevator because it felt too closed in and if the door didn't open quickly, I started to panic. I knew I was dealing with it as my mother had by avoiding situations that triggered the panic attacks, but that seemed to be the simplest solution.

As my anxiety worsened due to sleepless nights and constant worry, I was beginning to understand how my mother had succumbed to her anxiety, and I feared it would overtake me as well. Slipping into the abyss of depression or mental illness often seemed inevitable; possibly it was something genetic that would determine my destiny.

When I experienced pain and bruising in my legs and feet, one doctor told me there was nothing physically wrong and advised me, "Go home and think about what you are really upset about." I didn't have to think—I thought I already knew. I was constantly upset and frustrated at my inability to bring about change in Flynn or my mother.

But why didn't the knowledge of this alleviate the pain?

The antidepressant, Pamelor, eventually relieved this bout of chronic pain, which suggested a mental component. After an assortment of doctors and numerous medical tests on tingling and pain in my jaw during my thirties, I was diagnosed with "trigeminal neuralgia." With this condition, antidepressant drugs only seemed to "turn up the volume."

With the antidepressants no longer an option, whatever pain or illness developed might not respond to treatment. I imagined becoming totally incapacitated, with the specialists helplessly standing by with a medical puzzle on their hands.

While I urged my mother to seek psychiatric help, it was not an option for me. This is because I would have to admit my problems to Flynn. He was one who never took a sick leave day, even when he could barely drag himself out of bed. This failure to communicate served to further my feelings of isolation and despair.

Total Despair

I was driving myself to the brink of insanity over my son, my mother, my husband and problems experienced by my siblings. Had they all heeded my advice, it seemed all would be well. Peace or joy seemed unattainable unless my family members were willing to change.

Most of all I grieved for the worsening condition of the son who was once such a joy. Reasoning with someone in an altered state of mind was proving futile, but it didn't stop me from trying. My constant expressions of concern for his safety and freedom seemed ridiculous to him. "I know the consequences of what I'm doing," he would declare. "I'm prepared to go to jail. You just shouldn't worry about it."

Unfortunately, he couldn't tell me how to shut off my brain!

I struggled to maintain control, but Kyle's downward spiral was pushing me over the edge. I was desperate to find a way to focus on my normal daily activities. I wanted to be able to enjoy my other family members and friends, especially two young grandchildren, rather than centering my whole life on the undesirable behavior of a few.

Biblical Questions for Self-Examination

IDENTIFYING PROBLEMS

Use the *Journey to Recovery Through Christ: CASA's 12-Step Study Bible* or any other version of the *New American Standard Bible* © 1995 to fill in the blanks in biblical passages below.

Workbook material may be found following Chapters 2 through 15. There is no accompanying answer book. Rather, your solutions may be found by seeking God's will in your life. If there is something you don't understand or if you need assistance in some other way, ask a sponsor, spiritual mentor or pastoral counselor/minister.

IS THIS CONCEPT BIBLICAL?

Individuals involved in recovery often refer to addictions as being detrimental to people spiritually, mentally and physically. This is sometimes referred to as the threefold disease concept. Of course, a spiritual disease is the same as sin. Explore this concept with the questions below.

1. a. The Fifth Commandment is the first one with a promise: **Honor your father and your mother, that your days may be prolonged in the land which the Lord your God gives you** (Exodus 20:12).

   b. (circle one or more) To which does this verse relate: spiritual?   mental?   physical?

2. a. **My son, do not forget my _____ , but let your heart keep my _____ ; for length of _____ and _____ of life and _____ they will add to you** (Proverbs 3:1-2, p. 479).

   b. (circle one or more) To which do these verses relate: spiritual?   mental?   physical?

3. a. **The fear of the _____ _____ life, but the years of the _____ will be _____** (Proverbs 10:27, p. 490).

   b. (circle one or more) To which does this verse relate: spiritual?   mental?   physical?

4. As revealed in 2 Samuel 11 and 12, King David committed adultery with the wife of one of his best soldiers and as a part of the cover-up afterward, gave orders that resulted in the soldier being killed in battle. David later repented and faced the consequences of his sins. Read Psalm 38 that refers to that ugly episode.

   a. (circle one or more) To which does Psalm 38 (pp. 378-379) relate: spiritual?   mental?   physical?

5. a. Read Proverbs 23:29-35 (p. 508).

   b. (circle one or more) To which do these verses relate: spiritual?   mental?   physical?

6. a. Read 1 Corinthians 11:23-32 (p. 242).

    b. (circle one or more) To which do these verses relate: spiritual?   mental?   physical?

7. a. Reflecting on what Janet revealed about Kyle in the first two chapters, in what way(s) was he impacted by his addiction?

    b. Spiritually impacted? (circle one)   yes   or   no
       What led you to select this response? _____
       _____

    c. Mentally impacted? (circle one)   yes   or   no
       What led you to select this response? _____
       _____

    d. Physically impacted? (circle one)   yes   or   no
       What led you to select this response? _____
       _____

8. a. Thinking about what Janet revealed about herself in the first two chapters, in what ways was she impacted by Kyle's addiction:

    b. Spiritually impacted? (circle one)   yes   or   no
       What led you to select this response? _____
       _____

    c. Mentally impacted? (circle one)   yes   or   no
       What led you to select this response? _____
       _____

    d. Physically impacted? (circle one)   yes   or   no
       What led you to select this response? _____
       _____

9. Give three examples of how spiritual problems in your life have led to either mental or physical problems.

    1) _____
       _____

    2) _____
       _____

    3) _____
       _____

IN THE GARDEN

10. As detailed in Genesis 3:1-8, Adam and Eve were tempted by evil, ignored the command of the Lord God and ate the forbidden fruit. They then discovered that they were naked and attempted to hide from the Lord God among the trees in the Garden of Eden. He sought them out. **Then the Lord called to the man, and said to him, "Where are you?" He said, "I heard the sound of You in the garden, and I was afraid because I was naked; so I hid myself"** (Genesis 3:9-10).

   a. As Adam was motivated by fear, so was Janet. Name some of her fears. _____

   _____

   _____

   _____

   b. Name some of your own fears. _____

   _____

   _____

DETECTING BLAME

11. When things start going badly as a result of our own actions, we may blame others. People have been doing this for nearly as long as there has been sin in the world, starting with Adam.

   a. God asked Adam, **"Who told you that you were naked? Have you eaten from the tree of which I commanded you not to eat?"** (Genesis 3:11).

   b. Adam replied, **"The woman whom You gave *to be* with me, she gave me from the tree, and I ate"** (Genesis 3:12).

   c. Following Adam's logic, who deserved the blame for his sin?

      1) _____

      2) _____

12. Who did Janet blame for her problems? _____

   _____

   _____

13. Gives examples of when you blamed other people for your problems.

   _____

   _____

   _____

   _____

14.   a. Did you ever blame God for your problems? (circle one)   yes   or   no

      b. If yes to 14.a., give an example of it here. _____

      _____

      _____

      _____

15.   a. **"Why do you look at the _____ that is in your brother's _____ , but do not**
                _____ the _____ that is in your _____ _____ ? Or how can you
                say to your brother, 'Let me take the speck out of your eye,' and behold, the log is in your own
                eye?" (Matthew 7:3-4, p. 47).

      b. In Matthew 7:5 (p. 47) what does Jesus call a person who does this? _____

      c. What was included in the log that was in Janet's eye? _____

      _____

      _____

16.   a. Do you have a log in your eye? (circle one)   yes   or   no

      b. If yes, write about it here (and feel free to use extra paper if needed).

      _____

      _____

      _____

      c. If no to 16.a., give it some more thought and come back when you are ready.

Write down some insights you've gained from this lesson. To gauge your spiritual progress, in the future look back on what you've written here.

_____

_____

_____

_____

_____

_____

_____

Seeking a Solution

I jerked awake with the late-night ringing of the telephone, dreading the possibilities of what I'd hear when I answered. Had Kyle been in an accident? Was the morgue calling me to identify his body? Were the police calling to say he'd been arrested again?

It had reached a point where the ringing of a phone or the doorbell would create a pounding in my heart. Even distant sirens got me to wondering.

I reached over, picked up the phone and held it to my ear. It was a collect call from a local jail. On the other end was an unfamiliar voice. I hung up. Then I started wondering if it had been Kyle, after all. Perhaps he was locked in a jail cell unable to get to a phone and had recruited another prisoner to call on his behalf. I obsessed about it the rest of the night, unable to get another wink of sleep.

Only later did I find that Kyle had nothing to do with it. Evidently the man had dialed the wrong number.

Kyle's final year of high school should have been an exciting time of senior pictures, signing yearbooks, senior prom and applying for college. Instead, school officials and coaches were suspicious and concerned that he was still using drugs. Tardiness and detention hall were regular occurrences. His appearance and style of dress had not changed nor had his choice of companions.

We were advised that another attempt at rehab might be Kyle's only hope of being accepted back on the basketball team and graduating. He still loved basketball and seemed upset that he might not be allowed to play but seemed to take the prospect of losing this privilege as if it were inevitable.

The probation officer agreed that we should force rehab again before he turned 18 and legally lose any parental control.

By this time I had become more educated about addiction and knew that for recovery to be possible, it was necessary that the addict truly desire to change. That did not seem to be the case with Kyle. But we moved forward with inpatient rehab at the same facility where he'd been earlier. Flynn and I wanted to be sure that we had exhausted every possible effort to help him.

Kyle didn't resist and gave the appearance of thinking it was important to graduate and get back on the team. We obtained his schoolwork from his teachers and carried it to him when we went to visit each weekend.

By this time he had picked up some "recovery language," and I suspected that he was saying what everyone wanted to hear. The counselors had similar suspicions. My only hope was that later he might reflect on what he had heard there.

Financing His Habit

During family sessions Kyle admitted he was dealing marijuana in order to keep a stash on hand for personal use. This helped us to understand why he had refused to work in our family's lawn care business. Though he had not stolen from us as many addicts do, this revelation was shocking.

This time they only kept him at the recovery center for two rather than three weeks, as they had previously, probably because they realized he wasn't serious about recovery.

The day he was released we informed him that the boyfriend of one of his female friends had been charged with capital murder because of a drug-related incident. He seemed surprised but only slightly concerned.

Living in constant suspense and dread, Flynn and I attended outpatient family sessions once or twice a week for four months at the same place locally that offered outpatient treatment. This helped us to understand addiction and the importance of setting some boundaries for Kyle but didn't address our long-time communication problems, which made it difficult for us to agree on and implement rules.

When we were able to draw some lines he was not supposed to cross, Kyle had ways of getting around them. For example, we took the phone out of his room and a friend furnished him with a cell phone that he kept hidden. If we allowed him to go one place, he wound up somewhere else.

Various people shared during family sessions so we could learn from each other's experiences. One night a lady spent the majority of the meeting recounting her life story. Her mother had died and an alcoholic father had raised her. She and her siblings became aware that even if he was in a good mood, his anger could erupt at the drop of a hat. She had assumed the role of the adult in the family at the age of five—cooking, washing dishes and caring for a younger sibling.

Flynn remarked afterward that she could have been describing his family. This was both surprising and troubling. Though I knew he had grown up in a turbulent home, we really hadn't talked about it. Until then it never occurred to me that Flynn had been negatively impacted by growing up with an alcoholic parent and kept it all bottled up inside of him.

After the outpatient therapy ended, Flynn returned to working long hours, which seemed to be his method of coping rather than worrying himself to death the way I did.

Other family members from the outpatient facility seemed to have found help in the Al-Anon Family Groups. The main focus of Al-Anon, from what I had heard, was to improve one's self.

My main objective was to save Kyle from the "demon" that had possessed him. I had low expectations, then, when a Christian friend who had a drug-using daughter persuaded me to attend a meeting with her. Only one other lady showed up, and the three of us shared our stories. I was disappointed by the lack of attendees and didn't go back.

Months passed and nothing changed. Kyle was still hanging out with the drug crowd, while Flynn and I failed to put up a united front as to expectations for him.

I became desperate enough to try the Al-Anon program again. I walked into a different Al-Anon meeting one morning and was probably a bit more ready to hear what they had to offer.

I started attending regularly and was surprised at the different walks of life represented there. They ranged in age from newlywed women who had discovered their husbands were alcoholics to grandparents having to raise grandchildren because of the addiction of a son or a daughter. Some seemed of poor or average means while others appeared to be affluent, professional people. About 90 percent of them were women.

Many in Al-Anon held Christian beliefs while others expressed only a vague concept of God as a "Higher Power." Some were long-time members who attended regularly, while others came a few times and dropped out. What impressed me the most was that they were open about their own failures and shortcomings.

One member admitted to resorting back to her old controlling behaviors, yet she was able to laugh at herself and keep trying. As she described some of her antics, I felt myself beginning to relate. I had always tried to control family members and felt it was my duty to step in and try to fix every problem. This, I thought, was simply a part of my compassionate nature—not a possible character flaw.

Guidance for Our Marriage

Another member who still harbored resentment toward her alcoholic husband admitted that in some ways, she had trouble showing love to him—so she massaged his feet. I had to admit that I felt incapable of demonstrating affection to Flynn, even on happy occasions, because I was still too busy obsessing about what I perceived were his problems.

Several members who grew up in alcoholic homes admitted they were extremely angry. This helped me gain some insight into my husband. I realized that his anger was parallel to my anxiety issues.

I encouraged Flynn to attend Al-Anon with me, but he wasn't yet open to sharing our problems in front of a group of strangers. He agreed, however, to try another professional counselor. After the few sessions we had attended a few years before, our communication improved temporarily, but we soon fell back into the same pattern of frequent anger, sulking, sarcasm and criticism.

With the new counselor, we hoped to solve some of our marital issues, but we spent a lot of time discussing our frustration with Kyle. The counselor suggested we set up rules and consequences for Kyle. Kyle would argue, cry despairingly over our lack of understanding about his love for his girlfriend and his marijuana use, and then proceed to break whatever rules we made.

It was refreshing for me to attend the Al-Anon meetings, where I could tell others what was going on in my life and know that what I said would be kept confidential. Compared to my problems, some of the members were in the midst of monumental difficulties, yet there was an air of calmness about them.

Though we each got our turn to share, one member rambled a lot. She also lightened the meetings with humorous tales when it was her turn to share. I often wondered why she was in the group. I found her annoying until it was revealed that she had lost two sons in alcohol-related accidents within a short period of time. I then marveled that she was still vertical!

Other attendees had relatives who had gotten clean and sober and were staying that way, yet they were still involved in the program.

Compared to the Al-Anon group, the people at church generally seemed to be less open about their personal problems. Seldom did anyone openly confess a fault unless they went forward at the invitation song (known as an "altar call" at some churches) and admitted they had sinned but usually without naming any specifics.

The church members had always been helpful during sickness, after a death, or a calamity such as when our house burned. Yet they didn't seem to know how to respond to the problems we were facing with our son.

I spoke to the elders and preacher about visiting our home and talking to Kyle. My main concern was that he at least knew the church cared and might see it as a loving place where he might find solutions. Instead, they had the secretary type up a letter, which they all signed before putting it in the mail.

After reading it, Kyle responded, "They only wrote it because you told them to write it."

Guilty as charged!

A New Perspective

From attending the meetings I was beginning to see the role I played in spinning the merry-go-round of hopelessness. If I had been part of the problem, it seemed possible I could be part of the solution. I decided to take to heart the Al-Anon slogan, "Let it begin with me."

The focus of Al-Anon is to recognize and change one's own behavior rather than that of the addict or other "problem people" in one's life. Trying to force change on others had definitely become exhausting. It had become apparent that I was harming myself in a fruitless effort to control others.

This quote from Al-Anon literature sums up my solution: "Progress begins when we stop trying to control the uncontrollable and when we go on to correct what we have the right to change. If we accept a situation full of misery and uncertainty, it is no one's fault but our own. We *can* do something about it." [1]

I decided to start working the 12 steps advocated by Al-Anon. (For more information about the 12 steps that will be addressed individually in the chapters that follow, see the appendix that follows this chapter, "An Overview of the 12 Steps: An Appendix.")

Codependency

Many Al-Anon members identify themselves as being codependent, including me.

"Codependent relationships are a type of dysfunctional helping relationship where one person supports or enables another person's addiction, poor mental health, immaturity, irresponsibility, or under-achievement." [2]

A codependent is "one who has let another person's behavior affect him or her, and who is obsessed with controlling that person's behavior." [3]

Besides Al-Anon there are other groups for the loved ones of alcoholics and drug addicts that use the 12 steps to address codependency issues, including Codependents Anonymous, Families Anonymous, many Christian-oriented groups and others.

Biblical Questions for Self-Examination

DIRECTIONS IN LIFE

Use the *Journey to Recovery Through Christ: CASA's 12-Step Study Bible* or any other version of the *New American Standard Bible* © 1995 to fill in the blanks in biblical passages below.

1. **For the mind set on the flesh is _____ , but the mind set on the Spirit is _____ and _____** (Romans 8:6, p. 222).

2. a. According to Galatians 5:19-21 (p. 264), the acts of the sinful nature are obvious. Many of these may not apply to you, but list one that has most frequently surfaced in your life at times in the past.

   1) _____

   b. Why did you select this one? _____

   _____

   _____

   _____

3. a. Fruits of the Spirit may be found in Galatians 5:22-23 (p. 264). List three fruits of the Spirit that you would find most beneficial to exhibit in your life today, starting with the most important.

   1) _____

   2) _____

   3) _____

   b. Pick out any one of these and describe why you think it would be especially important in your life today.

   _____

   _____

   _____

   _____

A WRETCHED SLAVE?

4. a. **...for by what a man is _____ , by this he is _____** (2 Peter 2:19, p. 318).

   b. **Jesus answered them, "... everyone who _____ _____ is the _____ of _____"** (John 8:34, p. 160).

c. Based on the above two quotations, how many sins must a person commit before becoming a slave to sin?

_____

d. Why do you think that is true? _____

_____

_____

_____

_____

5. a. The most prominent New Testament author, the Apostle Paul, wrote, **For the _____ that I want,**
    I do not do, but I practice the very _____ that I do not want (Romans 7:19, p. 222).

    b. Paul then continues, _____ **man that I am! Who will set me free from the body of this**
    _____**?** (Romans 7:24, p. 222)

    c. Would you expect a very religious man to be writing things like this about himself? (circle one)   yes   or   no

    d. Why or why not? _____

    _____

    _____

6. a. In what way do you think that Janet identifies with what Paul wrote in the verses quoted in 5.a. and 5.b.?

    _____

    _____

    _____

    b. In what ways do you identify with Paul and with Janet? _____

    _____

    _____

    _____

THE BIGGEST LIE

Many Christian scholars believe the verse below refers to the devil. Read why Satan, originally an angel, was thrown from heaven. It is helpful to know that the word "star" is sometimes used to refer to an angel, and in the passage below Satan is the "star of the morning."

7. **How you have fallen from heaven, O star of the morning, son of the dawn! You have been cut down to the**
    earth, you who have weakened the nations! But you said in your heart, "I will ascend to heaven; I will raise

my throne above the stars of God, and I will sit on the mount of assembly in the recesses of the north. I will ascend above the heights of the clouds; I will make myself like the Most High" (Isaiah 14:12-14).

a. In the quotation above, how many times does Satan refer to "I will?" _____

b. How many times does he refer to God's will? _____

c. In the last line of the quotation above, Satan says he planned to make himself like God. In what way is this the biggest lie of all? _____

_____

_____

_____

HERE'S WHERE PRIDE FITS IN

8. It has been said that Satan was guilty of pride, but there is confusion over this word because it has both positive and negative meanings. The definition of pride in a positive sense has to do with dignity and self-respect. The kind of pride of which Satan was guilty is defined as having an overly high opinion of one's self and arrogance.[4]

a. Describe an example of something in your life causing you to have pride in the positive sense of the word.

_____

_____

_____

b. Describe an example of pride in your life, according to the negative definition of the word.

_____

_____

_____

c. Thinking about what you wrote in 7.b. through 7.c, why is "playing God" an example of pride in the worst sense? _____

_____

_____

_____

_____

IN THE GARDEN OF EDEN

Read about Eve's experience with Satan, who appears as a serpent in Genesis 3:1-5 and describes how sin entered the world.

9. **Now the serpent was more crafty than any beast of the field which the Lord God had made. And he said to the woman, "Indeed, has God said, You shall not eat from any tree of the garden?" The woman said to the serpent, "From the fruit of the trees of the garden we may eat; but from the fruit of the tree which is in the middle of the garden, God has said, 'You shall not eat from it or touch it, or you will die.'" The serpent said to the woman, "You surely will not die! For God knows that in the day you eat from it your eyes will be opened, and you will be like God, knowing good and evil."**

    a. In what way do the words of Satan demonstrate that he is a liar? _____

    _____

    _____

    b. In what way is this quotation from Satan in the last two sentences above consistent with the earlier quotation from Satan recorded above in 7.a.? _____

    _____

    _____

    c. How are the three words from Satan "For God knows…" consistent with the earlier quotation found in 7.a.? (Hint: See 1 Corinthians 2:16, p. 234) _____

    _____

    _____

10.   a. Speaking of Satan in John 8:44 (p. 161), Jesus said, **"…Whenever he speaks a _____, he speaks from his own *nature*, for he is a _____ and the father of _____."**

    b. Name at least five ways that you have been deceived by lies from Satan.

      1) _____

      _____

      2) _____

      _____

      3) _____

      _____

      4) _____

      _____

      5) _____

      _____

APPEARANCES CAN BE DECEIVING

11. Read Proverbs 23:29-35 (p. 508).

   a. Based on Proverbs 23:31, what appearance did the wine have and how did it taste?_____

   _____

   b. But what were the end results for the person who kept drinking it? (Proverbs 23:32-35, p. 508). _____

   _____

   _____

   _____

12. Read Proverbs 5:1-5 (p. 482).

   a. When the adulterous woman said something (Proverbs 5:3, p. 482) did it sound good or bad? _____

   _____

   b. But in the end what was she really like and where was she headed? (Proverbs 5:4-5, p. 482) _____

   _____

   _____

   _____

   _____

13. **When the woman saw that the tree was good for food, and that it was a delight to the eyes, and that the tree was desirable to make *one* wise, she took from its fruit and ate; and she gave also to her husband with her, and he ate** (Genesis 3:6).

   a. In the opinion of the woman (Eve) in the verse above, what were the three positive aspects of the forbidden fruit?

   1) _____

   2) _____

   3) _____

   b. Now consider Eve's three reasons that you listed in 13.a. in light of the following passage about the trees growing in the Garden of Eden: **Out of the ground the Lord God caused to grow every tree that is pleasing to the sight and good for food...** (Genesis 2:9).

   c. What does this reveal about Eve's perspective after dialoging with Satan?_____

   _____

   _____

_____

_____

d. Based on Genesis 2:9, what was Eve's actual reason for eating the forbidden fruit and how does this relate to Satan's statement in Genesis 3:5, "**...you will be like God...**"?_____

_____

_____

_____

e. How did the actions of Adam and Eve demonstrate pride in the negative sense?_____

_____

_____

_____

14. Eating fruit from that particular tree had been forbidden by God, and there were consequences to pay if God's word was not followed. See Genesis 2:15-17. As a result of their actions in the Garden of Eden, it is said that we live in a "fallen world." In other words, evil (Satan) is present. Why did God allow such a tree in the Garden of Eden? Because it shows that Adam and Eve had freedom of choice, the same as we do today. What was the result for Adam, Eve and us today?

a. God told Eve, **"I will greatly multiply your pain in childbirth, in pain you will bring forth children; yet your desire will be for your husband, and he will rule over you."** (Genesis 3:16).

b. In what ways does this still apply today? _____

_____

_____

c. God told Adam, **"...Cursed is the ground because of you; in toil you will eat of it all the days of your life. Both thorns and thistles it shall grow for you; and you will eat the plants of the field; By the sweat of your face you will eat bread, till you return to the ground, because from it you were taken; for you are dust, and to dust you shall return"** (Genesis 3:17-19).

d. In what ways does this still apply today? _____

_____

_____

15. a. Thinking about the lips and words of the adulterous woman, the appearance of the wine, and the forbidden fruit offered to Eve by the devil, you may conclude that Satan presents sin as being (circle one): a) very appealing; b) very unappealing.

b. Despite this, in the examples in 11.a. and 12.a. what were the longer-term effects? _____

_____

_____

_____

16. "Codependent relationships are a type of dysfunctional helping relationship where one person supports or enables another person's addiction, poor mental health, immaturity, irresponsibility, or under-achievement."[5]

a. Thinking about what you've read about Janet's story thus far, name some ways that her thoughts and actions correspond with the definition of codependency in 16.

_____

_____

17. A codependent is "one who has let another person's behavior affect him or her, and who is obsessed with controlling that person's behavior."[6]

a. Thinking about what you've read about Janet's story thus far, name some ways that her thoughts and actions correspond with the definition of codependency in 17.

_____

_____

_____

b. As a result of her codependency, in what way does Janet demonstrate pride in the negative sense?_____

_____

_____

_____

c. As we have seen, there is an initial seemingly positive payout to temptation that will harm a person in the long-term. What was the seemingly positive payout that Janet received from her codependency?_____

_____

_____

_____

d. What negative things in Janet's life are a result of her codependency?_____

_____

_____

_____

e. In what ways do you identify with the definition of codependency in 16?_____

_____

_____

_____

f. In what ways do you identify with the definition of codependency in 17?_____

_____

_____

_____

g. What are the seemingly positive payoffs to codependency in your own life?_____

_____

_____

_____

h. As a result of codependency, how have you been guilty of pride in the negative sense of the word?_____

_____

_____

_____

YOUR OWN WORST ENEMY

18.   Do you identify with Paul when he wrote to both people of both genders, **Wretched man that I am!**
      Who will set me free from the body of this death? Romans 7:24 (p. 222) (circle one)   yes   or   no

I know that I am a wretched slave to sin. (If you agree with this, sign your name on the following line and put today's date beside it.)

_____   _____

Your Signature   **Today's Date**

IN CONCLUSION

Satan-led, self-centered behavior brings about self-destruction. If you think that you have been your own worst enemy—whether your problem is or was codependency, alcohol, food, drugs, sex, gambling, envy, the list goes on and on—you have been self-centered and have allowed your addiction to supersede God in your life. Satan has been in charge. Rest assured that the 12 steps will lead you toward a life focused on God.

Write down some insights you've gained from this lesson. To gauge your spiritual progress, in the future look back on what you've written here.

_____

_____

_____

_____

_____

_____

_____

_____

_____

_____

_____

Self-centered ➡ ➡ ➡ ➡ ➡ ➡ ➡ ➡ ➡ ➡ ➡ ➡ **God**-centered

End Notes

1. *Hope for Today*, Al-Anon Family Group Headquarters, Inc., Virginia Beach, 1973, 86.
2. http://aspirace.com/you-are-not-required.
3. Melody Beattie, *Codependent No More: How to Stop Controlling Others and Start Caring for Yourself*, Harper & Row, New York, 1987, 31.
4. http://www.patheos.com/blogs/christiancrier/2015/05/22/what-is-the-biblical-definition-of-pride-how-is-pride-described-in-the-bible.
5. http://aspirace.com/you-are-not-required.
6. Melody Beattie, *Codependent No More: How to Stop Controlling Others and Start Caring for Yourself*, Harper & Row, New York, 1987, 31.

AN OVERVIEW OF THE 12 STEPS

AN APPENDIX

The 12 steps to which I referred in the previous chapter were originally written by the founders of Alcoholics Anonymous (AA) based on the influence of an organization known as The Oxford Group. The Oxford Group had been founded by a Lutheran minister in 1921 with the idea of recapturing the ideals of First Century Christianity. Emphasis was on Bible study, prayer and seeking guidance from God in all matters.[1] (For additional information on the background of the steps, the Oxford Group and the program of Alcoholics Anonymous, see *Journey to Recovery: CASA's 12-Step Study Bible*, Quarry Press, Dallas, 2015, pp. 6-8.)

One of the AA co-founders was Bill Wilson who had been a stockbroker on Wall Street during the 1920s. When the stock market crashed, he took solace in the bottle. Though he tried every possible means to stop drinking, alcohol dominated and then ruined his life. By 1934, Bill resigned himself to dying drunk. It was then that he applied a spiritual solution to his alcoholism. Based on the directive of James 2:17 (p. 308) that faith without works is dead, Bill stayed sober by attempting to help others suffering from alcoholism.[2]

As Bill attained sobriety and his life changed for the better, his wife, Lois, found herself in a new predicament explaining it in this way:

> After a while I began to realize that I was not as happy as I ought to be, that I resented the fact Bill and I had no life together anymore, and that I was left alone while he was off somewhere scouting up new drunks or working on old ones. My life's job of sobering up Bill, with all its responsibilities, which made me feel so needed, suddenly had vanished and I had not yet found anything to fill the void. There was also the feeling of being on the outside of a very tight clique of alcoholics, where no mere wife could enter. I did not fully understand what was going on within myself until one Sunday Bill asked me if I was ready to go to a meeting with him. To my own surprise, as well as his, I burst forth with 'Darn your old meeting'! And threw a shoe as hard as I could.

> This surprising display of temper woke me up to the fact that I had been wallowing in self-pity. In the light of this awakening I could see not only that Bill's feverish activity with alcoholics was absolutely necessary to his sobriety and that he had developed spiritually. I saw, too, that if I did not want to be left behind, I had better join the procession and strive for much more spiritual growth myself...[3]

Lois became the co-founder of the Al-Anon family groups. I was anxious to move forward in the same way that Lois did. In the chapters that follow, I will describe my spiritual journey through the 12 steps while dealing with other challenges, including a drug-addicted, drug-dealing son.

THE STEPS DEVELOPED BY ALCOHOLICS ANONYMOUS[4] (also used by Al-Anon*)

1. We admitted we were powerless over alcohol—that our lives had become unmanageable.

2. Came to believe that a Power greater than ourselves could restore us to sanity.

3. Made a decision to turn our will and our lives over to the care of God *as we understood Him*.

4. Made a searching and fearless moral inventory of ourselves.

5. Admitted to God, to ourselves, and to another human being the exact nature of our wrongs.

6. Were entirely ready to have God remove all these defects of character.

7. Humbly asked Him to remove our shortcomings.

8. Made a list of all persons we had harmed, and became willing to make amends to them all.

9. Made direct amends to such people wherever possible except when to do so would injure them or others.

10. Continued to take personal inventory and when we were wrong promptly admitted it.

11. Sought through prayer and meditation to improve our conscious contact with God *as we understood Him*, praying only for knowledge of His will for us and the power to carry that out.

12. Having had a spiritual awakening as the result of these steps, we tried to carry this message to alcoholics, and to practice these principles in all our affairs.

> * The lone exception in wording between these groups is in Step Twelve where Al-Anon substitutes "others" for "alcoholics."

THE SAME STEPS, DIFFERENT ADDICTIONS

Examining the steps above, you may be surprised to discover that there is only one reference each to alcohol and alcoholics. The word "alcohol" is found only in Step One where it is named as the substance over which alcoholics are powerless. "Alcoholics" is found only in the 12th step, "...we tried to carry this message to alcoholics..."

Some 200 different groups use the same 12 step model.[5] Members of these groups simply plug in the substance, behavior or pattern of thinking over which they are powerless in Step One and the similarly addicted individuals to whom they will carry the message in Step Twelve.

Here is a partial listing of groups using the 12 steps developed by Alcoholics Anonymous:
Adult Children of Alcoholics, Alanon, Alateen, Cocaine Anonymous, Codependents Anonymous, Clutterers Anonymous, Crystal Meth Anonymous, Co-Dependents Anonymous, Debtors Anonymous, Emotions Anonymous, Emotional Health Anonymous, Families Anonymous, Food Addicts in Recovery Anonymous, Food Addicts Anonymous, Gamblers Anonymous, Heroin Anonymous, Homosexuals Anonymous, Marijuana Anonymous, Narcotics Anonymous, Neurotics Anonymous, Nicotine Anonymous, Overeaters Anonymous, Online Gamers Anonymous, Sexaholics Anonymous, Sexual Compulsives Anonymous, Survivors of Incest Anonymous, Underearners Anonymous, Workaholics Anonymous.[6]

Several Christian groups also use the steps, including Christians Against Substance Abuse/Sexual Addiction (CASA) and Next Step Christian Recovery.

WHY THE SAME STEPS WORK FOR DIFFERENT ADDICTIONS

As written in the First Commandment: "I am the Lord your God, who brought you out of the land of Egypt, out of the house of slavery. You shall have no other gods before me" (Exodus 20:2-3). As you can see, this commandment makes reference to God (singular with capital G) and gods (plural with a lowercase g). What is the difference?

God is God Almighty who spoke the universe into existence (Genesis 1:1) and in whose image human beings are made (Genesis 1:27).

The gods named in the first commandment include any manifestation of self-will that takes precedence over God in a person's life. Lowercase g gods are the same as idols; they lead people away from God Almighty on a path of self-destruction. They cause people to lose perspective of their identity as children of God.

An idol may include an addiction to a substance, behavior or pattern of thinking. Based on the various types of addictions addressed by the 12 steps, it is clear to see that addictions are based on self-will continually trumping out God's will in their lives.

Why do the same 12 steps work for so many different types of addictions? The steps are designed to take people from self-will/self-centered (as it may manifest itself in any number of ways) to God's will/God-centered.

Al-Anon co-founder Lois W. reflected the same idea in regard to codependency.

Self-sufficiency caused by the habit of acting as mother, nurse, caretaker, and breadwinner, as well as always being considered on the credit side of the ledger with my alcoholic husband on the debit side, resulted in a smug feeling of rightness. At the same time, illogically, I felt a failure at my life's job of helping Bill to sobriety. All this made me blind for a long time to the fact that I needed to turn my will and life over to the care of God. Smugness is the worst sin of all, I believe. No shaft of light can pierce the armor of self-righteousness.[7]

Another Al-Anon author stated it this way:

When I took the First Step, I, for the first time, really looked to God for help. Before that I had been occupied with telling Him what to do, how to do it, and please to do it quickly. I'd always said "Thy Will be done" but hadn't thought I was still striving for my own will. My will, since I was asking only for peace, decency and a normal home, seemed all right to live by.

Now I am willing to believe I didn't earn congratulations for the way I had lived my life, and that God could do a better job of running it. I saw that if I hadn't fought against alcoholism, that problem might have been solved earlier. I had made Jim obstinate by pushing too hard. If I had just given up earlier in my efforts to control his drinking, our home would have been more tranquil, at least by the measure of my own acceptance and serenity.[8]

THE "HIGHER POWER" CONCEPT: A PROBLEM?

What is the difference between the numerous groups that use the 12 steps, such as Alcoholics Anonymous and Al-Anon, and Christians who utilize the 12 steps?

AA and the others often refer to God as a "Higher Power;" this terminology comes from Step Two which refers to "a Power greater than ourselves." Christians, of course, think of God as revealed in the Bible and His son, Jesus Christ.

Addressing criticisms of the "Higher Power" concept that sometimes come from the religious community, Christian writer Mark Parsec observed:

> Although AA does not claim to be a Christian organization and makes reference to what appears to be an ambiguous "Higher Power," its essential strength lies in its ability to reach atheists and agnostics, who otherwise might be completely predisposed to initially rejecting any "religious" solution to their problem. This propensity is common among addicts. The significant benefits of the 12-step approach are that it not only allows dialogue upon the subject of God that would otherwise be essentially unapproachable, but once dialogue has been commenced it provides a springboard for further evangelism, discipleship and Christian counseling.[9]

Step Three contains the wording, "God *as we understood Him*," which some people also find troubling. AA literature tells newcomers that if it is helpful, they may define God in a way that is comprehendible to them. This may be beneficial to anyone, because how else could a person think of God except for the way they perceive Him at that particular moment in their lives? The major concern would seem to be the spiritual direction in which any person is headed.

End Notes

1. *Dr. Bob and the Good Oldtimers,* Alcoholics Anonymous World Services, New York, 1980, 54.

2. Don Umphrey, *12 Steps to a Closer Walk with God: A Guide for Small Groups,* Quarry Press, Dallas, 2004, 18-19.

3. Lois W., *The Al-Anon Family Groups—Classic Edition,* Al-Anon Family Group Headquarters, Inc., Virginia Beach, 2000, 55.

4. Alcoholics Anonymous, Third Edition, Alcoholics Anonymous World Services, Inc., New York, 1976, 59-60.

5. Judy Howard, "12 Steps to Healing—Principles of Alcoholics Anonymous Help Clergy in Counseling Addicts," The Dallas Morning News, Aug. 30, 1990, 36.

6. http://en.wikipedia.org/wiki/List_of_twelve-step_groups.

7. Lois W., *The Al-Anon Family Groups,* Al-Anon Family Group Headquarters, Virginia Beach, 2000, 57-58.

8. "His Way, Not Mine," *The Al-Anon Family Groups,* Al-Anon Family Group Headquarters, Virginia Beach, 2000, 75.

9. http://searchwarp.com/swa226012.htm.

Letting Go with Love

Thinking about our tumultuous situation with Kyle brought to mind a near-tragic incident our family experienced during a camping trip 10 years earlier.

Along with my sister's family, Flynn, Kyle, Casey and I toured Fall Creek Falls State Park in Tennessee. We came upon a waterfall that emptied into a creek where people were swimming. A huge rock formed a natural waterslide to the joy of many who were sliding down. Kyle and the other older children with us joined in the fun.

Casey, then five years old, begged to try it. Though he had learned to swim the year before, for the sake of his safety, I decided to slide down first and stand at the bottom to catch him. What wasn't apparent to me was that I was standing on a ledge with a steep drop-off right behind me.

As I latched onto Casey at the bottom of the slide, the impact knocked me over the drop-off. We both went under. In panic he immediately started clinging to me, making it impossible to keep my head above water. Unable to call for help, it appeared we were both going to drown with people close by, yet unaware.

Thank God for Flynn! Sitting on the bank, he saw that we were in trouble and jumped into the water to rescue Casey. This enabled me to swim to safety.

Reflecting on this potential disaster, I've wondered what I could or should have done. One option would have been to push Casey away in hopes of getting my head above water to call for help or reach the shore for assistance. But what if Casey had then disappeared under the water and drowned?

That's all hypothetical, though. The bottom line is that it was impossible for me to let go of Casey. And vice-versa. Except for Flynn, we both would have died that day.

In my current situation with Kyle, it seemed we were both drowning, him in his addiction and me in my obsession to fix him. Was it possible for me to let go of Kyle, even though he was wallowing in shark-infested waters? Could I grab onto a lifeline and hope God would intervene on Kyle's behalf?

One of the conditions of Kyle's probation was that he continue to live at home. Despite this and against our wishes, he disappeared on several occasions. We finally told him if he did it again, we would report him. We would rather have seen him locked in the juvenile detention center than endangering his life with drug addicts. These threats kept him at home until he reached age 18 when, legally, he no longer had to answer to us.

Kyle Leaves

Shortly after his 18th birthday, I watched in despair as Kyle walked out the door and down the street. The car we never should have purchased after a couple of negative drug tests had been wrecked, so he left with the few belongings he could carry in a duffel bag. He disappeared from sight with me unsure of where he planned to stay or when—if ever—we would see him again.

My illusions of exercising any control over him disappeared down the street with him.

Of course I still had other responsibilities, including Flynn, our three other sons and two grandchildren. I also had to make long-term care decisions about my mother who had suffered a stroke that had claimed much of her physical and mental abilities.

As a result, I had to make the painful effort to follow another principle of the Al-Anon program to "detach" from Kyle. I loved him, prayed for him diligently, and attempted to keep the line of communication open, but otherwise let him live as he saw fit. He and I spoke occasionally, giving me temporary assurance that he was still alive.

The Parable of the Prodigal Son (prodigal is a word that means "spending money or resources freely and recklessly; wastefully extravagant"[1]) found in Luke 15:11-32 (pp. 133-134) took on personal meaning and gave me hope for something positive in an uncertain future. In the meantime, I had to take solace in the inactions of the father in that parable. He did not try to stop the son from packing his bag and walking down the road. The sad, wise father wasn't sure of the outcome, yet he knew there are some lessons that can only be learned by experience.

I also should have learned from previous experience that trying to change others is a mission of futility. I had spent many waking moments and sleepless nights trying to come up with the right words, the right plan or strategy to bring about change in my mother's mental state. I had suggested doctors, psychiatrists, drugs and books that explained her disorder. I had constantly recommended exercising, socializing and other self-improvement measures, but she came up with reasons for rejecting them all. Her thought processes did not correspond with mine and now in her present deteriorated condition, it was apparent that they never would.

When I had not been trying to "fix" her, I was obsessing about Flynn's anger issues, and how to convince him to confront his past and get the proper help to deal with it.

Other family members and friends had problems holding jobs, keeping house, managing their money and other problems that I was sure could have been resolved had they listened to me. But my efforts were all in vain.

Kyle proved to be my biggest challenge and his drug of choice was proving more powerful than any logic, reasoning, or potential consequences, such as imprisonment or death. He seemed blind to the direction his life was heading.

Facing My Futility

Come to find out, I was just like Kyle in terms of being blind to the direction of my life. We were each our own worst enemies. According to Proverbs 14:12 (p. 494), "There is a way *which seems* right to a man, but its end is the way of death." This is known as denial, defined as a "refusal to admit the truth or reality."[2]

Denial makes people blind to their own faults, and they often put the blame on others, as you have already seen that I did. People in denial may try to conceal their addictive behaviors and think they are succeeding while the truth may be obvious to everyone else.

Denial causes people to lose track of reality while lying to themselves not only about their addictions but also its negative effects in their lives, including (but not limited to) difficulties at work or school, unemployment, financial woes, family conflict, divorce, incarceration, depression, anxiety and sleeplessness. Some lose everything before they are willing to change; many never change and die in denial.

"Denial plays a formative role in all addictions. In fact, it seems that for a behavior to become addicting...
it must be denied. It's as if the mind conspires to help keep the addiction 'game' secret, according to Dr.
Archibald Hart.[3]

Author Don Umphrey traced the source of denial to Satan who is defined by Jesus as "the father of lies"
(John 8:44, p. 161).

> If someone wants to believe a lie and persists in doing so, denial takes over. Denial occurs when
> people lie to themselves and then believe their own lies. This self-delusion indicates that individuals
> are doing Satan's job for him as they continue on the road to self-destruction.[4]

The following quotation sums up my situation:

> When we come into Al-Anon, our main preoccupation is the alcoholism of someone who is
> important in our lives. We must sooner or later accept the fact that we have no way to stop the
> compulsion to drink. The desire for sobriety can come only from the alcoholic. We may guide or
> inspire by our example, but we cannot cast another person, however close to us, into the mold
> that we choose.[5]

As long as my attention was focused on fixing someone else, I had failed to see my contribution to the
cycle I was caught up in. My responsibility could be reduced to a more manageable size—MYSELF. The relief
of giving up a losing battle was overwhelming and liberating! I was ready to admit my inability to control or
change the behavior of others.

STEP ONE of the Twelve Step Recovery program states ▶

We admitted we were powerless over alcohol—that our lives had become unmanageable. (For additional
information on Step One and a listing of step reflections related to specific verses, see *Journey to Recovery
Through Christ: CASA's 12-Step Study Bible,* pp. 12-13.)

The 12 steps of Alcoholics Anonymous are repeated almost word for word in Al-Anon. (See the appendix
that precedes this chapter). Al-Anon members are also powerless over alcohol, drugs, or whatever substance,
behavior or pattern of thinking negatively impacts our addicted loved ones.

By owning up to my own powerlessness and unmanageability in attempting to control others, I was
admitting that I was codependent. Here's how Melody Beattie described her own codependency:

> ...I became so caught up in the chaos of a few alcoholics that I stopped living my own life. I
> stopped thinking. I stopped feeling positive emotions, and I was left with rage, bitterness, hatred,
> fear, depression, helplessness, despair, and guilt. At times, I wanted to stop living. I had no
> energy. I spent most of my time worrying about people and trying to figure out how to control
> them. I couldn't say no (to anything but fun activities) if my life depended on it, which it did. My
> relationships with friends and family members were in shambles. I felt terribly victimized. I lost
> myself and didn't know how it had happened. I didn't know what had happened. I thought I was
> going crazy. And I thought, shaking a finger at the people around me, it's *their* fault.[6]

I identified 100 percent with everything she wrote in that paragraph.

When a person puts the right label on his or her problem, it is the beginning of the end of denial. It is then
that an individual will start recognizing other self-destructive traits in themselves.

I was beginning to see that it was possible to allow others the dignity to make their own choices, experience the consequence of those choices and grow from them. Trying to force change on someone else was frustrating and futile. I could make the choice to work my recovery program and let Kyle find out for himself that using drugs was a dead-end street.

Finding a Sponsor

Though I was encouraged to make connections with a sponsor, initially I didn't choose one but kept attending meetings and soaking up the literature. There was one special lady I admired who had a daughter who had been addicted to drugs who eventually found recovery. I admired what I heard from her at Al-Anon meetings. She and I talked on the telephone occasionally, but I was hesitant to ask her to be my sponsor because I was always afraid of being a bother to someone. I was relieved and overjoyed one day when she offered to be my sponsor.

Sponsorship is a mutual and confidential sharing between two members. A sponsor is someone who is generally more advanced in the recovery program and one who can keep a confidence. The interchange benefits both parties.

My sponsor told me to call her day or night. Though she didn't give advice, she often shared what she had learned through her experience with her daughter. Her example gave me hope that I could survive and even thrive whether or not Kyle chose recovery.

Though Kyle was no longer living at home the last few months of his senior year, we were grateful he was still attending high school. Despite his determination to prove that marijuana did not affect his performance at school, he had trouble getting there on time, if at all. With only six weeks to go, it was still doubtful that he would graduate.

Would I Enable Him?

While I headed to the Al-Anon meeting one morning, Kyle called to inform me he was late to school again and needed me to come and make an excuse for him or he would be expelled. In my desperation for him to graduate and against my better judgment, I agreed to go there and provide an excuse. On the way, I tried to think of a way to word it so it wouldn't be an outright lie. I also pondered whether to confess at that meeting what would be considered "enabling the addict."

An enabler "is a person who by their actions, makes it easier for an addict to continue their self-destructive behavior by criticizing or rescuing." [7]

Enabling may include lying and making excuses, paying fines, hiring attorneys, bailing them out of jail, paying their bills, taking over other responsibilities and doling out money for food, gas, medicine and other requests when the money is likely being spent on an addiction.

The avoidance of enabling involves reverse logic. It is human instinct to reach out to catch someone who is falling. Love, however, must take an alternative route. Rather than doing what seems helpful in the moment, it is important to focus on the long-term positive result: An end to the addiction.

In allowing them to continue falling, the addicted individual may face incarceration, injury or even death. Yes, these are dire prospects, but they could also happen to an addict living at home, in jail, or sleeping on a park bench. In fact, I am personally aware of several addicts and alcoholics who died in their family home after years of being enabled by well-meaning relatives.

If I confessed at an Al-Anon meeting that I had enabled Kyle, the members would all understand, empathize and not judge me because they had to make similar decisions on a regular basis and "relapsed" as often as the addict. Perhaps my lapse would seem more excusable since I was not as far along in the program as others.

I had made excuses before to keep Kyle out of trouble at school. I had even lied for him when he backed our car into a pole after he had been suspended from our insurance policy and was not supposed to be driving.

Pondering all this on my way to the school, I finally made the choice to not enable him by shielding him from the consequences of his irresponsibility. Kyle had brought this problem on himself and my number one goal for him at that time was recovery rather than graduation. I was also convinced that even though it was less than a month until graduation, the same scenario would likely repeat itself. On arriving at the school I explained that it violated my conscience to lie for him. I told him I was sorry about his situation but refused to provide him an excuse.

School officials were also hoping Kyle would graduate and gave him another chance, but after more unexcused absences they felt they had no choice but to follow through on their threats. He was expelled two weeks before graduation.

I tried to avoid the graduation displays that lined the store aisles and parents who were excited about making plans for their children to head off to college. Graduation was a milestone that would provide a foundation for the future if and when Kyle chose recovery.

Biblical Questions for Self-Examination

WHERE IS MY FOCUS?

Use the *Journey to Recovery Through Christ: CASA's 12-Step Study Bible* or any other version of the *New American Standard Bible* © 1995 to fill in the blanks in biblical passages below.

1. Janet identified with the father in the story of the lost (or prodigal) son. Read the parable in Luke 15:11-32 (pp. 133-134) before starting to fill in the blanks below.

    a. In Jesus' story the younger of two sons asked his father for his inheritance. **"And not many days later, the younger son gathered everything together and went on a _____ into a _____ country, and there he squandered his _____ with _____ _____"** (Luke 15:13, p. 133).

    b. In what way is Kyle a prodigal son? _____

    c. In what way is Janet a prodigal daughter? _____

2. a. Matthew 14:22-31 (p. 59) tells about Jesus walking on water. Peter attempted the same thing.

But seeing the _____, he became _____, and beginning to _____, he cried out, "Lord, save me!" (Matthew 14:30, p. 59).

    b. As long as Peter's eyes were on _____, he was able to walk on the water. (See Matthew 14:28-30, p. 59.)

    c. According to Matthew 14:30 (p. 59), Peter started to sink because his eyes were focused on what?_____

    _____

3. According to Proverbs 23:30-31 (p. 508), where was the drunkard's focus? _____

    _____

4. Based on what you read about him thus far, where was Kyle's focus? _____

    _____

5. Based on what you read about her thus far, where was Janet's focus? _____

    _____

6. a. Can you see how having the wrong focus in your life has resulted in you heading in the wrong direction? (circle one) yes or no

    b. If yes to the above, describe those circumstances. _____

    _____

    _____

    _____

    c. If no to 6.a., give it some more thought.

PROBLEMS, PROBLEMS

7. The prodigal son was on a crash course with reality. **"Now when he had spent everything, a severe famine occurred in that country, and he began to be _____"** (Luke 15:14, p. 133).

8. a. As a result of having the wrong focus in life, list below six problems the drunkard had that are found in Proverbs 23:29 (p. 508).

    1) _____

    2) _____

    3) _____

4) _____

5) _____

6) _____

b. As things grew worse, what happened to the drunkard? **Your _____ will see _____ things and your _____ will utter _____ things** (Proverbs 23:33, p. 508).

9. What kinds of problems did Kyle have as a result of his drug addiction? _____

_____

_____

10. a. What kinds of problems did Janet have as a result of her codependency?_____

_____

_____

b. Name some ways that you identify with Janet.

_____

_____

_____

_____

BELIEVING YOUR OWN LIES

11. When you tell something untrue to someone else, that is a lie. But when you lie to yourself and believe it, that is denial.

a. What was creating problems for the man described in Proverbs 23:29-35 (p. 508)?_____

_____

_____

b. What was that man's solution to his problems? **...When shall I awake? I will _____ another _____** (Proverbs 23:35, p. 508).

c. Why is this an example of denial? _____

_____

12. What are the indications of denial in the woman described in Proverbs 5:3-6 (p. 482)?_____

_____

_____

13. a. If you had quoted Proverbs 16:25 (p. 500) to the prodigal son as he was getting ready to leave home, would it have caused him to change his mind and stay home? (circle one)   yes   or   no

   b. What reasoning did you use to answer the question above? _____

   _____

14. Describe some ways that Janet demonstrated denial in her life? _____

   _____

15. a. Have you ever been in denial?   (circle one)   yes   or   no

   b. If yes, describe it here. _____

   _____

   _____

   _____

ENABLING OTHERS

16. Enabling has been defined as:

   a. "Offering the wrong kind of help."[8]
      1) Did Janet do this? (circle one)   yes   or   no.
      2) Have you done this? (circle one)   yes   or   no

   b. "Anything that stands in the way of persons experiencing the natural consequences of their own behavior."[9]
      1) Did Janet do this? (circle one)   yes   or   no.
      2) Have you done this? (circle one)   yes   or   no

   c. "Rescuing your loved one so they don't experience the painful consequences of their irresponsible decisions."[10]
      1) Did Janet do this? (circle one)   yes   or   no.
      2) Have you done this? (circle one)   yes   or   no

17. If you responded with a "yes" to one or more of the above indications of enabling, give three examples of it below.

   1) _____

   2) _____

   3) _____

18. What did you think was going on in Janet's mind when she refused to lie for Kyle after he was late for school again? _____

_____

_____

19. Based on 2 Thessalonians 3:10-12 (p. 283), why would a refusal to give someone food be an example of not being an enabler? _____

_____

20. a. **Do not participate in the** _____ **deeds of** _____ **, but instead even** _____ **them** (Ephesians 5:11, p. 269).

   b. How did Janet participate in what is forbidden in this verse? _____

   _____

   c. Give examples of other forms of enabling that could be connected to the verse. _____

   _____

   _____

   _____

21. a. In the Parable of the Prodigal Son (Luke 15:11-32, pp. 133-134), why did the father allow his son to leave home and go to the far country?_____

   _____

   _____

   b. Why didn't the father journey to the distant country to bring his son home?_____

   _____

   _____

HITTING THE BOTTOM

22. If someone continues heading away from God through various forms of self-centered behavior, one of two things will happen: 1) the individual will grow increasingly uncomfortable to the point where he or she admits defeat and takes Step One; or 2) misery worsens along with ongoing negative consequences.

   a. Herod was responsible for the execution of James (Acts 12:1-2, p. 194) and the arrest of Peter (Acts 12:3-5, p. 194) and Herod also was guilty of pride in the negative sense. After he made a speech, the people cried out, ...**The voice of a** _____ **and not of a** _____ (Acts 12:22, p. 194).

b. Look what happened to Herod as a result of his pride. **And immediately an _____ of the _____ struck him because he did not give _____ the _____, and he was _____ by _____ and _____** (Acts 12:23, p. 194).

23. The lost son's journey took him to the verge of death. **"And he would have gladly filled his stomach with the pods that the _____ were _____, and no one was giving _____ to him"** (Luke 15:16, p. 133).

24. Based on what you've read so far, what do you think it will take for Kyle to give up marijuana? (No fair peeking ahead.) _____

_____

25. What led Janet to take Step One? _____

_____

NAMING IT

26. a. Has your codependency caused you to reach the point in life where you recognized that, like the prodigal son, you were starving to death in a pigpen? (circle one)   yes   or   no

    b. If yes, please describe that pigpen. _____

_____

_____

27. Read Mark 5:1-20 (p. 86-87).

    a. In what ways do you identify with the man described in verses 1-5? _____

_____

_____

    b. **And He was asking him, "_____ ____ _____ _____?..."** (Mark 5:9, p. 86).

It is important to put the right name on your literal or figurative demon or demons. If you've been pointing your finger, blaming others and staying in denial over the true nature of your problem, it is now time to put the right name on it by taking Step One.

Codependents and people with any addiction are sometimes confused at this point and may ask something like this: "There are many things over which I am powerless. Do I name them all in Step One?" The answer is no. Any form of self-centeredness that becomes addictive is always accompanied by plenty of collateral damage. This list may include, but is not limited to anger, resentments, judgmental nature, financial woes, mental and physical health problems, conflicts with family members and others, infidelity, promiscuity, conflicts in the workplace, inability to keep a job, the list goes on.

What people name in Step One is the one thing that brought them to their knees. The associated problems, such as those named above, will later be identified as defects of character and shortcomings and will be dealt with in Steps Four, Five, Six and Seven.

Some individuals may discover that they are cross-addicted. For example, codependency may be accompanied by drug or alcohol use. In these cases, the best advice would be to select the most destructive of their addictions and name it in Step One. Subsequently, they may return to Step One with one or more other addictions or may determine that what they initially thought was an addiction was actually a defect of character or shortcoming.

Take the first step below by filling in the blank and admitting this to yourself at the deepest possible level. The first step reads, "We admitted we were powerless over codependency, that our lives had become unmanageable." By making this confession, we also acknowledge that we will do our best to stop putting this poison (whether it be a substance, behavior or pattern of thinking) into our systems. Fill in the blank below.

Today I admit that I am powerless over _____, that my life has become unmanageable.

_____   _____
Your Signature   **Today's Date**

IN CONCLUSION

Someone once said that addictions are like a ride on a garbage truck; you can get off at any stop along the way or ride it to the dump. Denial keeps us on the garbage truck. Many people arrived at the dump before they even recognized where they were going. Whether or not we've reached the dump, what it takes for us to head in the right direction is the recognition of where we are, why we got there and that our arrival at that destination is the direct result of our own decisions. The good news is that we don't have to stay there. Naming your problem in the first step is the beginning of the road to recovery.

Write down some insights you've gained from this lesson. To gauge your spiritual progress, in the future look back on what you've written here.

_____

_____

_____

_____

_____

_____

End Notes

1. http://www.google.com/?gws_rd=ssl#q=definition+of+prodigal.

2. http://www.merriam-webster.com/dictionary/denial.

3. Dr. Archibald Hart, *Healing Life's Hidden Addictions*, Servant Publications, Vine Books, Ann Arbor, 1990, 67-68.

4. Don Umphrey, *Deliver Us I: Recognizing the Influence of Evil on the Road to Redemption*, Quarry Press, Dallas, 2012, 75.

5. *Hope for Today*, Al-Anon Family Group Headquarters, Inc., Virginia Beach, 1973, 167.

6. Melody Beattie, *Codependent No More*, Hazelden Educational Materials, Center City, 1992, 7.

7. http://www.asktheinternettherapist.com/index.php/content/what-is-an-enabler/

8. http://www.restorativeinterventions.com/wp-content/uploads/2014/11/newsletter-tc.pdf.

9. http://www.livingfree.org/index.php?option=com_content&view=article&id=560:enabling9&catid=33:when-help-is-harmful&Itemid=189.

10. http://www.livingfree.org/index.php?option=com_content&view=article&id=560:enabling9&catid=33:when-help-is-harmful&Itemid=189.

Rethinking Sanity

As a child, I always felt loved and cared for. If there were any problems in my family, they were not apparent to me.

Momma was a kind, generous "stay-at-home mom." She was always there for us, and our paternal grandmother came to our house and helped out a lot.

Daddy cherished my mother and never failed to kiss her, my two sisters, brother and me before leaving for work in the furniture business, initially as a salesman and later as the owner of a store. He was rarely away from the family except for work or when he visited the sick and elderly of our church.

My dad was an elder at our church, and it was evident that God took first place in his life. He lived out the words of Ephesians 6:4 (p. 270), "Fathers, do not provoke your children to anger; but bring them up in the discipline and instruction of the Lord." I don't remember a time when he was not kind, loving and gentle. Even at a young age, I realized how blessed we were and how different we were from my cousins who frequently stayed at our house after their parents divorced.

Home was a safe haven. My childhood was spent happily playing with my siblings, cousins and the neighborhood kids.

We attended every service of the church a few blocks from our home in my birthplace of Russellville, Alabama, and when I was eight, we moved 30 miles to Muscle Shoals, Alabama, and became involved in a church there.

I have many happy memories of friendships that were made through the church—potluck meals together, visiting in the homes of other Christians, home Bible studies, and visiting ailing members and those who were new to our congregation. Because I trusted and respected my parents, a preacher we adored and the other leaders of the church, I accepted everything they said at face value.

We thought people who worshipped the way we did were the only ones going to heaven. This was apparently based on an assumption that we had interpreted the Bible correctly. Excluded from salvation were people who attended churches that reportedly taught "grace only" or "faith only."

What went on within the walls of the church, such as acceptable modes of worship, seemed to receive the greatest emphasis at the churches we attended. Special attention was paid to the church treasury being spent in a way that was deemed as pleasing to God. Forbidden were things not authorized in the Bible, such as the support of children's homes or Christian colleges. Churches with the same name as ours that didn't see eye-to-eye with us on the distribution of church funds were considered as "erring brethren" and likely hell-bound. Included in this category were those who practiced a "social gospel," the ones who supposedly spent their time and the church treasury on "food, fun and frolic."

Though our church could hire a secretary and people to do cleaning and lawn maintenance (neither of which are specified in the Bible), we did not believe in hiring a youth minister or having a youth group. The church was clear in its belief that the church was there for spiritual enrichment and not for the entertainment of children.

Religious Questions

These and several other inconsistencies were increasingly confusing to me but questioning of the church leadership seemed to be discouraged. I also wondered if a youth minister or youth group as found in other churches might have benefitted Kyle and his older brother, Brian, who had left the church.

I had raised my children according to the pattern my parents and teachers instilled in me. We attended every service of the church and participated in all additional activities. I had always listened to the preaching and teaching, took notes, studied my Bible class lessons, and even taught children's Bible classes. I thought of the Bible as our "rule book" and if we could follow the rules, we could be saved.

Despite all of this, I could never truly measure up and doubted my salvation but held out hope that I could get it right before judgment day. I had tried to teach my children to follow the rules, but they were not measuring up to the standard very well, either.

As high school graduation day approached for Kyle's classmates, the associate minister at our church delivered a sermon giving advice to graduates as they ventured into the world. Even though he had been expelled and was not eligible to graduate with his class, Kyle was listed among the graduates. I tried to hide my tears. Though the people at church were surely aware of Kyle's drug problem, just about everyone avoided the topic.

Privately, I talked to our minister about helping Kyle. He was baffled and asked something to this effect: "What would you have me to do about it?"

The elders did not know Kyle personally and had never made an attempt to talk with him. I requested that they seek him out for some face-to-face spiritual counseling and offered to set up a meeting.

Kyle Dis-fellowshipped

Later, after his name had appeared in the newspaper on charges related to possession of marijuana, Kyle received another letter from the elders. This one said he would be dis-fellowshipped from the church if he didn't repent within a certain amount of time. Since he was no longer attending, Kyle didn't care. A few Sundays later Flynn, Casey and I were at church when, much to our embarrassment, it was announced that the church was officially withdrawing fellowship from Kyle.

One member of the church who formerly had a drug problem wrote a personal letter to Kyle. This effort meant little or nothing to Kyle at the time, but it meant a whole lot to me.

In the midst of all this, my involvement in the Al-Anon group continued. Earlier, I had wondered about some of the beliefs of my church, but now started questioning them. For example, why did the church never elaborate on scriptures that were so helpful in daily living and frequently discussed in Al-Anon, such as "So do not worry about tomorrow; for tomorrow will care for itself. Each day has enough trouble of its own" (Matthew 6:34, p. 46)?

I was able to apply this principle as my mother's health continued to deteriorate. Trying to care for her while juggling family responsibilities was wearing me out. Even with family members helping, we still had to pay caregivers. The difference between mother's income and outgoing expenses showed that a financial crisis was coming. It was only possible to stay sane by dealing with it all on a daily basis and trusting God to provide.

Focusing on the present was also of great help in my worries about Kyle and other family matters. I had often lain awake at night contemplating what it would be like to visit Kyle in prison or planning his funeral. I also obsessed about what I might have done differently in raising my children or handling marital conflicts.

I began striving to stop allowing my mind to rewind or fast-forward while staying focused on living in the present.

Al-Anon also emphasized that each member focus on his or her own shortcomings rather than focusing on the faults of others as I had so often seen in church. Why did the church never stress the passage on judging found in Matthew 7:1-5 (p. 47)?

Those in the Al-Anon group seemed to think that God guided and strengthened them in a personal way. This contrasted with a seeming assumption of my religion that I could only move forward spiritually by my own strength and determination.

Other subjects we discussed in meetings such as forgiveness, compassion, peace and humility weren't emphasized in church as much as warnings against such sins as drinking, smoking, sexual sins, immodest dress, dancing and so on, things that were primarily of an outward nature.

I often wished there had been some church lessons on dealing with anger because it seemed to be the primary problem in our home.

In the Al-Anon group we were all considered to be in a process of spiritual growth. "Progress, not perfection" was the goal. It was also stressed that we should allow others the liberty to grow spiritually at their own pace without criticism.

At the end of each Al-Anon meeting, we joined hands and prayed The Lord's Prayer, and we were all united as one.

Having said all of this, please don't get the idea that I believe a 12-step group should take the place of the Lord's church. The purpose of recovery groups is to address specific Step One problems via a very practical spiritual approach. Many people who stopped attending church while acting out in various addictions have rededicated their life to Christ and became faithful church members after joining a recovery group. The idea of seeking a power greater than one's self is also a good start for unbelievers.

There are some people who attend 12-step groups, however, who seem to use their recovery group as church; perhaps the future holds a change of heart for them. (For additional information on this topic, see the Recovery Insight "Victory Over Death," related to 1 Corinthians 15:12-58 in *Journey to Recovery Through Christ: CASA's 12-Step Study Bible*, p. 247.)

An End to Kyle's Denial?

We were warned that addicts had to "hit bottom" and hoped that each incident would bring the inevitable crash. I thought this might occur after one of Kyle's best friends was shot in the head during a drug deal.

Kyle and the rest of the gang congregated at the hospital as the wounded teen hovered near death. They seemed to reflect on the possible consequences of their behavior for a few days. The doctors were unable to remove the bullet that remained deeply imbedded in the boy's brain. Though they couldn't predict whether complications might arise later, he eventually recovered without any obvious effects.

Kyle and the rest of them then returned to business as usual.

Since I had admitted powerlessness over what Kyle and others did with their lives, my job was to keep moving forward in addressing the co-dependency issues that drove me to the brink of insanity. That took me to **STEP TWO ▶ Came to believe that a Power greater than ourselves could restore us to sanity.** (For additional information on Step Two and a listing of Step Reflections related to specific verses, see *Journey to Recovery Through Christ: CASA's 12-Step Study Bible,* pp. 14-15.)

I had always assumed that God had just left us a book of rules to obey and then returned to His throne in heaven. He would eventually come back to judge us on whether we had kept the rules.

Had I been putting God "in a box" by placing limitations on His ability to do things in my life of which I was incapable of doing for myself? Would He actually work with me on a personal level and return me to a place of normalcy, if there was such a place?

I began to rethink my viewpoint of God. I wanted to find out who He was and what He expected.

I was initially uncomfortable with the "Higher Power" concept but could see that it was a good starting point, applying not only to non-believers but also to Christian people like me who needed to evaluate their spiritual beliefs. If anyone could restore my sanity, it would have to be Father God, Jesus Christ and the Holy Spirit as described in the Bible. I certainly didn't have the power or knowledge to do so. My best thinking had gotten me into a miserable predicament!

Don Umphrey's explanation of Step Two applied to me:

> After taking the first step, we can see that through our self-centered behavior, we attempted to put ourselves at the center of the universe by our actions. This was done via our attempts at pleasing ourselves—instead of pleasing God—and manipulating other people to our own ends. Certainly we did not say on a conscious level that we were the biggest, most important being in the universe; nevertheless, we sometimes expected the universe and everything in it to march to the drum we were beating. Thus, in our own way, we may have tried to displace God. The admission of the existence of a power greater than one's self is a step toward humility and a recognition that we have been playing God; it is a step away from self-centeredness and toward God-centeredness.[1]

I had never thought of myself as being self-centered or playing God, but by assuming I had all the answers for everyone else, that's what I was doing. Recovery groups explain insanity as "doing the same thing over and over and expecting different results." I was certainly guilty of that.

A sticking point for some may be the last word of this step: "sanity." By asking people to admit that God could restore them to sanity, someone might reply that they have never been locked in an insane asylum or fitted for a straitjacket. But definitions of insanity also include "extreme foolishness, folly, senselessness, foolhardiness."[2] Based on these definitions, I can honestly say that my previous behavior, especially with my husband, could be labeled as insane. I can think of plenty of other examples, too.

Alcohol (or drugs) can affect the family member in much the same way as it does the alcoholic or addict. As a devotional writer explained:

In Al-Anon I've learned that even without ever taking a drink, I struggle with the effects of the disease of alcoholism. They can rob my life of the joy each day holds. Denial steals from me the ability to see my situation clearly and honestly. Stubborn self-reliance wipes out the guidance and comfort available from my Higher Power. Resentment erodes love and goodwill in my relationship with others. Obsessive worrying raids my willingness to accept and enjoy life as it is. Hope comes in the words of the second step. My Higher Power can restore to me what I once believed to be irrevocably lost—my sanity and serenity.[3]

Even though my husband was not addicted to drugs or alcohol, he had been raised in a home where drinking was prevalent. From the sharing of Al-Anon members, it was becoming clear that this had profoundly affected his perception of the world, along with our relationship and the raising of our children.

Step Two meant opening my mind to the idea that help is available. In the Bible God spoke to people in various ways and orchestrated certain events, but it never occurred to me that He would do that in the here and now. I became ready to open my mind to the possibility that God was a source of power, strength and healing that was available to each person who chooses to seek Him.

My side of the equation is to trust that He is available. That can begin by trusting that these biblical principles, and the 12 steps based on them, could work for me as they have worked for others.

Scripture confirms that finding sanity and serenity are attainable goals. "Be anxious for nothing, but in everything by prayer and supplication with thanksgiving let your requests by made known to God. And the peace of God, which surpasses all comprehension, will guard your hearts and your minds in Christ Jesus" (Philippians 4:6-7, p. 274).

I came to believe that God could restore my sanity regardless of the behavior of others. It was foolish to assume there would ever come a time that everyone would act in such a way that would never cause me stress and worry.

As written in Al-Anon literature, "…we *do* have a power, derived from God, and that is the power to change our own lives. *Acceptance* does not mean submission to a degrading situation. It means accepting the fact of a situation and then deciding what we will do about it."[4]

As I contemplated attending another church, primarily seeking a place my youngest son might grow spiritually, I decided to study the Bible along with my Al-Anon meditations. Of course, I wanted to find a church that aligned with the Scripture.

New Perspectives

In the past I had relied on the judgment of men who claimed to have interpreted the Bible correctly. With all the lengthy, complex explanations that we heard at the church we attended, I had assumed that only educated, spiritual giants could understand biblical principles and present it to us.

It now seemed logical that if a common person could not understand the Bible, then the majority of people could be easily deceived. It became crucial to know what I believed!

I had only read through the Bible once before (out of a sense of duty) in my 45-plus years of life, but managed to read through the New Testament twice within a few weeks. I was quite perplexed when my search raised more questions than answers.

I decided to talk to a long-time friend from our church who had always seemed very spiritually minded. She and her husband had moved to a town about an hour away and reportedly had gone "off the deep end" by attending a religious group with different beliefs than ours.

She told me that the pain of some intense marital problems had prompted her to seek solutions via prayer and Bible study, leading her to reach some new conclusions about God's truth in her life.

Rather than trying to persuade me to join her new church, her advice was, "Forget everything you have learned; start over and just listen to God." It seemed like a sensible idea. If God did guide us personally, perhaps He would show me what I had missed.

I had no idea that I was on the verge of making the greatest discovery of my life and embarking on an amazing spiritual journey.

Biblical Questions for Self-Examination

THAT SINKING FEELING

Use the *Journey to Recovery Through Christ: CASA's 12-Step Study Bible* or any other version of the *New American Standard Bible* © 1995 to fill in the blanks in biblical passages below.

1. a. When Peter tried to walk on water, he didn't have ice skates and the lake wasn't frozen. **But seeing the wind, he became** _____... (Matthew 14:30, p. 59).

    b. Describe how you started sinking and were filled with fear when your "higher power" was your Step One problem. _____

       _____

2. a. What does Peter have in common with the prodigal son? As a reminder, see Luke 15:11-32 (p. 133-134).

       _____

       _____

    b. What does Janet have in common with Peter and the prodigal son? _____

       _____

       _____

THIS IS CRAZY

3. Which better describes the situation of the prodigal son? (circle one)

    1) He first lost his sense and then his cents.

    2) He first lost his cents and then his sense.

4. a. As quoted by Janet, what are some words used to define insanity. _____

    _____

    _____

    b. Thinking of insanity in these terms, describe how they apply to the prodigal son. _____

    _____

    _____

    c. Give some examples of insanity in Janet's life. _____

    _____

    _____

5. Name some examples of how insanity applies to some attitudes and actions in your past . _____

    _____

    _____

6. "Repeating the same behaviors and expecting different results." This is one way people in recovery programs sometimes define insanity.

    a. Give examples of how this definition of insanity has been true in your life. _____

    _____

    _____

    _____

7. a. David wrote, **The fool has said in his heart, "**_____ _____ _____ _____**"**
        (Psalm 14:1, p. 355).

    b. Thinking of the definitions of insanity discussed above, why would a fool say this? _____

    _____

    _____

    c. In what ways did you think and act as if there were no God?_____

    _____

    _____

    _____

    _____

MOMENTS OF CLARITY

8. After people take the first step, they will often be able to put aside some of their denial and see themselves much more clearly. This is known as a moment of clarity; it enables them to start heading in the right direction.

    a. Go back to Matthew 14:30 (p. 59) and fill in the blanks pertaining to Peter. **But seeing the wind, he became frightened, and beginning to sink, he cried out, "_____, _____ _____!"**

    b. Right after the prodigal son realized he was starving to death and powerless, he had his moment of clarity. **"…when he came to his _____, he said, 'How many of _____ _____ hired men have more than enough _____, but I am dying here with _____!'"** (Luke 15:17, p. 133).

    c. How does the moment of clarity for both Peter and the prodigal son relate to Step Two? _____ _____ _____

9. Read about Saul of Tarsus in Acts 9:1-22 (p. 190-191).

    a. **Saul got up from the ground, and though his eyes were open, he could _____ _____; and leading him by the hand, they brought him into Damascus. And he was three days without _____, and neither _____ nor _____** (Acts 9:8-9, p. 190).

    b. What do you think was going through Saul's mind during those three days?_____ _____ _____

    c. What are the indications that Saul had a moment of clarity? _____ _____ _____

10. What led up to Janet's moment of clarity? _____ _____

11. a. Have you had a moment of clarity? (circle one) yes or no

    b. If yes, describe it here. _____ _____ _____ _____

A CHANGE OF MIND

12. a. **The younger of them said to his father, "**_____, _____ _____ _____
     _____ **of the** _____ **that falls to me"** (Luke 15:12, p. 133).

     b. What is the attitude of a son toward his father who goes to his father and asks for his inheritance while his
        father is still alive? _____
        _____
        _____

     c. How does that attitude toward his father compare to the one expressed above by the son in 8.b.?_____
        _____
        _____
        _____

13. a. What was Saul's attitude toward Christians before his moment of clarity? (See Acts 9:1-2, p. 190). _____
        _____
        _____

     b. What was Saul's attitude toward Christians after his moment of clarity? (See Acts 9:10-22, p. 190-191).
        _____
        _____

14. How did Janet's moment of clarity impact her religion and her view of God? _____
     _____
     _____
     _____

15. a. If you answered "yes" to 11.a., how has your moment of clarity impacted your spiritual life?_____
        _____
        _____
        _____

     b. If you answered "no" to 11.a., what do you think it will take for you to have a moment of clarity?_____
        _____
        _____
        _____

OUR SOURCE OF POWER

16. **"For My thoughts are not your thoughts, nor are your ways My ways," declares the Lord. "For as the heavens are higher than the earth, so are My ways higher than your ways and My thoughts than your thoughts"** (Isaiah 55:8-9).

    a. How do these verses apply to your approach to Step Two? _____

    _____

    _____

    b. **In the beginning God created the heavens and the earth** (Genesis 1:1).

    c. Have you ever done anything like what God did in Genesis 1:1? (circle one)

        1) Yes

        2) No

        3) Please don't ask such obvious questions.

        4) Okay, okay, I'm getting the point.

        (If you answered "Yes" to the above question, seek help immediately.)

    d. With that established, how much power do you have in relationship to God's power?_____

    _____

    _____

    _____

17. As detailed in 2 Samuel 11, King David had an affair with Bathsheba, the wife of one of his best soldiers. This was Uriah the Hittite who was away at war. Discovering that Bathsheba was pregnant, David launched a plot that would make Uriah think he was the father. Failing at this, David had Uriah killed, and he remained in denial about his sin until the Nathan, a prophet, did an intervention on him that is detailed in 2 Samuel 12:1-15.

    Once he was out of denial, David must have been thinking about God's power and his relationship with God when he wrote Psalm 51 (pp. 390-391). Read it and respond to the questions below.

    a. What is David seeking in Psalm 51:1 (p. 390)? _____

    _____

    b. What are two characteristics of God named by David in verse one?

        1) _____

        2) _____

c. What does David ask God to do for him in Psalm 51:2 (p. 390)? _____

_____

_____

d. In Psalm 51:7(p. 390)? _____

_____

_____

e. In Psalm 51:8 (p. 390)? _____

_____

_____

f. In Psalm 51:9 (p. 390)? _____

_____

_____

g. In Psalm 51:10 (p. 390)? _____

_____

_____

h. In Psalm 51:11 (p. 390)? _____

_____

i. In Psalm 51:12 (p. 390)? _____

_____

j. In Psalm 51:14 (p. 390)? _____

_____

k. In Psalm 51:15 (p. 390)? _____

_____

l. Quite clearly, David knew who had the power in his relationship with God. David knew there was nothing he could do (such as offering sacrifices) that would restore his relationship with God. (See Psalm 51:16, pp. 390-391). What did David know was his starting point in re-establishing a relationship with God, a Power greater than himself? **The sacrifices of God are a** _____ _____ ; **a** _____ **and a** _____ _____ ... (Psalm 51:17, p. 391).

m. Based on Psalm 51, what do you most need to apply to your life from David's prayer about God's power? Starting with what you think is the most important, list five things from his prayer that you desire in your life.

1) _____

2) _____

3) _____

4) _____

5) _____

OUR TRUE NATURE

18. When the prodigal son "came to his senses," (Luke 15:17, p. 133) he realized that he had believed his own lie, that he had not been true to himself, that he had been "beside himself." He realized his true nature dictated that he be at home with his father.

    a. **Then God said, "Let Us make man in Our image, according to Our likeness; and let them rule over the fish of the sea and over the birds of the [a]sky and over the cattle and over all the earth, and over every creeping thing that creeps on the earth"** (Genesis 1:26). (a Genesis 1:26 Lit *heavens*)

    b. Based on the passage above, how would you describe your true nature? _____

    _____

    _____

19. a. **The one who does not _____ does not know _____, for _____ is _____** (1 John 4:8, p. 322).

    b. What does this verse tell you about your ideal behavior? _____

    _____

LISTEN

20. a. **The way of a _____ is _____ in his own eyes, but a _____ man is he who listens to _____** (Proverbs 12:15, p. 492).

    b. **_____ to _____ and accept _____, that you may be _____ the rest of your days** (Proverbs 19:20, p. 502).

    c. To learn more about the value of being a good listener, see the Recovery Insights, "Taming the Tongue" on page 308 and "A Time to Listen" on page 476 of *Journey to Recovery: CASA's 12-Step Study Bible.*

    d. Newcomers to recovery programs sometimes hear this: "It's time to take the cotton out of your ears and put it in your mouth."

Does this statement apply to you? Circle one:　True　or　False

(The correct answer is True.)

e. To whom do you need to listen? _____

_____

_____

THE GREAT PHYSICIAN

21.　Read Matthew 9:10-13 (p. 50).

a. How do these verses relate to Step One? _____

_____

_____

b. How do these verses relate to Step Two? _____

_____

c. How do these verses relate to you? _____

_____

THE FIRST COMMANDMENT

22.　a. Here is what God said to the children of Israel after He delivered them from being slaves in Egypt for 400 years. **"I am the Lord your God, who brought you out of the land of Egypt, out of the house of slavery.**[a] **You shall have no other gods**[b] **before Me"** (Exodus 20:2-3). (a Exodus 20:2 Lit *slaves*; b Exodus 20:2 Or *besides Me*).

b. What did God do for the children of Israel? _____

_____

_____

c. To what was God referring when He used the word "gods" (note lower-case letter g)? _____

_____

_____

d. Based on what God said in the First Commandment, what can God do for you in terms of your codependency?

_____

_____

_____

_____

IN CONCLUSION

Though we may not have done this on purpose, we turned our back on God and ran our lives on self-will. This was a form of insanity that put us on a crash course with reality. We started recognizing this after landing in our own personal pigpen (or at least getting close enough to smell it). Since we are made in God's image and He is our Creator, we recognize that not only does He have the power to help us but that He loves us and wants to help us. By taking Step Two, we embark on a new way of living. We start putting ourselves in a position to receive God's blessings as we make every possible effort to stop indulging ourselves in our Step One problem.

I have now come to believe God and His Son Jesus Christ are a Power greater than myself with the power to restore me to sanity. (circle one)   yes   or   no

_____   _____
              Your Signature   **Today's Date**

Write down some insights you've gained from this lesson. To gauge your spiritual progress, in the future look back on what you've written here.

_____

_____

_____

_____

_____

End Notes

1. Don Umphrey, *12 Steps to a Closer Walk with God, Third Edition: A Guide for Small Groups*, Quarry Press, Dallas, 2004, 37-38.
2. http://www.dictionary.com/browse/insanity.
3. *Hope for Today*, Al-Anon Family Group Headquarters, Inc., Virginia Beach, 1973, 12.
4. *Hope for Today*, Al-Anon Family Group Headquarters, Inc., Virginia Beach, 1973, 86.

Seeking God's Truth

Though Kyle had escaped the confines of home, he continued to involve us in his life from time-to-time. He dropped in briefly for holiday family gatherings and even called to ask us to pick him up for church once or twice.

He decided to go back to school in the fall and finish his senior year, which would take only one semester. An ounce of hope flared up briefly, but he fell back into the same pattern of tardiness and absences and quit within a month. It seemed like the original Kyle was still in there somewhere and wanting to break free, but his new lifestyle was holding him back.

Bloodied and bruised from a fight, he stopped by early one morning requesting that I take him to the emergency room. He said that as he was leaving his cousin's apartment late the previous night, someone had assaulted him for no apparent reason. By this time, I knew that if his explanation didn't seem reasonable, there was probably more to the story.

I told him that based on his daily choices, he would have to learn to deal with these situations on his own. I refused to take him.

Love normally dictates that we help when our loved ones are sick or injured. This "tough love" felt unnatural and caused me to feel tremendous guilt. It took a giant leap of faith to relinquish my own judgment and trust the advice and experience of Al-Anon members.

It is doubtful I could have followed through if it had been a serious injury, but my sponsor's experiences had strengthened my resolve and courage. At one point, her drug-addicted daughter was hospitalized for several days. Having already lived through one crisis after another created by the daughter, my sponsor refused to go to the hospital. Losing the support of her last ally turned out to be the young woman's turning point.

I had no expectations that it would be the same for Kyle in this particular situation, but maybe it was another step downward that would lead to his ultimate surrender. In this case the best way up was down.

Though Kyle's formal education had ended for the time being, mine was just beginning. I was determined to find out exactly what the Bible said. For the first time ever, I determined to test the religious doctrine I had been taught. I prayed before beginning to read the New Testament again and asked God to guide me in understanding whatever important points I'd been missing.

"But if any of you lacks wisdom, let him ask of God, who gives to all generously and without reproach, and it will be given to him" (James 1:5, p. 307). This was a promise of God I had never taken personally.

It also propelled me into **STEP THREE ▶ Made a decision to turn our will and our lives over to the care of God as we understood Him.** (For additional information on Step Three and a listing of Step Reflections related to specific verses, see *Journey to Recovery Through Christ: CASA's 12-Step Study Bible*, pp. 16-17).

When I opened my Bible that morning at the kitchen table, it was as if the scriptures were illuminated, almost as if I were wearing a new pair of glasses. I found it fascinating that even when Jesus was first conceived, prophecies were being fulfilled and continued through each phase of His life.

The words and actions of the apostles took on a new meaning as they shared their experiences with the living Christ.

The horror that Jesus went through at the cross was heart-wrenching, and He dreaded the mission that God had set before Him. Yet Jesus followed through because of His love for His people, even though most of the sinners for whom He died were oblivious to the meaning of what occurred that day.

Throughout the Bible, the theme of love leaped out at me. "A new commandment I give to you, that you love one another, even as I have loved you, that you also love one another. By this all men will know that you are My disciples, if you have love for one another" (John 13:34-35, p. 169). This scripture seems like it should have been number one on our list of identifying marks of a scriptural church, yet it was not all that familiar to me.

I hungrily tried to absorb it all, even carrying my Bible with me in the car so I could read a few verses while stopped at the train tracks or stalled in traffic. I read through the New Testament in a week and faced the shocking revelation: "It's all about *Jesus!*"

Though desperately wanting to call my zealous friend who had told me "unlearn everything" and share my discovery, I decided not to be influenced by anyone for a while but to just continue with God as my teacher. I immediately started reading through the New Testament again.

What's Most Important?

In church certain scriptures had been emphasized repeatedly. They were based on what was handed down from previous generations as the five-point plan of salvation: hear, believe, repent, confess and be baptized.

Certainly, these things are important, but confessing to a church that Jesus is the son of God and being baptized are both things that may be observed by people. Believing and confessing also occur in one's heart where only God can see. "…if you confess with your mouth Jesus as Lord, and believe in your heart that God raised him from the dead, you will be saved; for with the heart a person believes, resulting in righteousness, and with the mouth he confesses, resulting in salvation" (Romans 10:9-10, p. 226).

Faith is another thing that only God can measure. As it turns out, this word (faith) may be found 458 times in the *NIV* Bible and 378 in the *NASB*.[1]

In a scripture that especially struck a nerve, Jesus accused the Pharisees of hypocrisy. The Lord quoted Isaiah when saying, "'THIS PEOPLE HONORS ME WITH THEIR LIPS, BUT THEIR HEART IS FAR AWAY FROM ME. BUT IN VAIN DO THEY WORSHIP ME, TEACHING AS DOCTRINES THE PRECEPTS OF MEN.' Neglecting the commandment of God, you hold to the tradition of men" (Mark 7:6-8, p. 90).

This was the result of the Pharisees lavishly donating money to God in the sight of others while refusing to care for their own elderly parents. Although it was a somewhat different scenario, our church refused to organize a visitation group to see that the needs of the elderly were being filled because this was not specifically commanded in the Bible to be done in this way.

The *New American Standard Bible* includes the phrases "do not fear" 57 times and "do not be afraid" 46 times, often from the lips of Jesus Christ.[2] Plus, there are many lessons dealing with the dangers of fear that paralyzes people into inaction, such as the parable of the talents (see Matthew 25:14-30, p. 74) and the children of Israel refusing to enter the Promised Land (Numbers 13 and 14).

Fear is the polar opposite of faith.

I could see that my mother lived with numerous irrational fears, and I had followed in her footsteps. Why weren't lessons about fear ever mentioned at church?

Jesus' parable of the Pharisee and the tax collector was told "to some people who trusted in themselves that they were righteous, and viewed others with contempt" (Luke 18:9, p. 136). At our church we spent a lot of time talking about us being right and everyone else being wrong. How did we conclude that we were the only ones going to Heaven? Did God tell this to someone or was it a conclusion based on following a man-made check-list?

After reading with my eyes opened for the first time, I was absolutely certain God would not have wanted us to interpret the Bible in such a selective fashion.

Our family began to visit other congregations.

God As We Understood Him

When I first encountered Step Three, the phrase "God as we understood Him" was offensive to me. Christians viewing the steps for the first time often have similar thoughts because the wording seems to conjure up images of people creating false gods in their own image. Both then and now my belief was/is that the God of the Bible is the only true God.

One man said he picked the radiator in his apartment as his "higher power" because at least it continued to function—it turned on and shut off when it needed to. Ridiculous!

Thinking about the "higher power" concept over a period of time, however, I came to see that it was beneficial. It can be used as a starting point for people with any religious background, even those who have never stepped foot in a church. After all, people can't understand that to which they have never been exposed.

It also became obvious that the concept was helpful to someone who had been going to church all of her life, like me. You can see that when I started truly seeking God with an open mind, my blinders started being removed.

As I awakened to the spiritual, it was as if I was seeing nature for the first time. I was intrigued as to how God had programmed the tiny brains of insects to fulfill specific roles. I stopped to examine them and to "smell the roses" along my daily walk, marveling at the design and delicacy of plants and flowers.

As I comprehended the idea of grace, I understood that my powerlessness over worry and my inability to solve the problems of others was rooted in a belief system that left me dangling by my own willpower. Seeking to put God at the helm of my life, my attitude gradually changed from bitterness and resentment to having greater compassion.

It gave me great comfort to know He could do the same for Kyle, Flynn and others.

I was overwhelmed with gratitude for all of God's blessings, especially for Jesus and His sacrificial offering for us. I had taken so much for granted! I wanted to pass this spiritual message on to others, but I knew that it was important that they see Christ through me. My efforts at improving my attitude and relationships were driven by a higher motivation.

Through my early stages of growth, I started taking to heart the Al-Anon slogan "Live and Let Live."

Though Al-Anon is crucial in dealing with addictions on a daily basis, it was proving to be quite helpful in other areas of my life. My fears had eased about caring for my mother. We began to look for options rather than full-time sitters. I was praying and trusting God with the outcome. I treasured the time mom and I spent just sitting on the porch or watching our favorite television shows together.

After searching all the long-term care facilities available, we were growing concerned because none of them seemed like the solution due to her mental state. We had one more stop, which we hadn't considered an option because of the distance involved and other factors. The moment we walked into the private assisted-living home and met the owner, we knew it was the place for mom.

The detailed requests I had petitioned God for—to find a place that seemed more like her home—had been answered. She could see the people in the kitchen from her room, which helped ease her panic about being alone. The owner resembled an old friend of ours. Even the wallpaper border in her room was similar to her bedroom.

As I locked the door each night, the uneasy feeling was still present of Kyle being out in the darkness (in more ways than one) rather than safe at home. People do go to prison and even die as the result of irresponsible and sinful acts, even though people are praying for them. Yet a family might find more of a sense of peace and closure with death than with some other tragic circumstance. It could all even be part of some greater plan that I could not fathom.

It was also possible and highly probable with God in control that a miraculous outcome may be just as likely as a tragic one. Author Barbara Johnson, in her book, *Stick a Geranium in Your Hat and Be Happy* (Thomas Nelson Publishers, Nashville, 2004), tells of the shock when her son reappeared on Mother's Day after disappearing into the gay lifestyle for 11 years. He came to ask her forgiveness and let her know he had turned his life over to God.

Rather than lying awake letting my imagination run wild with every worst case scenario, I prayed for God's protection and guidance for Kyle in detailed requests. One prayer was that if he were arrested again, it would be in a neighboring county where it was reported that the probation officer enforced the rules (unlike the one in our county). Yet I always prayed that God's will be done, realizing finally that my judgment was quite limited.

Made a Decision

It is important to note that Step Three is not about turning one's life over to God, per se. (That occurs in Step Eleven). It is about *making a decision* to do that, a decision that is likely to be taken back on a regular basis due to long-time habits of running on self-will.

"What a relief it is to finally make that decision and to realize that I don't have to do or fix everything," [3] wrote an Al-Anon devotional writer, and I identified completely.

"Making a decision" was not something I did once and accomplished it. It was something I had to do regularly by making a decision to have a "quiet time" with God each morning by reading from both the Bible and my Al-Anon devotional to glean whatever insight I needed for the day. It also involved daily prayer for guidance in whatever situation that arose and asking for God's help in my responses and reactions to others as I went about my daily routine.

"Spot prayers" were also helpful throughout the day when I needed an extra measure of patience, kindness, tolerance or boldness.

In case you were starting to wonder whether I viewed myself as St. Janet of Assisi, I can assure you that my actions proved otherwise. Self-will often crept back into my life, and I wasn't even aware of it.

I would still get caught up in obsessing about the self-destructive behaviors of other people and how I might fix them.

For example, one of my family members held deeply to their legalistic beliefs. I continually exchanged letters and emails with him trying to convince him I was right in my interpretation of the scriptures. Our continuing argument about it accomplished very little, and I discovered it only worsened my tension which aggravated my back and neck pain.

Some mornings I might get up late and skip my morning devotional. Then, before breakfast, Flynn might say or do something that irritated me, and I would respond in a way that was not beneficial to our relationship.

When we started attending a new congregation, they would announce some activities that I had been indoctrinated to believe were not according to scripture. I would start to feel a bit uncomfortable and wonder if I should express my concerns to the elders. Instead, I vowed to hold my tongue. As it turned out, many things frowned upon at our previous church, such as youth rallies, turned out to be very positive from a spiritual standpoint.

For the first time in my adult life, I experienced periods of peace when I was able to trust God with the outcome and to simply wait as His plan unfolded.

Biblical Questions for Self-Examination

OUR SOURCE OF STRENGTH

Use the *Journey to Recovery Through Christ: CASA's 12-Step Study Bible* or any other version of the *New American Standard Bible* © 1995 to fill in the blanks in biblical passages below.

1. a. Jesus said, **"I am the _____, you are the _____; he who abides in Me and I in him, he bears _____ _____, for apart from Me you can do _____. If anyone does not abide in Me, he is thrown away as a _____ and dries up; and they gather them, and cast them into the _____ and they are _____"** (John 15:5-6, p. 170).

    b. In the passage above, you can see what happens to a branch when it stays attached to the vine. Then you can see what happens to a branch that becomes detached. As one of the branches, give three examples from your own life of times when you knew you were attached to the vine.

    1) _____

    2) _____

    3) _____

c. Give three examples of when you were detached from the vine.

1) _____

2) _____

3) _____

d. From one of the examples in 1.c., describe how you got detached and how you recognized that you were detached from your source of spiritual strength. _____

_____

_____

_____

_____

_____

A NEW PAIR OF GLASSES

2. a. What was Janet's initial reaction to the "God as we understood Him" wording found in Step Three? _____

_____

_____

b. What was your longer-term reaction to that wording? _____

_____

3. a. Janet wrote this: "I was determined to find out exactly what the Bible said. For the first time ever I determined to test the religious doctrine I had been taught. I prayed before beginning to read the New Testament again and asked God to guide me in understanding whatever important points I'd been missing." List at least five things that Janet discovered as a result of this quest.

1) _____

_____

2) _____

_____

3) _____

_____

4) _____

_____

5) _____

_____

LOST AND FOUND

4. a. In our studies of Step One and Step Two, we drew upon Jesus' Parable of the Prodigal Son from Luke 15: 11-32 (p. 133-134). As a review, describe the son's circumstances when he took Step One. (See Luke 15:16, p. 133). _____

    _____

    b. What do you think was going through his mind when he took Step Two? (See Luke 15:17, p. 133). _____

    _____

    _____

    c. As a review from the Step Two lesson, what was the difference in the son's attitude "before" and "after"? ___

    _____

    _____

    d. The son said, "'**I will get up and** _____ _____ _____ _____...'" (Luke 15:18, p. 133).

    e. In what way does the quotation immediately above parallel Step Three? _____

    _____

    _____

WHAT GOD THINKS ABOUT YOU

5. Not only does Jesus' story tell about the attitude of the lost son, but it also demonstrates the attitude of his father. In this parable the father represents God.

    a. "**So he got up and came to his father. But while he was still a** _____ _____

    _____**, his father saw him and felt** _____ _____

    _____ ..." (Luke 15:20, p. 133).

    b. Which more accurately reflects the attitude of the father? (circle one)

    1) If that ingrate son ever came home, the father was planning to make him beg at the door like the dirty pig that he was.

    2) The father really missed his son and was watching for him in the distance.

    c. The father "**...ran and embraced him and** _____ **him**" (Luke 15:20, p. 133).

    d. Which more accurately reflects the attitude of the father? (circle one)

    1) The father in this story was a Mafia godfather and was running to give his son the kiss of death.

    2) The father wanted the son to beg at the door for a few hours and really learn his lesson before the door would be opened for him.

3) No matter what his son had done in the past, the father loved him anyway.

e. **"But the father said to his slaves, 'Quickly bring out the _____ _____ and put it on him, and put a _____ on his hand and _____ on his feet; and bring the fattened calf, kill it, and let us _____ and _____;'"** (Luke 15:22-23, p. 133).

f. Which more accurately reflects the attitude of the father? (circle one)

1) The father fitted the son with tight-fitting shoes to rub blisters on his feet and was planning to force-feed him spoiled leftovers.

2) What his father gave him were symbols of the young man's restoration as a son and heir, and he threw a banquet in his honor.

g. **"…for this son of mine was _____ and has _____ to _____ again; he was _____ and has been _____"** (Luke 15:24, p. 133).

h. In what way do you think that Janet identifies with the prodigal son in her new understanding of Father God?

_____

_____

_____

_____

i. In what way do you identify? _____

_____

_____

_____

_____

MORE REMINDERS OF GOD'S ATTITUDE

6. a. Turning back to another familiar passage, Peter started sinking when he switched his focus from the solution (Jesus) to the problem (the windy seas). He then cried out to Jesus for help. Here's what happens next: _____ **Jesus stretched out His _____ and took _____ of him, and said to him, "You of little faith, why did you doubt?"** (Matthew 14:31, p. 59).

b. Which more accurately reflects the attitude of Jesus? (circle one)

1) Jesus wanted to teach Peter a lesson for his weak faith by letting him nearly drown before saving him.

2) Jesus didn't want Peter to even get his feet wet and rescued him right away.

7. a. In the words of Jesus, **"Or what man is there among you who, when his _____ asks for a _____, will give him a _____? Or if he asks for a _____, he will not give him a _____, will he? If you then, being evil, know how to give _____ _____ to your children, how much more will your _____ who is in _____ give _____ is _____ to those who ask Him!"** (Matthew 7:9-11, p. 47)

    b. Give examples of gifts from God that you believe Jesus would define as "good gifts?" _____
    _____
    _____

    c. Name some of the gifts that you would like to receive from God. _____
    _____

8. a. Name three fears and/or anxieties that you have today.

    1) _____

    2) _____

    3) _____

    b. **Therefore humble yourselves under the _____ _____ of _____, that He may exalt you at the proper time, casting all your _____ on Him, because He _____ for you** (1 Peter 5:6-7, p. 315).

    c. **Cast your _____ upon the _____ and He will _____ you; He will never allow the _____ to be _____** (Psalm 55:22, p. 393).

    d. **When I am _____, I will put my trust in You. In _____, whose word I praise, in God I have put my_____; I shall not be _____. What can mere man do to me?** (Psalm 56:3-4, p. 394).

    e. Give specific examples of how you can apply the verses from 8.b., 8.c., and 8.d. to the fears/anxieties you named in 8.a.

    _____
    _____
    _____
    _____

9. a. **No** _____ **has overtaken you but such as is** _____ **to man;**

   and _____ **is faithful, who will not allow you to be** _____ _____

   what you are able, but with the _____ **will provide the** _____ **of**

   _____ **also, so that you will be able to** _____ **it** (1 Corinthians 10:13,

   p. 240).

   b. Thinking about the biblical passage in 9.a., what do you learn in regard to having thoughts, feelings or

   situations that seem to be more than you can handle? _____

   _____

   _____

   _____

   _____

   c. What do you learn from the verse in 10.a. about being tempted to return to your Step One problem? _____

   _____

MADE A DECISION

10. Even though we have recognized God as a power greater than ourselves and made a decision to put Him at the

    helm of our lives, self-will can frequently divert us. As a result, our decision is one that we may take back with

    alarming regularity. The fill-ins below are guides to helping you stay on course.

    a. **Hear, my son, and** _____ **my sayings and the** _____ **of your** _____

    will be _____ (Proverbs 4:10, p. 481).

    b. Have you ever seen years taken away from someone's life because that person was not following the right

    path? (circle one) yes or no

    c. If yes, describe it here. _____

    _____

    _____

11. a. **I have directed you in the way of** _____; **I have led you in upright** _____.

    When you _____, **your** _____ **will not be** _____; **And**

    if you _____, **you will not** _____. **Take hold of** _____;

    do not let go. _____ **her, for she is your** _____ (Proverbs 4:11-13, p. 481).

    b. **But the path of the** _____ **is like the** _____ **of** _____, **that shines**

    _____ **and** _____ **until the full of** _____ (Proverbs 4:18, p. 482).

c. What sticks out in your mind when thinking about the path described in 11.a. and 11.b.? _____

_____

_____

12. a. **The way of the _____ is like _____; They do not _____ over what they _____** (Proverbs 4:19, p. 482).

b. Describe some times in your past when you did not know what was causing you to stumble through life.

_____

_____

_____

_____

13. a. **Do not enter the _____ of the _____ and do not _____ in the way of _____ men. Avoid it, do not _____ by it; turn _____ from it and _____ on** (Proverbs 4:14-15, p. 481).

b. Who are the people described in these two verses? Describe how they might be some of your friends and associates who are still acting out in their addictions.

_____

_____

_____

14. The verses of Proverbs 4:20-27 (p. 482) tell how to stay on the straight path. Starting with the one you believe is the most important, then second most important, etc., pick out five of these and list them below.

1) _____

2) _____

3) _____

4) _____

5) _____

TURNING IT OVER

In addition to staying on the right path, how else might you go about putting yourself in God's hands?

15. a. **Be _____ for nothing, but in everything by _____ and _____ with _____let your requests be made known to _____. And the _____ _____ _____, which surpasses**

all comprehension, will guard your _____ **and your** _____ **in** _____
_____ (Philippians 4:6-7, p. 274).

b. What have you been anxious about? _____

c. What does this passage say to do about this? _____

d. What will you receive? _____

16. (a) _____ **always; (b)** _____ **without ceasing; (c) in everything give**
_____ **; for this is** _____ _____ **for you in Christ**
Jesus (1 Thessalonians 5:16-18, p. 281). Comment in the spaces below as to how you can improve in each
of these three areas as a part of Step Three.

a. _____

_____

b. _____

_____

c. _____

_____

17. a. **Finally, brethren, whatever is** _____ **, whatever is** _____ **, whatever is**
_____ **, whatever is** _____ **, whatever is** _____ **, whatever**
is of good _____ **, if there is any** _____ **and if anything worthy**
of _____ **, dwell on these things** (Philippians 4:8, p. 274).

b. **Set your mind on the things** _____ **, not on the things that are on** _____
(Colossians 3:2, p. 277).

c. Be specific in describing what was mostly on your mind when you were indulging in your Step One problem?

_____

_____

_____

d. How has that changed since you took Step One? _____

_____

_____

e. Thinking about the passages in 17.a. and 17.b., name some ways that your thought processes could still be
improved. _____

_____

_____

18. a. **All Scripture is _____ by _____ and profitable for**
     (a) _____, for (b) _____, for (c) _____, (d) for training
     in _____; so that the man of God may be adequate, equipped for every good
     work (2 Timothy 3:16-17, p. 290).

     b. Think about the three words and one short phrase that you put in the blanks a through d above. Describe how
        you can use the Bible to apply each of those to yourself.

        a. _____

        _____

        b. _____

        _____

        c. _____

        _____

        d. _____

        _____

19. How has your understanding of God changed as a result of working Steps One, Two and Three and studying God's
     word? _____

     _____

     _____

     _____

20. Contrast your initial reaction to the Step Three wording of "God as we understood Him" that you wrote in 2.b. to
     your current understanding of that wording. _____

     _____

     _____

PRACTICING TOUGH LOVE

21. a. Janet wrote that she had refused to be an enabler of Kyle and practiced "tough love" when he came to her
        with a phony story about how he had been injured and requesting that she take him to the hospital. Was her
        refusal to take him (circle one)   difficult   or   easy   for her?

b. In the Parable of the Prodigal Son (see Luke 15:11-13, p. 133), did the father (circle one)

1) Run down the road in an attempt to prevent his son from leaving

2) Journey to the far country to try to persuade his son to come home so that he would not have to suffer the consequences of his poor decisions

3) Stay at home with hopes that his son would return

c. If the father had run down the road in an attempt to prevent the son from leaving, what do you think the son would have said to him? _____

_____

d. If the father did journey to the far country while the son was in the midst of "loose living" and tried to beg the son to come home, what do you think the son would have said to him? _____

_____

_____

e. What did it finally take for the prodigal son to realize he had made a mistake by leaving home? _____

_____

_____

22. a. Read Hebrews 12:5-11 (p. 305) and describe how these verses apply to tough love.

_____

_____

b. Read 2 Timothy 4:1-5 (p. 291) and describe how these verses apply to tough love.

_____

_____

23. a. How does practicing tough love benefit the loved one of the addicted person? _____

_____

_____

b. How might an addicted person be helped by being on the receiving end of tough love from a loved one?

_____

_____

IN CONCLUSION

Our understanding of God is starting to expand. We now know that not only does God have the power to help us, but He is anxious for us to come to Him. Considering where we have come from, we recognize that self-will often will divert us from being closer to God. So we don't expect perfection. But now having made this decision, we need to renew our decision when we discover that we have lost focus and started to stray.

I have made a decision to turn my will and my life over to the care of God as I understand him. (circle one) yes or no

_____   _____
Your Signature   **Today's Date**

Write down some insights you've gained from this lesson. To gauge your spiritual progress, several months from now look back on what you've written here.

_____

_____

_____

_____

_____

End Notes
_____

1. http://www.ask.com/world-view/many-times-word-faith-used-bible-76f634e381e600fd.
2. http://www.reference.com/world-view/many-times-bible-say-fear-7bca141376d0ed13.
3. *Hope for Today*, Al-Anon Family Group Headquarters, Virginia Beach, 2002, 365.

Taking Inventory

It had been my dream to see a big write-up about Kyle in the sports section of the newspaper such as "player of the year" or as an NBA draft pick. Instead, I picked up our local paper one morning to see Kyle's picture plastered on the front page after being arrested for drug trafficking with a couple of his friends.

My prayer for him to be arrested in a neighboring county had been answered in short order, but it was not one in which I rejoiced. I had hoped a few days in jail might be a chance for him to "sober up," but this was a serious charge which carried a mandatory three-year prison sentence.

Kyle's friends had bailed him out, and he called to warn me that it would be in the newspaper. My hopes of a small, obscure article were dashed. Now everyone would know the seriousness of Kyle's drug involvement.

It was still incomprehensible that my little boy who once loved the Muppet Babies, excelled in every sport and attracted friends like a magnet, might actually end up in prison.

How could we have gone so horribly wrong?

The "Three C's" were continually stressed in Al-Anon: "You didn't cause it. You can't control it. You can't cure it."

I accepted that the addiction was beyond my ability to control or cure, but I wrestled with the cause of his problems. Pondering the words of the psalmist, "Like arrows in the hands of a warrior, so are the children of one's youth" (Psalm 127:4, p. 461), I wondered if I had played a part in pointing him in the wrong direction. And now that the arrow had left the bow, was there no stopping it?

A part of my grief came from my new understanding of the Bible. I had taught my children that we must belong to a church that was correct on each doctrinal point and to live by an impossible moral code by our own strength, yet with no absolute certainty of eternal security.

Rather than wondering why two children had strayed from that belief, I could only wonder "why not?" I had blamed my husband for being absorbed in work and television and not taking time for home Bible study with the family. Now I wondered what had prevented me from setting the example of studying for myself and setting aside a time to teach them whether or not he participated.

Counter to these obsessive thoughts about the past was the fact that I could not go back to undo past mistakes, but I could take steps to improve my present situation and future by taking Step Four.

It was becoming glaringly obvious that I had been focused on trying to point out and correct the faults of other people and then rescue them from their self-made messes. While doing this, I was shockingly blind to my own faults.

STEP FOUR ▶ Made a searching and fearless moral inventory of ourselves. (For additional information on Step Four and a listing of Step Four Reflections related to specific verses, see *Journey to Recovery Through Christ: CASA's 12-Step Study Bible*, pages 18-20.)

A personal inventory must be searching in order to probe deep enough to locate spiritual problems that may be lurking well below the surface. Fearlessness enables people to face painful aspects of their pasts that might arouse emotional pain or feelings of guilt or anger. It must be moral in that it necessitates delineating right from wrong.

The Bible encourages and requires self-examination.

"For if anyone thinks he is something when he is nothing, he deceives himself. But each one must examine his own work, and then he will have *reason for* boasting in regard to himself alone, and not in regard to another. For each one will bear his own load." (Galatians 6:3-5, p. 264).

"But a man must examine himself, and in so doing he is to eat of the bread and drink of the cup" (1 Corinthians 11:28, p. 242).

Theodore W. Jennings, Jr. wrote the following that applies to the self-examination process:

> (This) must not become a random recitation of imagined faults but instead must be a sober assessment of our condition... Quite simply we are concerned with the particular ways we resist the freedom for which Christ has set us free...the ways with which we are continually at war with the summons to freedom, the ways we are bound up by resentment, envy, and enmity.[1]

According to AA literature,

> These instincts so necessary for our existence, often far exceed their proper functions. Powerfully, blindly, many times subtly, they drive us, dominate us, and insist upon ruling our lives. Our desires for sex, for material and emotional security, and for an important place in society often tyrannize us. When thus out of joint, man's natural desires cause him great trouble, practically all the trouble there is. No human being, however good, is exempt from these troubles... Step Four is our vigorous and painstaking effort to discover what these liabilities in each of us have been, and are. We want to find exactly how, when and where our natural desires have warped us. We wish to look squarely at the unhappiness this has caused others and ourselves.[2]

Though we are all defective to some extent, we are each blessed with unique talents, abilities, and spiritual traits. Our inventory must also include assets, lest we judge ourselves too harshly. Assets can be used as a foundation to build upon.

Recognizing My Faults

I began my personal inventory by filling out an inventory questionnaire booklet designed by Al-Anon Family Group Headquarters called "Blueprint for Progress." It was a thin paperback booklet with "yes and no" questions on areas of life such as attitudes, responsibilities, self-worth, love, maturity and other character traits. In the "Attitudes" chapter, there were questions such as: "Am I realistic about my abilities and limitations?" "Do I avoid judging the alcoholic's motives and behavior?" "Can I take a stand and express my opinions diplomatically?" "Am I pleasant to my loved one's friends?"[3]

At the end of the booklet, we were to summarize our positive and negative behaviors and other conclusions we derived from the questions. Putting the answers to the questions in writing was therapeutic and beneficial to me in understanding my past and how it had affected my adult life. I was able to recognize patterns of behavior by looking back at previous answers.

According to an author dedicated to recovery work, "It is strongly recommended that this step be written. As you start to write about your past, many related things will come to mind. You'll find yourself saying, 'I hadn't thought of that in years.' By writing, we take something from abstract in our minds to the concrete." [4]

This inventory caused me to have to think seriously about my feelings and attitudes about different people in my life. Though I could answer positively to many questions, there were numerous others that suggested needed improvement and patterns that needed to be broken.

Here are some things I discovered about myself:

I was not assertive enough and failed to express my opinions and feelings. I had trouble demonstrating affection to others. I took on too much responsibility for others, doing what they could have done for themselves. I focused more on the negative than the positive in most situations. I tended to criticize rather than praise. A word of praise often ended in a "but" (you should have done better).

I fixed meals for the family on a daily basis, but there were times when it would have been helpful for them to fix themselves a sandwich, waffle or something easy when I was in the midst of a busy day. Though my youngest son, Casey, was certainly old enough to prepare something for himself, he would sit and wait for me to fix him something, which I continued to do even though I sometimes resented it. Casey really loved and missed Kyle. I probably pampered Casey trying to make up for his loss.

I also recognized some assets. One was compassion. I truly cared about people and wanted them to realize their potential, not get hurt or find themselves in difficult situations. However, it was one of those misguided notions that also caused me frustration and grief. Out of concern for others, I spent more time trying to manage, control and fix their problems rather than seeking answers for my own. My faults were likely as glaring to others as theirs were to me, which is probably why they didn't take my advice seriously.

Though concern and compassion were positive traits, it was important for me to learn how to use these assets in a more effective way and know when to set boundaries.

One period of my life was spent trying to help a Christian woman through a divorce. We suspected her husband of cheating, and I felt it was crucial that we prove he was the guilty party and make sure "adultery" was listed on the divorce decree. This was because our church stressed that adultery was the only biblical reason for divorce, so it seemed of utmost importance that he be listed as the guilty party. We spent a great deal of time spying outside his apartment, secretly following him and using a scanner to record his phone conversations.

Obviously, the focus should have been on meeting the emotional needs of her and her children.

As I learned the concept of "enabling" addicts, I could see how my dad's kindness and compassion toward my mother crossed the boundary into "enabling." She was never compelled to seek help for her anxiety and panic disorder. When he died, I picked up right where he left off.

Beneath the Surface

Certain inventory questions also helped me see where I had gone wrong in my relationship with Kyle and my other children in not perceiving that they had different needs. With the other children, there were occasional displays of anger or emotional turmoil, but Kyle always appeared well-adjusted and happy, usually smiling and fun-loving. Until we were in family counseling due to his addiction, I had not been aware of how our tumultuous home life had affected him.

Until becoming involved in Al-Anon, I had been unaware that my father-in-law's alcoholism was likely at the root of Flynn's behavior. Therefore, I was completely unaware that alcoholic traits could be passed to future generations.

I also discovered that I had never taken criticism well. I had always thought along the lines of "How dare this person with faults much worse than mine criticize me?" Rather than pondering the criticism to see if it actually applied, I was defensive and found ways to defend and excuse all my actions.

I had often feared potential suffering and hardship. This traumatic period of my life had driven me to seek God, and I was grateful despite the pain and worry it had caused. I could understand what the apostle Paul meant when he wrote, "...we also exult in our tribulations, knowing that tribulation brings about perseverance; and perseverance, proven character; and proven character, hope; and hope does not disappoint, because the love of God has been poured out within our hearts through the Holy Spirit who was given to us" (Romans 5:3-5, p. 220).

A section about "fear" in the inventory guide was especially troubling. My constant fear of being stricken with a terrible disease or disability was especially embarrassing since I knew these fears were irrational and that my fear probably contributed to my health problems. I normally kept these types of fear locked inside and tried to make it appear to others that I was trouble-free.

King David came to realize that he was the villain after the prophet Nathan confronted him in a story that paralleled David's adultery with Bathsheba and the subsequent murder of her husband. (See 2 Samuel 11 and 12:1-15.) "You are the man!" (2 Samuel 12:7) Nathan told him before spelling out the consequences that David would face. This prompted David to finally come out of denial.

"You are the woman!" applied to me. I had allowed my children to be emotionally damaged by the problems in our home. My role in the ongoing problems was becoming increasingly obvious. Though Flynn's occasional anger outbursts lasted only a few minutes, my anger at him seethed within, causing tension in the home for days or weeks on end. My way of reacting and responding was counterproductive in finding a genuine solution. I had failed to teach my children through word or example how to handle and resolve conflict.

Regardless of the behavior of others, it was now my responsibility to learn to behave in such a way that was pleasing to God.

Resentments Abound

Examining myself, I could also see that I had plenty of resentments. These occur when people "re-feel" past hurts and perceived damages to ego, even though they may have occurred years or even decades earlier. According to one definition, "Resentment typically includes anger, ill-feeling, or even hatred, and desire to punish the perpetrator."[5]

An approach to Step Four recommended by Alcoholics Anonymous is a resentment list because, according to their program, "Resentment is the 'number one' offender."[6] As you might suspect, I had resentments toward Flynn, my mother and others, including Kyle.

I could only hope that Kyle might have a moment of clarity. For now, he and his accomplices still had plenty of money and were able to hire a prominent attorney. Sure enough, the charges were reduced. He received youthful offender status and a two-year sentence which would be suspended if he wasn't arrested again.

Though the police were aware of their illegal activities, Kyle and his friends continued on the same course that was underpinned by their delusions of invincibility.

I mentioned to Kyle that between the bail money and lawyers, the "overhead" of his business was cutting into the profits, and he might be better off getting a regular job. He flashed a thick wad of money in my face and yelled, "Do you think I'm going to flip burgers for minimum wage when I can make this?"

I knew the end was coming, just not how or when. God was in control. Kyle's foolish words didn't reduce me to hopelessness as they had previously. I just prayed more specifically. Since incarceration seemed inevitable, I prayed he would be caught locally. (I preferred not to know why they made several trips out-of-state.)

I also prayed that somehow God could help him escape the two-year sentence he would be facing if caught again. I prayed God would allow his punishment to be short but effective, though I had no idea how that could be accomplished. I trusted that even if he were 25 or 30 years old, we would someday put this behind us.

Since another crisis seemed inevitable, I continued to work my program hoping to be strong enough to handle it when it occurred.

Biblical Questions for Self-Examination

Use the *Journey to Recovery Through Christ: CASA's 12-Step Study Bible* or any other version of the *New American Standard Bible* © 1995 to fill in the blanks in biblical passages below.

DO YOU IDENTIFY?

1. a. Janet listed several things in her Step Four inventory where improvement was needed. In what ways do you identify with what Janet wrote in her inventory? _____

   _____

   _____

   _____

   b. In what ways do you not identify? _____

   _____

   _____

   _____

2. a. How did Janet's self-perception impact her perspective of the world around her? _____

   _____

   _____

b. Do you identify with the idea that your self-perception has impacted the way you have viewed the world around you? (circle one) yes or no

c. If yes to 2.b. describe it here. _____

_____

_____

_____

d. If no to 2.b. think about it for a while and later revisit 2.b.

3. a. The Step Four inventory needs to be "fearless." Why would a person fear what he or she might discover about self when conducting a moral inventory? _____

_____

_____

_____

b. Give examples of how fear and forgetting your Step Three decision to let God run your life has prompted you to return to thoughts and behaviors that you wished to avoid. _____

_____

_____

_____

THE ULTIMATE SOLUTION TO FEAR

4. Read 1 John 4:7-21 (p. 322).

a. **"There is no _____ in _____; but perfect _____ casts out _____..."** (1 John 4:18, p. 322).

b. Who has perfect love? _____

c. **"We have come to _____ and have believed the _____ which _____ has for us. _____ is _____, and the one who abides in _____ abides in _____, and _____ abides in him"** (1 John 4:16, p. 322).

FAITH—THE OPPOSITE OF FEAR

5. a. The word "faith" is defined in this way: **"Now faith is the _____ of things _____ for, the _____ of things _____ _____"** (Hebrews 11:1, p 303).

b. Please read the rest of Hebrews 11 (pp. 303-304) to see some examples of faith. From what you have read, list your three favorite examples of faith in action.

1) _____

2) _____

3) _____

c. Give an example of when you have demonstrated faith in spite of fear. _____

_____

_____

6. a. Let's return once again to Peter attempting to walk on water and being saved by Jesus.

"Immediately, Jesus stretched out His hand and took hold of him, and said to him, 'You of little _____, why did you _____?'" (Matthew 14:31, p. 59).

b. Give an example of when your fear was stronger than your faith. _____

_____

_____

c. When you have doubts, list three things that have occurred in your life that would be most helpful for you to remember.

1) _____

_____

2) _____

_____

3) _____

_____

SELF-EXAMINATION IN THE BIBLE

7. We come out of denial about our wrongs when we recognize them for what they are. As we seek God, a self-examination process begins, and this is what Step Four is about. As you will see, self-examination precedes confession, which is the topic of Step Five. Read Luke 18:9-14, p. 136.

a. Who was the Pharisee examining? _____

b. Who was the tax collector examining? _____

c. As she surveyed her past, what similarities did Janet find between herself and the Pharisee?

_____

_____

_____

d. Thinking about yourself prior to taking Step One, itemize some similarities between the Pharisee and yourself.

_____

_____

_____

e. Thinking about yourself since you started working the steps, name some similarities between you and the tax collector. _____

_____

_____

8. a. **"Let us examine and probe our ways, and let us return to the Lord. We lift our heart and hands toward God in heaven. We have transgressed and rebelled..."** (Lamentations 3:40-42).

    b. **"_____ yourselves _to see_ if you are in the _____; _____ yourselves! Or do you not recognize this about yourselves, that _____ _____ is in you—unless indeed you fail the test? But I trust that you will realize that we ourselves _____ _____ fail the test"** (2 Corinthians 13:5-6, p. 259).

    c. Thinking about the two verses above, name some self-examination habits that you already have.

    _____

    _____

    _____

    _____

    d. Is there any room for improvement? (circle one)   yes   or   no

    e. If yes, how might you accomplish this? _____

    _____

    _____

    _____

9. Let's return again to the prodigal son. After deciding to return home to his father, the son examines himself and plans what he will say to his father when he sees him face-to-face.

    a. **"I will get up and go to my father, and will say to him, 'Father, I have _____ against _____, and in _____ _____; I am no longer**

_____ **to be called your _____; make me as one of your** _____

men'" (Luke 15:18-19, p. 133).

b. What does the son now have in common with the tax collector from Luke 18:9-14 found in number 7 above.

_____

_____

_____

c. On the basis of what the son says in Luke 15:18-20, how can you tell that his attitude about his role in his father's house has changed since he first left home? _____

_____

_____

d. How has your attitude about yourself in relationship to God changed in the time since you took Step One?

_____

_____

_____

A MEASURING STICK FOR SELF-EXAMINATION

10. Read Ephesians 4:17-5:21 (pp. 268-269). Based on what you read, list at least five things you have identified about yourself that will become a part of your Step Four inventory.

1) _____

2) _____

3) _____

4) _____

5) _____

YOU SPOT IT, YOU'VE GOT IT

11. a. According to Matthew 7:3-5 (p. 47), what are you most apt to have in your eye? _____

b. Since this obstructs your view, it stands in the way of you seeing others objectively. Therefore, when you judge others, the things you see in them are faults that you possess yourself. This prompts the saying, "You spot it, you've got it." This is sometimes paraphrased in this way, "When you have a finger pointed at someone else, you have three fingers pointed back at yourself." Also, "it takes one to know one." Give an example from your own life when you were pointing a finger at someone else and later realized you had three fingers pointing back at yourself. _____

_____

_____

_____

c. Even though we all have a tendency to focus on the faults of others, God will allow us to use this for good. Here's how: When we recognize a fault in someone else, we try to see how that fault applies to us. In the next few days, try to apply the principal of "You spot it, you've got it." When you start mentally criticizing someone, think of how that very same fault applies to you. When you are successful in recognizing one of your own faults in this manner, write about it here. _____

_____

_____

_____

_____

_____

RELIVING THE BAD OL' TIMES

12.   Janet wrote about her problem with resentments. The first two letters of the word "resentment" mean "again" and the rest comes from the Latin word *sentire* which means "to feel." [7] Putting these things together, we re-feel and re-live old pains from the past. For example, a 40-year-old man may burn with anger every time he thinks back to the seventh grade when a bully humiliated him in front of a large group of fellow students. The 40-year-old man sometimes finds himself fantasizing of finding where the bully lives, hiding in the bushes near his home and beating him over the head with a baseball bat. But, thankfully, he never does this.

   a. In the example above, who is being hurt by the resentment harbored by the 40-year-old man? (circle one)

      1) the guy who was the bully 27 years ago;

      2) the man with the resentment;

      3) the baseball bat.

   b. Name three examples of resentments that you harbor today.

      1) _____

      _____

      _____

      2) _____

      _____

      _____

3) _____

_____

_____

c. Pick one of these resentments and tell how it has been detrimental to you. _____

_____

_____

_____

_____

d. In the words of Jesus, **"But I say to you, _____ your _____ and _____ for those who _____ you."** (Matthew 5:44, p. 44).

e. Why do you think Jesus commanded you to do that? _____

_____

_____

_____

_____

13. a. Jesus also stated, **"…you have heard that it was said, 'AN EYE FOR AN EYE, AND A TOOTH FOR A TOOTH.' But I say to you, do not resist an _____ _____; but whoever _____ you on your _____ _____, turn the other to him also. If anyone wants to _____ you and take your _____, let him have your _____ also. Whoever _____ you to go _____ _____, go with him _____"** (Matthew 5:38-41, p. 44).

b. This passage has meaning beyond giving away your coat to an enemy or walking an extra mile. What are the implications of these words in your life? _____

_____

_____

_____

c. Thinking of the words of Jesus from 12.d. and 13.a., name at least one way you can practice these principles in your life starting today. _____

_____

_____

THE BIG TWO

14. a. Jesus summarizes the Law with the following statement, **"YOU SHALL LOVE THE** _____ **YOUR** _____ **WITH ALL YOUR** _____ **, AND WITH ALL YOUR** _____ **, AND WITH ALL YOUR** _____ **; AND YOUR** _____ **AS YOURSELF"** (Luke 10:27, p. 123).

   b. According to these words, what is your first priority? _____
   _____

   c. How will you accomplish this first priority in your life? See John 14:15 (p. 169) and John 14:23 (p. 169).
   _____
   _____
   _____
   _____

   d. According to Luke 10:27 (p. 127) what is your second priority? _____
   _____

   e. While you were wallowing in codependency, what was number one in your life and how did this affect your relationship with other people? _____
   _____
   _____

   f. Looking at the 12 steps, identify by number which steps deal with our relationships with God and which deal with our relationships with other people. (Note: some steps may cover both).

   1) Steps that apply to your relationship with God. _____

   2) Steps that apply to your relationships with people. _____

   g. **If someone says, "I** _____ _____ **," and hates his** _____ **, he is a liar; for the one who does not** _____ **his** _____ **whom he has seen, cannot** _____ **God whom he has not seen** (1 John 4:20, p. 322).

   h. To summarize, how does your relationship with God impact your relationship with other people? _____
   _____
   _____

   i. What have you learned from 14.a. through 14.h. that will apply to your fourth step? _____
   _____

_____

_____

_____

_____

_____

IN CONCLUSION

As a part of our self-centered pasts, we've done many things that were wrong and have justified them as being right. In order for us to move toward God, we have to examine ourselves to recognize these things. Through God's grace, once we recognize them, maybe we won't have to repeat them. While we may stray off the straight and narrow path, God will give us a compass to get us going in the right direction again.

I now understand the need for self-examination and a Step Four inventory. (circle one)   yes   or   no

_____   _____
Your Signature   **Today's Date**

Write down some insights you've gained from this lesson. To gauge your spiritual progress, several months from now look back on what you've written here.

_____

_____

_____

_____

_____

End Notes

1. Theodore W. Jennings, Jr., *The Liturgy of Liberation—The Confession and Forgiveness of Sins*, Abingdon Press, Nashville, 1988, 65-66.

2. *Twelve Steps and Twelve Traditions*, The A.A. Grapevine, Inc. and Alcoholics Anonymous Publishing (now known as Alcoholics Anonymous World Services, Inc.), New York, 1953, 42-43.

3. *Blueprint for Progress*, Al-Anon Family Group Headquarters, Inc., Virginia Beach, 1976, 10-11.

4. Don Umphrey, *Journey to Recovery Through Christ, CASA's 12-Step Study Bible*, Quarry Press, Dallas, 2015, 18.

5. http://www.oxfordreference.com/search?q=resentment&searchBtn=Search&isQuickSearch=true

6. *Alcoholics Anonymous, Third Edition*, Alcoholics Anonymous World Services, Inc. New York, 1976, 64.

7. http://www.barefootsworld.net/aaresentments.html.

APPENDIX TO STEP FOUR

SOME APPROACHES TO TAKING A WRITTEN INVENTORY

If you are ready to take your fourth step, below are some guidelines. Use any one of them, a combination of them, or all of them. Also consider other sources for fourth step ideas.

A PERSONAL HISTORY

When you think about your past, your mind probably arranges it by various milestones in your life, such as when you moved from one place to another, completed a segment of formal education, marriage, divorce, the death of a loved one and job changes.

Thinking about your life in these terms on a chronological basis, start writing about the first section of your life. You may use a spiral notebook or a computer. When you finish the first part, go on to the next. With this method, you'll find that the writing process really stimulates a lot of memories.

Cite specific examples where your self-centered behavior caused problems for others and yourself. List personal liabilities as well as assets. Include a resentment list (as found on the next page) for each section of your life.

Don't try to do your entire history in one day. That would be draining, and the quality would suffer. If you devote a period of time to working on your inventory each day, even 20 or 30 minutes, you will find that in the midst of other activities, you will remember many things that could be included.

QUESTIONS FOR EVALUATION

Some questions that may be used as a part of a fourth step are reprinted below. These were printed in *The Messenger* (Alamo City Church of Christ, July 3, 2005) and have been reprinted in numerous church bulletins over the years, always without attribution to their original source.

1. Am I so CRITICAL that I see only a person's failures and not his/her good points?

2. Am I so CHILDISH that people must handle me gently lest I be offended?

3. Am I MATURE ENOUGH to handle hurts and disappointments without feeling mistreated and making everyone else miserable?

4. Do I HURT people while boasting, "I believe in saying what I think?"

5. Can I be completely TRUSTED with confidential information?

6. Am I guilty of making SARCASTIC REMARKS about the success of others?

7. Am I big enough to admit when I am wrong, or do I seek to excuse myself by BLAMING OTHERS?

8. Do I excuse my sins while self-righteously CONDEMNING OTHERS?

9. Are others UPLIFTED AND ENCOURAGED through their association with me?

10. Do I follow after peace or do my words and actions PROMOTE STRIFE?

RESENTMENT LIST

As found in AA's "Big Book," this method contains three columns.[1] However, many people add a fourth column, consistent with suggestions from the text of "The Big Book." The fourth column tells how the individual is at fault in that particular incident. Below is a partial resentment list from our author, Janet.

I'm Resentful at	The Cause	Affects My	How I Was Wrong
Mother	Would not seek help for mental issues	Home life, peace of mind	I chose to enable her
Flynn	Mood swings, angry outbursts	Emotional well-being, physical health, children	I refused to seek help for my own issues
Church leaders	Refusal to help, wrong teaching, failed in their responsibilities	Emotional well-being, peace of mind	I didn't study the Bible myself or seek help earlier
Kyle	Worry, heartache	Physical, mental health	Enabling him
Former employer	Not allowing me to return to work after child-birth	Self esteem, finances	I was too introverted to greet clients and didn't make an effort to improve

ACTS OF THE FLESH

This method comes from a friend, Kathy M. She recommends that we look at the acts of the sinful nature as found in Galatians 5:19-21 (p. 264) and examples of godlessness in 2 Timothy 3:1-5 (p. 290). For a listing of positive things, you could also add a listing of the fruits of the Spirit found in Galatians 5:22-23 (p. 264). The example below is not complete, so please see the appropriate verses for complete listings. If necessary, use a dictionary for the definitions.

Word/Phrase	Definition	Example(s) from My Life	Consequences to Others & Self
Sexual immorality			
Debauchery			
Jealousy			
Selfish ambition			
Lover of money			
Boastful			
Unforgiving			
Love			
Patience			
Self-control			

MORAL INVENTORY GUIDE

The following moral inventory guide was developed by James Group Ministries and gratefully reprinted here via permission of Steve Steele, executive director of that ministry.

The idea of a "moral inventory" is to take stock of ourselves, including our personality traits. We must quit lying to ourselves and have the courage to look thoroughly and honestly at *all* of our personal characteristics. This inventory is a voyage of self-discovery. The object is to discover which character traits we allow to control us and which ones serve us well. We will find out whom we are and why we behave the way we do. After we identify our defects of character, the steps that follow will allow us to eliminate them so that we can live the life that God has planned for us. As you answer the questions below, try to look at yourself clinically, as if you are looking at another person; in a way, you are working toward being another person. The person you become will be happier and more fulfilled than the person you leave behind.

It is important that the answers to these questions be written. This helps to trigger the release of feelings and memories. A strictly mental exercise will do little or no good. Write out all resentments, fears, hates and hang-ups that you can remember. List separately each of your character defects as they surface. The list of character defects that start at the end of the questions may help you. Answer the questions completely and honestly.

1. Were you wanted at birth? In what ways did you learn this and how did you feel about it?

2. Were you an only child? If so, how did you feel about this? Did you resent it or enjoy it? If not an only child, how old were you at the birth of brothers and sisters? How did you feel about the new arrivals?

3. Did you grow up in a home with both parents? If not, describe the circumstances. How did you feel?

4. Were you closer to one parent than the other? Do you still have unresolved issues with one or both parents?

5. In your home, was there laughter, arguing, depression? Describe what you can remember of your early home life and the feelings that were frequent.

6. Describe what you *think* your family thought of you.

7. How did your parents punish you? Did they try to reason, or was it physical? How did you react to punishment? For what were you punished the most?

8. What kind of marriage do you *think* your parents had? If they fought, did you resent it? Did it scare you? Were you used to breaking up their fights? Were you encouraged to (or did you take) one side or the other? Were they so close you couldn't feel a part of them?

9. Did your family move often? Did you make friends and then have to break off the relationships? Were you afraid to get too close?

10. Did you get in many fights? Were you afraid to fight? Were you afraid *not* to fight? Did you feel pressure from parents, brothers, sisters or others on this subject?

11. Did your appearance (looks, dress, etc.) embarrass you? Did you feel that you were "different" from your classmates?

12. List the first time you stole anything. Inventory all your thefts. Why did you first steal? How did you feel about it afterwards?

13. How old were you when you first masturbated? Were you ever caught and made to feel guilty? Did you feel guilty even though you weren't caught?

14. Did you have friends? What kind of friend were you? What kind of friends did you have?

15. Were you undependable as a friend—breaking off relationships without any explanation when something or someone who seemed better came along?

16. Were you jealous or envious of others? For what reasons?

17. How did you get the attention of your family? Did you pout, sulk, be a good child, have temper tantrums, etc.?

18. Do you remember the kind of lies you told? What did your parents do when they caught you lying? How did you feel when you got caught lying?

19. Were you ashamed of your parents? Were they too old, too fat, too sloppy, too drunk, too whatever?

20. Were you the kind of child you would want to have?

21. Some girls are taught that men are only interested in sex, and some boys that they must be the greatest of all time. Have you experienced either of these attitudes? Is there a pattern? How has it affected you?

22. What was the best experience you had? The worst? In school? At home? In public? With friends? With your family?

23. What was the *most* embarrassing incident of adolescence? Were there any others that you really remember?

24. Do you gossip or cut other people down? Do you make up things about other people's behavior? Is it to feel superior to them? Do you do it to get ahead, to remove the competition? Relate any incidents of this behavior. Were you put down by parents, boyfriends/girlfriends, etc.?

25. Do you use people to get what you want? Do you pretend to be their friend as long as you want something, then dump them when you have gotten what you wanted? Write out any instances of this type.

26. Do you feel superior because you have more education, brains, money, social background, job or any other seeming advantages? List your feelings of superiority.

27. Do you feel inferior because you have any less of any of the above? List your feelings of inferiority.

28. Do you think you are superior to the general run of people? List in what ways you are different.

29. Is your personal appearance particularly careless and sloppy, or prideful and vain?

30. On sight, do you judge people by their appearance? Do you form an opinion of them because they look sloppy, neat, preppie, freak, or punk?

31. Do you avoid looking at yourself by making statements like "at least I'm not that messed up" or "others do it too"? List instances of this.

32. Are you still judging the outside of others by the inside of yourself? Give some examples of this from your own experiences.

33. Do you argue with people? Is it important for you to be "right"? Do you become angry when people don't see things the way you do? Relate incidents and your feelings about them.

34. Are you scornful of or do you put down ideas that aren't your own? Elaborate on this.

35. Do you resent others who don't seem to have problems finding happiness? Have you asked people who seem happy how they got that way?

36. About what things do you feel greedy, envious or angry?

37. How do you presently get people's attention? Pouting, sulking, temper tantrums, being extra good (and letting them know it), frustrating others' activities, complaining so that others know how bad you feel? What reactions do you get most frequently? Can you tell why you feel the need to do this?

38. Do you tell others how bad you are? (This is pride in reverse; a good tool if you like self-pity and depression). Or do you go to the other extreme and tell people how great you are? (A good way to give yourself a false sense of security; however, when the security topples you are back in depression). What do you tell others about yourself?

39. Do you have the need to "one up" everyone? Do you always have a better story to tell? Why do you do this?

40. What kind of things do you lie about most? How do you feel when lying? Do you almost believe your own lies? What do you get from lying?

41. Are you a tightwad or stingy? Do you spend money with no thought for tomorrow? How do you handle your money?

42. What are your fears concerning money?

43. In work relationships, write out your resentments toward bosses and co-workers.

44. List all the negative feelings you have about people in your work life.

45. Do you over-rate yourself and play the "big shot"?

46. Do you feel that no one really understands you? (If they only knew what you had been through they wouldn't expect so much from you).

47. Have you reacted with frustration in sexual matters? In what situations or events are you sexually frustrated?

48. When denied sex, do you become angry or depressed?

49. Have you been involved in an affair, even an imaginary one? How close have you come to having an affair?

50. If you are or have been involved in a relationship with a cold and unloving person, ask yourself why you chose that person. Is that person like one of your parents? Are you trying to get the love that you didn't get from that parent through someone like them?

51. Did you have sex earlier or later than your peer group? How do you feel about that? How do you feel about that first relationship?

52. Do you feel you entered your first relationship for the right reasons? Were you honest with yourself about what you wanted or expected? Were your expectations reasonable?

53. If you are or were married, why did you get married? Was it for the right reasons? Did you marry earlier or later than your peer group? Do you, or did you resent the responsibilities of marriage and family?

54. If you are not married, why not?

55. Do you use sex as a punishment or reward? Why?

56. What is your sex life like? Is it as mature as you would like it to be? Are you careless of your partner's feelings?

57. Write out your idea of a healthy sex life. Why isn't your sex life like that?

58. Are you afraid of being sexually rejected? Are you ashamed of your body or the way you look? Write out what's wrong with you. Who told you what was wrong with you? Why do you believe them?

59. Write out the things about yourself of which you are ashamed and why.

60. If you are divorced, or are getting one, write out the negative feelings about your relationship with your spouse and children.

61. If married, write out exactly how you feel about your spouse and children.

62. Is your family living up to your expectations? What are your expectations? Are they reasonable?

63. How do you think you would be different if your family were out of your life? In what ways do they affect the person you are?

64. Have you been so busy trying to make money that your family sees little of you? Do you say "I give my family everything they want, but they are never satisfied"?

65. How much time do you spend with your family? Do you take at least one night a week for the family only? What do you do together? Is the time spent in fun or fighting?

66. Define love. What do you feel it is?

67. Are you working to build your ego? Describe the difference between ego and self-esteem.

68. If you are married and your spouse turns cold, do you spend more time with him or her, or do you turn to someone more understanding?

69. What is your greatest fear, relating to your family? Your friends? School or work? The future?

70. Are you afraid of getting too close to another person for the fear of being rejected? Do you reject others before they can reject you? What are your fears in this regard?

71. Do you find yourself punishing others the way your parents punished you? In what ways?

72. Are you cold and indifferent to your family, friends, work, your own needs? What do you get from this? What fear keeps you from trying something different?

73. Are you hostile because you don't like the hand life has dealt you? Did you think your life would turn out differently? In what ways?

74. What are your present fears? List them.

75. Resentment is caused by failed expectations. Unresolved resentment breeds bitterness, which leads to depression. List your greatest resentment.

76. If revenge were possible right now, who would be the top people on your list? Why?

77. As children, we develop ways to avoid being hurt by others. These methods rarely work as adults. What methods do you still use to avoid being hurt?

78. Which childish behaviors do you use to get what you want from others? Do they still work?

79. What are your hopes and goals?

80. What do you like most about yourself?

81. What do you like least about yourself?

82. What do you *think* people think of you? Do they think you are rude, obnoxious, boring, fun-loving, outlandish, refined, impulsive, shy, up-tight, driven or angry? How do *you* see yourself? Who is right?

83. In what ways are you a responsible person?

84. Are you a perfectionist? In what ways does this manifest itself?

85. Are you easily offended? Why?

86. What social situations make you uncomfortable? Why?

87. Do you enjoy being the center of attention? Are you a show-off? Do others look to you for leadership or do you just take it?

88. What are your obsessions or compulsions? How do they manifest themselves?

89. Are you addicted to anything? Drugs, alcohol, sex, money, television, exercise, the Internet?

90. What do you waste more time worrying about: the future or the past?

91. What kinds of things still stir guilt feelings in you?

92. Looking at both the past and the present, what situations have caused you anxiety, bitterness, frustration or depression? Is there a pattern?

93. Appraising each situation fairly, can you see where you have been at fault? Did these things upset you because of selfishness or unreasonable demands?

94. If your anxiety was seemingly caused by the behavior of others, ask yourself: why am I unable to accept conditions I cannot change?

The most common symptoms of emotional insecurity are resentment, worry, anger, self-pity and depression. Resentment often causes the *most* damage to us and others. Consider carefully *all* personal relationships which bring continuous or recurring troubles.

Things that offend us, or cause resentment, anger, or uneasiness can often be traced to a particular character defect. For example, in order to feel good about himself or herself, a perfectionist must see order reflected in the world around him. Disorder brings uneasiness. A person who demands control may become angry or resentful when he or she is unable to control his environment.

Many of us have so much shame about our past we wince at the memories. The past controls who we are today, because we can't seem to shake how we feel about it. A personal inventory helps release us from our past. Owning up to who we are is the first step toward putting the past behind us, once and for all. Only then can we begin living the abundant life that God promises His people.

The following is a list of defective character traits and what those defects steal from us. Each group of character traits should be considered as a whole. Individual traits on the left do not necessarily correspond to individual traits on the right.

CHARACTER TRAITS

THESE DEFECTS:	ROB US OF:	THESE DEFECTS:	ROB US OF:
false pride	humility	greed	generosity
vanity	modesty	overindulgence	hospitality
arrogance	gratitude	selfishness	moderation
perfectionism	acceptance	gluttony	
egotism			
		hostility	compassion
envy	happiness	indignation	peace
jealousy	kindness	need to control	
distrust	sincerity		
dissatisfaction	trust		
		sloth	spirit
		sloppiness	pride
dishonesty	authenticity	irresponsibility	accomplishment
rationalization	genuineness		
manipulation	integrity		
people-pleasing	joy	intolerance	tolerance
		opinionated	patience
		overbearing	empathy
self-pity	courage	sarcasm	
pessimism	strength		
despair	hope		
over-sensitivity	optimism	sexually abusive	respect
self-hatred	self-reliance	indecency	decency
low self-esteem	confidence	uncaring spirit	restraint
		self-gratification	consideration
		infidelity	sincerity

Endnote

1. *Alcoholics Anonymous, Third Edition,* Alcoholics Anonymous World Services, Inc, New York, 1976, 65.

A Time to Confess

The nightmare began unfolding that I had anticipated since Kyle's arrest and sentencing a few months earlier.

Flynn, Casey and I had been visiting a new church and found a great connection with the people there. One Sunday morning, a family had invited us over for dinner after evening services, and we looked forward to becoming better acquainted with them.

A phone call from Kyle's new girlfriend, Shelley, interrupted a family lunch. Kyle and a buddy were traveling to Montana supposedly to visit his friend's mother. The police had pulled them over for speeding in Centennial, Colorado. A background check revealed an outstanding warrant in Alabama. Kyle was arrested, and his "best friend" resumed his travels.

I had the feeling that another arrest would be inevitable since he had continued on the same self-destructive course, but I had prayed he would at least be arrested locally. Though doubt crept in momentarily, it dawned on me that his being alone in a jail some 1,200 miles away could be part of God's plan to get him clean and sober.

It would take diligent prayer seeking God's guidance and all my Al-Anon "tools" to get through this.

We went through the motions of attending the Sunday evening service and visiting with our new friends. We were able to manage polite conversation, but unbeknownst to them, my mind was in a Colorado jail.

It took all the strength I had to not make the journey to help him.

Attempting to rescue Kyle, however, was not an option at this point. I had prayed for God's will to be done, and I had to trust that He could accomplish it without my input or interference.

My hope was that Kyle would "hit bottom." I wanted my son back, and this was a possible step toward a destination he had to reach to begin the journey upward.

As I pondered the situation, I was well aware of my many failures as a parent and continued to grapple with the Al-Anon principle that I didn't cause it. To move forward spiritually I would have to own and accept my failures as a human being, wife, and mother, even if some were unintentional.

Having completed Step Four, I knew that I would not experience true relief until these things were brought into the light.

I fell to my knees one morning and recounted specifically every sin and shortcoming that came to mind and begged God's forgiveness. I hadn't really planned to start work on Step Five that day, but it seemed to occur naturally as my Step Four inventory weighed upon me heavily.

STEP FIVE ▶ Admitted to God, to ourselves and to another human being the exact nature of our wrongs. (For additional information on Step Five and a listing of Step Five Reflections related to specific verses, see *Journey to Recovery Through Christ: CASA's 12-Step Study Bible*, pages 21-22.)

There are three parts to this step. 1) Admitting to God; 2) Admitting to self; 3) Admitting to another person. Let's look at each part individually.

Admitting to God brings us into closer fellowship with Him. "If we say that we have no sin, we are deceiving ourselves and the truth is not in us. If we confess our sins, He is faithful and righteous to forgive us our sins and to cleanse us from all unrighteousness" (1 John 1:8-9, p. 320).

A Christian author explains the importance of first making a Step Five confession to God: "With this confession we grasp the knowledge of where we stand as sinners in relationship to our all-knowing Heavenly Father. When we make our confession to God, we know that God knows everything. We must, therefore, be as honest as possible." [1]

Prayer Life Impacted

Many of my former prayers had been of generic form, such as "forgive me of my sins," "help me become a better person," and "heal the sick." I now felt the need for my prayers to include greater precision, "the exact nature of our wrongs" as specified in Step Five, just as Step One requires that we specifically identify the addiction over which we are powerless.

Admitting these faults to myself was a sign that I was coming out of denial and self-deception.

A devotional writer explains this part of Step Five:

> Next, I learn to be at peace with myself. I wake up with myself every morning and go to sleep with myself every night. I spend 24 hours a day with that one person, so it is important that I'm at least tolerable, if not downright enjoyable company. I can't be that person when I'm overly controlled by guilt, fear, and resentment and negligibly aware of my gifts and talents. [2]

Finally, Step Five requires that our faults be confessed to another human being. "Therefore, confess your sins to one another, and pray for one another so that you may be healed..." (James 5:16, p. 311).

People often go before the church assembly to make confession, which is beneficial and necessary at times, but seldom do they actually bare their souls (or have time to).

My previous reasoning had been, "My behavior may not be ideal, but I sure wouldn't have to act this way if it weren't for the obnoxious behavior of _____." I had to own up to the fact that my bitterness and resentment toward Flynn had compounded our problems.

In finding an individual to hear my confession, I wanted someone who could be trusted to keep it confidential. I also wanted a person who was open about her own faults and with whom I had much in common. (Same gender confession partners are preferred.) To meet these goals I knew that I would need to select a woman from my Al-Anon group who had been in recovery for a long period of time and who was serious about working her program.

One's sponsor is always a possibility to hear a fifth step, but my original sponsor had dropped out of Al-Anon, and we had not communicated for over a year. It was past time for me to get a new one.

As I prayed about whom I might select and weighed the options, my mind kept coming back to one person. She had experienced similar communication problems with her husband and made significant strides toward improving her marriage. The successes she shared in the meetings inspired hope that Flynn and I could continue to make positive changes. I asked her and she agreed to be my sponsor and be on the listening end of my fifth step.

We met for one hour before the meetings for several weeks. I first read the typewritten summary of my inventory. We discussed it and in subsequent weeks we talked about specific sections of the questionnaire booklet.

One major topic included my fears, especially the fear that I would be permanently disabled or fall victim to a serious disease.

Resentment Problems

We discussed my resentments. My mother was on the list even though she was now deceased. I had been resentful of her for years because she would not seek help for her anxiety, creating stress in my life. My resentments toward Flynn and others in my past also stemmed from their refusal to acknowledge wrongdoing or seek the help they needed. I knew I could never experience any level of serenity until I let go of these resentments and allowed people to either grow at their own pace or not grow at all.

When I confessed my shortcomings to my sponsor, she was understanding, non-judgmental and usually echoed many similar sentiments. She had been raised in a dysfunctional family similar to my husband's and shared some of the same insecurities. I could identify with the way she described her husband. In explaining her need for affection and attention from her husband, she helped me to understand simple ways to cope with Flynn's insecurities.

This confession gave me a deeper comprehension of the truth of this passage. "No temptation has overtaken you but such as is common to man…" (1 Corinthians 10:13, p. 240). As it turned out, I wasn't as evil or insane as I thought.

Coming out of denial during Step Four and confessing in Step Five is also a sign of repentance which is defined in this way:

> That divinely wrought conviction of sin in the heart that the soul is guilty before God, and a resolute turning away from sin in which the sinner identifies himself with the gracious act of God in redeeming him. Repentance involves both a change of mind about sin, and a change of heart-attitude toward sin. It is at the time a renunciation of sin and an acceptance of the Holy Spirit's enablement to holy living.[3]

"Therefore repent and return, so that your sins may be wiped away, in order that times of refreshing may come from the presence of the Lord" (Acts 3:19, p. 183).

My repentance included listing the ways I had gone wrong in Step Four, admitting them to God and myself, and having a desire to do better. This made me ready for the confession to another person in Step Five.

In addition to the spiritual benefit, repentance and confession are acts of emotional cleansing. I could now face my wrongdoing, accept that I could not change the past and move forward in my spiritual growth. A huge burden was lifted from me. I had done all within my power to do, and the rest was in the hands of the Lord.

The current crisis with Kyle would have been unbearable had it not been for my belief that God was working in this situation and hearing my prayers. Having realized that God was in control, rather than having to work it all out myself, I was able to trust and wait. I prayed for Kyle to understand that this ordeal could prove to be the end of his self-will run riot. It was my hope that him "bottoming out" would guide him toward Step One.

The paradox of recovery is that it is necessary to surrender in order to win.

To escape my own personal "merry-go-round," I had to face the fact that my way was never going to produce the results for which I had hoped. Kyle would have to realize that drugs were his problem rather than his solution. Circumstances seemed to be leading in that direction as arrests, bail money and attorney fees continued to mount.

Even though I knew better, it still took every ounce of strength I possessed to not board a plane and bail him out of this current dilemma (even though flying was near the top of my list of fears). God was telling me, in this case, that real love meant letting him tough it out.

In the meantime Kyle's "nervous stomach" returned with a vengeance without his self-prescribed drug of choice. Upset and crying, he was phoning anyone who would accept his collect calls. Rather than portraying his usual tough gangster façade, he was my little boy again and acknowledging his need for help.

As the prodigal son acknowledged his powerlessness in the pig pen, I hoped that Kyle's pain would bring about his willingness to take Step One.

Help from a Minister

After considerable prayer it occurred to me that there might be a church in that area that would help. Internet research produced the closest one to the jail. The preacher there admitted to frequently getting calls for assistance but was surprised to hear from someone as far away as Alabama. Yet he was compassionate to the plight of a mom with a 19-year-old son in jail many miles away from home. The minister promised to visit him and assist in any way possible; he ended up providing tremendous relief to both Kyle and me.

What a nice lesson it was for Kyle to get help from a Bible-toting preacher.

I continued to take care of each day's business, sometimes like a "walking zombie." I had no idea how long this ordeal would last or what would happen when he returned to Alabama.

Communicating with God on an hourly basis and sharing it with Al-Anon friends gave me the extra strength I needed to cope. Trusting that this was His will helped me to sleep at night with some measure of peace, even though any time I awoke my thoughts immediately went to Colorado.

After two weeks Kyle was informed he would be released on the following Monday unless a van showed up to transport him back to Alabama. Since his charge involved selling marijuana to an undercover officer, it seemed unlikely they would go to such trouble and expense. The minister was informed and agreed to provide transportation to a bus station.

I only hoped Kyle would make good on the promises he made during our emotional phone conversations. He had admitted to me that he should have listened, that my warnings had come true, and that he was praying like never before. I was still hoping God would somehow, in His wisdom, help him avoid the two-year suspended sentence. He might have to stay in jail locally but the worst would soon be over, or so we thought.

Biblical Questions for Self-Examination

Use the *Journey to Recovery Through Christ: CASA's 12-Step Study Bible* or any other version of the *New American Standard Bible* © 1995 to fill in the blanks in biblical passages below.

TURNING TOWARD THE TRUTH

1. Thinking of the way repentance was defined and discussed in this chapter, what was the sign of repentance in the life of the prodigal son? (See Luke 15:11-24, p. 133). _____

   _____

   _____

   _____

2. a. **"For the sorrow that is according *to the* _____ *of* _____ produces a repentance without _____, *leading* to _____, but the sorrow of the world produces _____"** (2 Corinthians 7:10, p. 253).

   b. Based on what you know about repentance, describe the difference between sorrow according to the will of God and worldly sorrow. _____

   _____

   _____

   _____

   c. Describe some worldly sorrow that you have experienced in the past. _____

   _____

3. a. How did Janet demonstrate repentance in her life? _____

   _____

   _____

   b. Give some examples from your own life that demonstrate repentance. _____

   _____

   _____

   _____

4. a. The people listening to Peter's sermon in Acts 2:14-36 (p. 180-181) at least knew about or had taken part in the recent crucifixion of Jesus Christ. What was their response in Acts 2:37 (p. 181)? _____

_____

_____

_____

b. **Peter *said* to them, "_____, and each of you be _____ in the name of Jesus Christ for the _____ of your sins; and you will receive the gift of the _____ _____"** (Acts 2:38, p. 181).

c. In Acts 2:39 (p. 181) Peter relates that the promise is for those who are "far off." To whom do you think this promise applies? (circle one)

   1) Those who were geographically removed from him on that day.

   2) People in the future, including us.

   3) Both 1 and 2.

d. How does Acts 2:38 (p. 181) apply to you? _____

_____

_____

_____

WHO'S IN CHARGE?

5. a. **"So then _____ one of us will give an _____ of himself to _____"** (Romans 14:12, p. 229).

   b. Before you took Step One, to whom (or what) were you accountable? _____

_____

_____

   c. To whom are you accountable now? _____

_____

_____

THE NEED FOR CONFESSION

6. The Bible shows that the necessity of God's people to confess their sins goes back at least to the time of Moses more than 3,000 years ago.

   a. **So it shall be when he becomes guilty in one of these, that he shall confess that in which he has sinned** (Leviticus 5:5).

b. **"If we say that we have no _____, we are _____ ourselves and the**

_____ is not in us. If we _____ our sins, He is _____

and _____ to _____ us our _____ and to

_____ us from all _____" (1 John 1:8-9, p. 320).

c. In what way does denial about an addiction or codependency prevent a person from confessing that he or she

has sinned? _____

_____

_____

d. Was there ever a time in your life when you either claimed to be without sin or never even gave it a thought?

(circle one)   yes   or   no

e. If yes, describe why. _____

_____

_____

f. If any person claims to be without sin, why is that person a liar? (See Romans 3:23, p. 218). _____

_____

_____

g. Which do you believe is more likely? (circle one)

1) God wants His people to confess their sins because He has a need to hear people confess.

2) God wants His people to confess because in order to grow spiritually, they have a need to confess to Him.

BURDENS OF NOT CONFESSING

7. David's sin with Bathsheba and the ramifications of it (2 Samuel 11 and 12) were discussed earlier. According
to the story, at least nine months elapsed between David's adultery and the time when he was finally confronted
by the prophet Nathan. Have you wondered how David felt when he was in denial about all of this? He tells you
in the passage below:

a. **When I kept silent *about* my _____, my body _____ away through my**

_____ all day long. For day and night _____ hand was heavy upon

me; My _____ was drained away *as* with the fever heat of summer. *Selah.*

I _____ _____ _____ to You, and my iniquity I did not hide;

I said, "I will _____ my transgressions to the Lord;" and You _____

the guilt of my sin. (Psalm 32:3-5, p. 370).

b. **"Therefore, _____ your sins to one another, and pray for one another so that you may be _____. The effective _____ of a righteous man can _____ much"** (James 5:16, p. 311). While you are there, it would be helpful to read James 5:13-18 (p. 311).

c. What kinds of problems have you experienced as a result of your failure to recognize and confess your sins?

_____

_____

d. How might your unconfessed sins affect your relationships with other people? _____

_____

_____

_____

_____

A FAMILIAR CHARACTER

8. So far we have talked about the prodigal son in conjunction with every step. As a review, record the number for the verse or verses from Luke 15:11-24 (p. 133) when the son:

a. Demonstrated that he was his own worst enemy. _____

b. Took Step One. _____

c. Took Step Two. _____

d. Took Step Three. _____

e. Took Step Four. _____

f. What follows is equivalent to the son's Step Five: **"And the son said to him, 'Father, I have _____ against _____ and in your_____; I am no longer _____ to be called your _____'"** (Luke 15:21, p. 133).

g. There is a difference in what the son planned to say to his father while he was still in the far county (his fourth step in Luke 15:18-19, p. 133) and what he actually did confess to his father upon his arrival at home (his fifth step in Luke 15:21, p. 133). What is it? _____

_____

_____

_____

_____

h. Which of the following most likely explains that difference described in 8.g.? (circle one)

   1) The son forgot the last part of his Step Four before he had a chance to confess it in Step Five.

   2) The son didn't forget it but decided not to humble himself any further.

   3) When the father heard the son say he was no longer worthy to be called his son, he'd heard enough and was anxious to demonstrate that this boy was worthy to be called his son.

ACCEPTING GRACE

9. a. Do you think there is anything the son could have done in the far country—any sin he could have committed—that would have caused the father to not welcome him home? (circle one) yes or no

   b. If yes, please give some examples of sins the son could confess to his father that would have caused the father to turn his back on the son and slam the door in his face. _____

    _____

    _____

    _____

   c. Is there any sin you've committed that you think God would not forgive? (circle one) a) yes; b) no; c) unsure

   d. Read the listing of sins below and circle the ones you think that God would not forgive.

    fornication

    idolatry

    adultery

    homosexuality

    theft

    covetousness

    drunkenness

    reviling (use of abusive language)

    swindling

   e. **"Or do you not know that the _____ will not inherit the kingdom of _____? Do not be _____; neither _____, nor _____, nor _____, nor _____, nor _____, nor _____, nor *the* _____, nor _____, nor _____, nor _____, will inherit the kingdom of God. Such were some of _____..."** (1 Corinthians 6:9-11, p. 236). (This means that some of the Christians in the church at Corinth had done these things. And that everyone in the church at Corinth knew about their past sins.)

f. Now keep going with the rest of that verse. "...**but you were** _____, **but you were**

_____, **but you were** _____ **in the name of the** _____

_____ _____ **and in the** _____ **of our** _____ "

(1 Corinthians 6:11, p. 236).

g. What do these verses confirm? _____

_____

10. a. David was guilty of a variety of sins in connection with his sexual relationship with Bathsheba, including
adultery and murder. Did he believe that God forgave him of those sins? Re-read Psalm 32:5 (p. 370) (circle
one) yes or no

b. Here is something else David wrote on the same subject. "**He has not** _____ **with us**

according to our _____, **nor** _____ **us according to our**

_____. **For as high as the** _____ **are above the** _____,

so great is His lovingkindness toward those who fear Him. As far as the _____ **is**

from the _____, **so far has He** _____ **our** _____

from us" (Psalm 103:10-12, p, 434).

c. "**Come now, and let us reason together,**" **says the Lord,** "**Though your sins are as scarlet, they will**
be as white as snow; though they are red like crimson, they will be like wool" (Isaiah 1:18).

d. What did Jesus say to the thief on the cross next to him? **And He said to him,** "**Truly I say to you,**

_____ **you shall be** _____ _____ **in** _____ "

(Luke 23:43, p. 146).

e. "**For I am convinced that neither** _____, **nor** _____, **nor** _____,

nor principalities, nor things _____, **nor things to come, nor** _____, **nor**

_____, **nor** _____, **nor any other created thing, will be able to separate**

us from the _____ **of** _____, **which is in** _____ _____

our Lord" (Romans 8:38-39, p. 224).

11. a. After reading all of the above, do you now believe that you've committed an unforgivable sin? (circle one)
a) yes; b) no; c) unsure.

b. If yes or unsure, explain your thoughts about it here and then discuss this with God in prayer and with the
person who listens to your fifth step. (Remember, though, that if you think your ability to sin exceeds God's
ability to forgive, that would be an example of pride in the negative sense.) Here is my explanation of why I
think my sin(s) is/are beyond God's ability to forgive: _____

_____

_____

_____

IN CONCLUSION

The practice of confession has been an integral part of living a godly life for thousands of years. As a part of our self-centered pasts, we've done many things that were wrong and have justified them as being right. We've examined ourselves to discover these things and are now going to get them out in the open through confession. This will help to end our isolation and will move us closer to letting God make us into new men and women.

I have made a decision to admit to God, to myself and to another human being the exact nature of my wrongs. (circle one)   yes   or   no

_____   _____

Your Signature   **Today's Date**

I have completed Step Five by confessing these wrongs to God, admitting them to myself and confessing them to another human being.

_____   _____

Your Signature   **Today's Date**

Write down some insights you've gained from this lesson. To gauge your spiritual progress, in the future look back on what you've written here.

_____

_____

_____

_____

_____

End Notes

1. Don Umphrey, *12 Steps to a Closer Walk with God: The Workbook, 2nd Edition,* Quarry Press, Dallas, 2015, 54.

2. *Hope for Today,* Al-Anon Family Group Headquarters, Inc., Virginia Beach, 2002, 326.

3. Merrill C. Tenney, *The Zondervan Pictorial Bible Dictionary,* Zondervan, Grand Rapids, 1967, 711.

Another Step Toward Faith

When a day had passed without either us or Shelley receiving one of his many distraught phone calls from the Colorado jail, we became alarmed. Upon inquiry, we found he had been picked up to be carried back to Alabama and would be out of contact until he arrived at the local jail. We didn't know the means of transportation, but at the very least Kyle would be handcuffed, shackled and definitely having problems with nausea.

I assumed it would take two or three days to get him back and figured this would be my toughest challenge yet in trusting God to keep him safe.

When Kyle still wasn't back after the third day, I inquired at the local sheriff's office and was told that he was on a van that carried prisoners all over the U.S. They stopped at random jails along the way to sleep at night, and he predicted it could take up to 10 days. I fell to the floor and literally screamed! I had heard horror stories of what happened to young men placed in close confinement with hardened criminals.

This was my lowest moment.

As long as he was in jail, even a great distance away, I had the idea that I could intervene on his behalf. I hoped he would stay there long enough to come out of denial and get clean and sober.

Of course, I started to get a handle on "powerlessness" when I took the first step. But with Kyle on a prisoner van or in jail somewhere between Colorado and Alabama, the realization of powerlessness took on a whole new meaning. It was similar to when my dad died and my vocal chords could not form the words, "Daddy is dead."

Trying to explain my predicament to my Al-Anon group was impossible without me going to pieces.

I did my best to muster up enough faith in God to protect Kyle through this, knowing full well that God allows people to face the consequences of their sins. I prayed diligently several times a day, especially that the officers would have compassion on him. It provided some comfort to realize that my earlier prayers – punishment that was effective but of a relatively short duration – were being answered.

Finally on the seventh day he called from the local jail to say he had arrived.

I don't know who was more thrilled for him to be back, him or me. He seemed delighted and didn't elaborate much on his trip except to mention that the officers had treated him better than the other prisoners.

I sent up a heartfelt "thank you" prayer.

It has been said that if you allow Satan in the driver's seat, he will "take you further than you want to go, keep you longer than you want to stay and it will cost you more than you are willing to pay." Kyle's "road trip" had been a lesson in experience.

A Comforting Admission

He admitted that while he sat in that Colorado jail, his intention was to sell his remaining inventory and retire from the drug business. Somewhere during his seven-day journey alongside hard-core criminals and even murderers headed to death row, he had concluded, "I would rather be poor and live in a cardboard box than be in jail."

What had started out as abandoning God's laws, parental authority and the laws of the land to pursue an entirely self-centered agenda had ended in the same way that Satan's false promise of freedom always does. Though Kyle had often boldly proclaimed that he was willing to suffer the consequences of his behavior, he realized the folly of this belief and that being in the hands of law enforcement was no trivial matter.

In my youth I also envied what seemed like true freedom – to do whatever the other young folks were doing, get up when I wanted, eat and drink what I wanted, go wherever the road led and come home when I was ready. It had seemed like the ideal situation would be to live in the flesh until you were old and give your life to Christ at the last possible moment. Thankfully, I was much too fearful of my strict parents, the police and of going to hell to just abandon all the rules. Even then, a few times I pushed the limits as close as I could.

As I had concluded as an adult (and Kyle was in the process of learning), the progression of sin will lead to situations that have the potential to spin totally out of control.

In one of several phone conversations from the jail, he had admitted, "You warned me this could happen, but I never seriously thought it could come to this. I should have listened to you. Where I'm at now, there is no one but me and God. I've spent more time praying than I ever have."

I replied, "You haven't yet done anything you can't get past. You are still young. You can start now and live your life God's way."

Though I had been seeking God's way in my own life, I realized that there was still plenty of room for progress. Though I had made the decision to let God run my life in Step Three, I had wavered a lot in this decision.

Step Four helped me to uncover numerous other problems beyond Step One. The Step Five confession brought them out into the open. As I pondered the main point of Al-Anon, which is to "let change begin with me," I was ready for additional changes in my life that would be initiated by moving forward in my recovery program.

STEP SIX ▶ Were entirely ready to have God remove all these defects of character. (For additional information on Step Six and a listing of Step Six Reflections related to specific verses, see *Journey to Recovery Through Christ: CASA's 12-Step Study Bible*, pp. 23-24.)

The defects mentioned above may be deeply ingrained and a part of our very identities. They may be characterized as invisible crutches on which we have leaned to the detriment of our relationship with the Lord. It is difficult to extricate one's self from certain relationships, behaviors and habits because people in addiction and codependency are more comfortable in that which is familiar as opposed to stepping out into uncharted territory.

The "Big Red Book of Adult Children of Alcoholics" explains this step.

> Our defects of character usually include self-centeredness, judgmentalness, envy, greed, lust, jealousy, feeling superior, dishonesty, and pettiness. As we sit and think about our shortcomings, we do not judge ourselves. Our character defects and survival traits are old friends we are beginning

to bid farewell… We are seeking our wholeness with what we are about to do. By now we have stopped punishing ourselves. We are asking God, as we understand God, to help us become entirely ready to have these defects of character removed. We must realize that good intentions do not work in removing our defects of character. Likewise, will-power or self-determination is no match for these flaws in our thinking and reacting. We need help from a power greater than ourselves to achieve Step Six results.[1]

"Do you wish to get well?" (John 5:6, p.154) was a question Jesus asked a man who had been an invalid for 38 years. Does the question seem too obvious to ask? Apparently not when you consider who was doing the asking.

What are some possible reasons this man would respond negatively to Jesus' question? Had he made a living by begging and couldn't imagine himself working a normal job? Had he always been dependent on others for his basic needs? Had he been in the habit of always receiving and never giving? Would he have to make new friends? What other responsibilities would he have to assume as a healed individual? (See four reasons why individuals might want to cling to their character defects on p. 23, *Journey to Recovery Through Christ: CASA's 12-Step Study Bible.*)

Was I Entirely Ready?

The question Jesus posed is one that I had to ask myself in regard to Step Six. Was I entirely ready to get well? (In this case the word "entirely" is not understood to mean absolutely or perfectly, which is not humanly possible, but rather to the best of one's ability.) Was I willing to give up spiritual blindness and depend on the Great Physician for guidance? If yes, I would be stepping out of my comfort zone and growing in faith (probably painfully).

For example, it would have been totally out of character for me to yell and scream obscenities. Yet offering a word of praise or repenting of my wrongdoing to someone I loved but often resented still made me uncomfortable. Of course, this included my husband, Flynn.

I wanted to start responding to him in a way that was healthier and more productive. My association with others in the Al-Anon group who had experienced similar childhood trauma helped me understand the origin of his anger. It had little to do with the trivial issues that usually set him off.

My contribution to the cycle had to end for me to be at peace with myself. The angry, sarcastic comments I made in response to his criticism or outbursts were no longer acceptable. Yet when caught off guard, I still responded in the same manner.

To some extent I had overcome my severe shyness by dealing with my four sons, their teachers, coaches and other parents. However, I was still uncomfortable with any type of public speaking. I wanted to be rid of this defect and be able to speak calmly or assertively when the need arose, whether in general conversation or through public speaking. I wanted to be able to convey to others God's amazing truths that had become apparent to me.

When making comparisons between myself and others, I frequently encountered people to whom I felt inferior. In reality, this had nothing to do with the other person and had everything to do with my own negative self-perception. I wanted God to guide me in overcoming this.

I was also very concerned about carrying on "the family curse" and being like my mother and grand-mother whose lives were characterized by constant pain and illness. It always seemed that there must be a psychological basis to their physical ailments. Since I thought a healthy diet and exercise could have helped them, I was very self-disciplined in those areas. But this did little to eliminate the pain, and I constantly worried that it was some genetic trait. I desperately wanted to be independent, strong and healthy.

My current problem was debilitating back pain that started with a severe strain but had lingered for years. At times I would feel it had responded to treatment, but no sooner than the thought entered my mind that it was cured, any seemingly harmless movement – even reaching in the car to turn up the radio volume – could cause muscle spasms to return with a vengeance for days or weeks on end.

A psychiatrist had no clear answers, and all medical doctors could do was prescribe muscle relaxers, physical therapy or steroid injections. I became ready for God to help me understand and take the necessary steps to remove this particular character defect, psychological issue, or whatever might define it.

Of course, it is always possible that someone (including me) will answer negatively to the question about getting well, spiritually speaking. A biblical example is the rich young ruler whose story is found in three of the gospels (Matthew 19:16-22, p. 66; Mark 10:17-22, p. 94; Luke 18:18-25, p. 137). While he gave the appearance of having it all together in terms of the world's standards, his dependence on his riches prompted him to turn his back on Jesus.

Emmet Fox offers insight on the story of the rich young ruler.

> This is really the story of mankind in general. We reject the salvation that Jesus offers us – our chance of finding God – because we "have great possessions," not in the least because we are very rich in terms of money, for indeed most people are not but because we have great possessions in the way of preconceived ideas – confidence in our judgment and in the ideas with which we happen to be familiar; spiritual pride born of academic distinction; sentimental or material attachment to institutions and organizations; habits of life that we have no desire to renounce; concern for human respect, or perhaps fear of public ridicule; or vested interest in worldly honor and distinction. And these possessions keep us chained to the rock of suffering that is our exile from God.[2]

Though I still had a long way to travel on the road to spiritual maturity, I had made tremendous progress. I was trusting more and more in God's wisdom, especially concerning the consequences Kyle would have to face.

We didn't know if he could be released on bail or would have to immediately begin serving his sentence that had earlier been suspended. But I was thankful he was where we could visit and possibly provide some essentials for him. We had no plans to bail him out but figured that one of his friends might if it was possible.

I was cautiously optimistic that was the turning point for which I had prayed. However, I knew there was still a strong possibility of relapse and that his attitude might change if he was released again. Considering all his previous charges and the fact that court-ordered inpatient and outpatient treatment had not helped, there didn't seem to be much option left for the judge but to finally sentence him to jail or prison.

Biblical Questions for Self-Examination

FOCUSING ON THE RIGHT PATH

Use the *Journey to Recovery Through Christ: CASA's 12-Step Study Bible* or any other version of the *New American Standard Bible* © 1995 to fill in the blanks in biblical passages below.

1. a. **"And do not be _____ to this _____, but be _____ by the _____ of your _____, so that you may prove what the _____ of _____ is, that which is good and acceptable and _____"** (Romans 12:2, p. 228).

    b. Name some ways that you have conformed to the pattern of this world. _____
    _____
    _____
    _____

    c. In what way will Step Six guide you in the "renewing of your mind?" _____
    _____
    _____

2. a. **"But if any of you lacks _____, let him ask of _____, who gives to all _____ and without _____, and it will be given to him. But he must _____ in _____ without any _____, for the one who _____ is like the surf of the sea, driven and tossed by the wind"** (James 1:5-6, p. 307).

    b. Name three times when you have been "like a wave of the sea, blown and tossed by the wind" and describe how this came about.

    1) The example: _____
       How it came about: _____

    2) The example: _____
       How it came about: _____

    3) The example: _____
       How it came about: _____

3. a. As a reminder about faith, please revisit what you wrote in Step Four, items 5.a. – 6.c. Why is faith so very

important in your approach to Step Six? Make sure your answer includes your recognition of the way faith is defined in your response to Step Four, item 5.a. _____

_____

_____

_____

_____

DO YOU IDENTIFY?

4. Janet listed several defects of character, including angry, sarcastic responses to her husband, resentments toward her husband, feeling inferior to others, fear of speaking up, concerns about being like her mother and grandmother in regard to pain and illness as well as back pain. With which of these do you most identify and tell why you selected it. _____

_____

_____

_____

5. a. As it was described in this chapter, what is the meaning of the word "entirely" as it applies to Step Six?____

_____

_____

   b. In what ways are you entirely ready to let God remove your defects of character?_____

_____

_____

_____

_____

NO THANKS, I'LL KEEP MY CHARACTER DEFECTS

6. As mentioned earlier, one man's sad story is told in three of the gospels. We will use the rich young ruler as a bad example, but let's first look at his demographics.

   a. **"But at these words he was saddened, and he went away grieving, for he was one who owned**
   _____ _____ **"** (Mark 10:22, p. 94).

   b. **"A _____ questioned Him..."** (Luke 18:18, p. 137).

   c. **"The _____ man said to Him, 'All these things I have kept...'"** (Matthew 19:20, p. 66).

d. Based on the three blanks you filled in above, which do you think would be most apt to be true? (circle one)

    1) This elderly man had spent most of his life in a leper colony.

    2) He had recently been seen on a street corner holding a sign that read, "Will wash your camel for food."

    3) He had recently appeared on the cover of *New Testament Times Magazine* as a man who "had it all."

e. Read the man's story in Matthew 19:16-22 (p. 66). As indicated in verses 21 and 22, what was standing in the way of this man's closer walk with God? _____

f. It could be said that this man: (circle one)

    1) Had something else in his life that was more important to him than God.

    2) Wanted to serve God and secretly planned to give his money to the poor the next day.

g. Suppose you were present when this story occurred. As the man started to walk away, what would you want to say to him? _____

_____

_____

h. What does the man seem to gain by walking away from Jesus? (Remember, there always seems to be a payoff when indulging in self-will.) _____

_____

_____

i. What does the man lose by walking away from Jesus? _____

_____

_____

j. Describe a time in your life when you made a conscious decision to walk away from God. Be sure to name what was more important to you than God at that particular moment. _____

_____

_____

_____

_____

THINGS HOLDING YOU BACK

7. a. After taking Steps Four and Five and having examined yourself and made a confession, list at least five defects of character that you've discovered. *Please do not proceed with this lesson until you have listed the defects here.*

    1) _____

_____

2) _____

_____

3) _____

_____

4) _____

_____

5) _____

_____

POOLSIDE WITH JESUS

8. We'll come back to those defects of character you listed above. But before we do, let's look at another biblical character. Read John 5:1-15 (p. 154).

   a. There was a pool where sick people went to be healed. One of the people at the pool was an invalid who had been there for 38 years. When Jesus saw him lying there, He asked him, **"Do you _____ to _____ _____?"** (John 5:6, p. 154).

   b. What are some reasons why the man would answer "no" to this question? (Janet covered some of these excuses in this chapter.) _____

_____

_____

_____

   c. John 5:3 (p. 154) lists the people who were at the side of the pool wishing to be healed. They included the sick, blind, lame and withered. Besides the actual physical maladies, it is possible to be spiritually blind, emotionally lame and mentally sick and/or withered. Earlier you listed five defects of character that you discovered in your fourth and fifth steps. Tell here in what way each of these makes you spiritually, mentally and/or emotionally handicapped.

   1) _____

_____

   2) _____

_____

   3) _____

_____

   4) _____

_____

5) _____
   _____

d. Now suppose that Jesus asks you, "Do you want to get well?" and Jesus is talking about your character defects. If you answer, "No thanks, Jesus. I'm going to hang onto these defects of character," describe how your life is seemingly more comfortable living with the spiritual, mental and emotional handicaps that go along with each of the previously listed defects of character?

   1) _____
      _____

   2) _____
      _____

   3) _____
      _____

   4) _____
      _____

   5) _____
      _____

e. By answering "Yes, Jesus, I wish to be made well," tell what kind of adjustments you'll need to make in your life to live without each of the defects of character.

   1) _____
      _____

   2) _____
      _____

   3) _____
      _____

   4) _____
      _____

   5) _____
      _____

9. a. "...let us also lay aside every _____ and the _____ which so easily
      _____ us, and let us _____ with _____
      the _____ that is set before us, fixing our _____ on _____,

the _____ and _____ of _____ ..."
(Hebrews 12:1-2, p. 306).

b. Thinking of what you've learned so far, tell what the scripture above means to you in regard to Step Six.

_____

_____

_____

c. What are some of the hindrances in your life today? _____

_____

_____

IN CONCLUSION

With our reliance on self instead of God, we have become spiritually, mentally and emotionally handicapped. We discovered these things in our first, fourth and fifth steps. Sadly, we are often accustomed to living with these spiritual handicaps as we use them to provide us with a false sense of security. In Step Six we have becoming willing to live without these burdens. We know we can't take these away ourselves, but that God can. We are now ready to let Him do this.

I have become entirely ready to let God remove my defects of character.

_____   _____
Your Signature   **Today's Date**

Write down some insights you've gained from this lesson. To gauge your spiritual progress, in the future look back on what you've written here.

_____

_____

_____

_____

_____

End Notes

1. *Adult Children Alcoholic/Dysfunctional Families*, ACA World Service Organization, Torrance, 2006, 215.
2. Emmet Fox, *The Sermon on the Mount—The Key to Success in Life*, Harper & Row, New York, 1934, 22.

The Role of Humility

When Kyle was transported home, we thought he would have to remain in jail locally, but instead he was released immediately. That morning Flynn, Shelley and I went with him to the drug house. We stayed in the car while he went in to gather his belongings. Of course, I had high hopes that this was the end of association with that bunch.

Kyle begged Flynn and me to temporarily keep one of several pit bull dogs that were at the drug house until he could move into his own place and take the dog with him. I had sworn I would never own a dog of that breed, but we went along with his request. We wound up keeping Lecter for 11 years; he was apparently named for the villain Hannibal Lecter in the movie, *The Silence of the Lambs*. Though Flynn had never cared much for pets, Lecter became as much a part of our family as any dog can be.

After spending some time with Kyle, I sensed that for the first time in four years he was actually experiencing a change of heart.

Of course, even clean and sober, he still had to face consequences for past mistakes. Besides possible jail time, there were fines to clear up, his drivers license was suspended and could not be reinstated until he could purchase expensive insurance. After all that was accomplished, he would need to buy a car.

Kyle didn't try to apply for a regular job until his forthcoming court date, but he did find several odd jobs. I knew it must be quite frustrating for him to know he was going to have to work indefinitely with little, if any, discretionary income. Would he be tempted to return to the big bucks associated with drug dealing?

I hoped he would become involved in a recovery program, but he just seemed to want to get on with his life and put his drug life behind him. By this time I had accepted that I was powerless over his choices.

Though I didn't know much about her, Shelley, the girl he had been involved with for the past few months, came from a good, Christian family. The few times I had been around her or talked with her on the phone, she seemed sweet and kind of quiet. She expressed her desire to see Kyle escape from the drug lifestyle.

While Kyle was trying to clean up the mess from his destructive choices, I still had to work toward cleaning up my own mess. In Step Six, I did my best to become entirely ready to have God remove my defects of character. I now hoped to move forward from there.

STEP SEVEN ▶ Humbly asked Him to remove our shortcomings. (For additional information on Step Seven and a listing of Step Seven Reflections related to specific verses, see *Journey to Recovery Through Christ: CASA's 12-Step Study Bible*, pp. 25-26.)

The shortcomings named in Step Seven are the same as the defects of character from Step Six. And similar to a Step One problem, these things stand in the way of us growing closer to God.

The idea of being humble is often misunderstand as weakness, but the actual definition of the word sounds as if it were written for Step Seven: "having a consciousness of one's defects, modest."[1]

Interestingly, the words humble and humiliation both come from the same Latin base, *humilus*, which means "low."[2] In short, if we don't humble (or lower) ourselves in our own opinions of self, pride takes over and we will be humiliated (lowered).

Pride is the polar opposite of humility. The word "pride" is sometimes confusing because it has multiple, nearly opposite, meanings. For example, there is nothing wrong with having pride in a job well done. But the definition of pride that clashes with humility is this one: "an overly high opinion of oneself; haughtiness, arrogance;"[3] this is the type of pride that is often associated with Satan.

"When pride comes, then comes dishonor, but with the humble is wisdom" (Proverbs 11:2, p. 490).

Parallel to that proverb, Jesus concluded his Parable of the Wedding Feast (Luke 14:7-11, p. 130-131) by saying, "For everyone who exalts himself will be humbled, and he who humbles himself will be exalted" (Luke 14:11, p. 130).

The bottom line is that humility involves a comprehension of the magnitude of difference between God and self. It is important for me to grasp that He is the potter; I am the clay. He has all wisdom; I have little, if any. He is in control; I am powerless. God is wholly Spirit and His character and nature are perfect; I am a spiritual being dwelling in a physical body with conflicting natures.

I must be in submission to God—not because He is a harsh taskmaster but because He loves me and wants what is in my best interests.

Humility is a necessary prerequisite to answered prayer. "…to this one I will look, to him who is humble and contrite of spirit, and who trembles at My word" (Isaiah 66:2).

The authors of the book *Serenity* say that we need humility for three reasons:

1. So that we can recognize the severity of our character defects. One aspect of our addictions is that we tend to deny and minimize the pain they inflict. Therefore, as we try to assess our character defects, we may, unless we take a very humble approach, underestimate their severity.

2. So that we can acknowledge the limits of human power in addressing these character defects. We cannot do it on our own. We cannot do it by sheer willpower. We cannot do it by our own intellect and reasoning.

3. So that we can appreciate the enormity of God's power to transform lives.[4]

New Perspective on Prayer

While trying to pray during my legalistic past, my shortcomings often came to mind and caused me to wonder if God would even hear my prayers because I had not managed to overcome them. I found that I can be honest with God, confess that I still have problems and continue to ask for His help in removing them. Each shortcoming that is removed brings me a step closer to Him, opens the flow of communication and enhances that Father/child relationship.

When defects of character/shortcomings have been exposed and are ready to be removed, what happens next may be compared to entering the hospital to have a cancerous tumor surgically extracted. It requires great trust in the physician with the faith that complete healing is possible, although there may be pain involved in the post-op recuperation.

Instant relief is a definite possibility. Many people testify to immediately losing their craving for drugs or alcohol, instant relief from illness and other events that are unexplainable by science. Yet others may go through a long period of time fighting temptation.

Don Umphrey offers an explanation on why instant removal might not occur in every case.

> It could be that God wants to see some action on our part. Perhaps He will remove them if we first show we were indeed earnest in Step Six when we became ready for these things to be removed. Or it could be that we are consciously or unconsciously trying to put up a smokescreen and have skirted our true defects of character in Steps Four, Five and Six. Or maybe God has something completely different in mind, the magnitude of which we are not capable of even perceiving at the present time.[5]

An Al-Anon devotional writer sums up her experience.

> I begin to learn humility when I take the First Step. By admitting I am powerless, I make room for the possibility that a Power greater than myself can do all things that are beyond my reach. In other words, I begin to learn about what is, and is not, my responsibility. As this becomes clear, I am better able to do my part, for myself and for others, and better able to ask God to do the rest.[6]

When approaching God in prayer, asking Him to remove shortcomings or for guidance in any situation, it is important to believe and expect answers. "If you then, being evil, know how to give good gifts to your children, how much more will your Father who is in heaven give what is good to those who ask Him!" (Matthew 7:11, p. 47).

While struggling with Kyle's addiction and praying fervently each day, I was advised repeatedly to continue seeking help in Al-Anon meetings.

On another occasion, while studying the "fruit of the Spirit" (Galatians 5:22, p. 264), I found myself to be particularly lacking in peace and began to pray for peace. While visiting a young lady who attended our church, though I had not made mention of my lack of peace, she offered me the book, *21 Ways to Finding Peace and Happiness: Overcoming Anxiety, Fear and Discontentment Every Day* by Joyce Meyer.[7] I could have considered this to be a strange coincidence or conclude that God's providence might be at work. The book provided tremendous insight and food for thought.

My Thorn in the Flesh

When Paul petitioned God on three occasions for relief from his "thorn in the flesh," he was reminded, "My grace is sufficient for you, for power is perfected in weakness" (2 Corinthians 12:9, p. 257). I had prayed multiple times for my thorn of chronic pain of trigeminal neuralgia to be removed. I had approached my chronic back pain from every conceivable angle. God's grace was proving to be sufficient in that enthusiasm and joy dominated my life more so than the pain. Was this the final answer?

When I first had symptoms of "panic disorder" about five years earlier, simply learning what physiological changes took place in the body and understanding what was happening in a panic attack had aided in overcoming them. Though I still felt panic occasionally, I had not had any full blown attacks in a couple of years.

I had thought that if I could learn exactly what was going on in my brain and body the same might be true with the chronic pain, but the doctors I had questioned only advised me that my problem was muscular rather than a disc or nerve. They had no idea why the spasms returned with a vengeance every few weeks.

Though still embarrassed that so much pain might be caused by my own mental state, I confessed these fears at the Al-Anon meeting one morning. I was surprised at what others confessed, one even admitting to having engaged in prostitution; the group never seemed shocked or judgmental.

The closing statements read at meetings declare that, "whatever your problems, one of us has had them, too." Sure enough, a lady approached me afterwards who had a similar problem and recommended books by Dr. John Sarno. He had studied and proven through numerous patients the "mind-body" connection to back pain. I purchased his books immediately.

Mine turned out to be a textbook case of the pain syndrome. By applying his theory, my pain decreased significantly. Every flare-up had increased my fear of another so that I began to avoid anything that would trigger a return of muscle spasms (quite similar to the strategy my mother used to control panic attacks). As what seemed to be becoming the "norm," I had to take the opposite approach by pretending to be well though the pain persisted.

It required moving forward with Dr. Sarno's method without knowing if it would actually work. To my surprise, his theory was that the primary mental component to back pain was repressed anger. This was quite shocking, as I never considered myself the one with the anger problem. Through Christian meditation and journaling, it became obvious that there was a tremendous amount of repressed anger that I was internalizing. I am still trying to learn to express (rather than suppress) my anger by learning to communicate my needs and feelings more effectively. I assume this will be a life-long process.

After a few less severe recurrences, the muscle spasms all but disappeared. Though I'm not totally pain free, it is mostly tension-related and significantly less debilitating. I can now ride bikes and enjoy activities with my grandchildren, as well as mow the yard and perform other chores that I had concluded were a thing of the past. My prayers would not likely have been answered had I not been honest about my problems and kept my mind, eyes and ears open.

"Listen and learn" is an Al-Anon slogan.

I had asked God to help me overcome my fear of speaking out when the need arose, whether it was expressing a need or opinion to an individual or speaking publicly. I felt this would require some effort on my part. I faced my fear of public speaking first by volunteering to lead Al-Anon meetings. The leader speaks for less than 10 minutes and then asks each person to share his or her personal experiences. I had become comfortable sharing with the group so this seemed like a good place to start.

Books that were instrumental in my growth process appeared out of nowhere. One was left on my doorstep by a friend. Two were left on the side of the road as garbage that I found on my morning walk. And yet another was found at a thrift store. If I had left those books lying where they were or failed to read them, I would have never received the insight God was providing.

Insights on Personal Relationships

I began to notice when I said something inappropriate. God seemed to be making me aware of how my words, actions and body language might be causing others to feel hurt, frustrated or angry. Awareness seemed to come through the voice of conscience or from words spoken by others that may have been previously ignored. "Many a truth is spoken in jest."

My children often jokingly described me as being "negative." I thought of myself as a positive thinker and tried to focus on the good in others. When I took this criticism to heart, it became apparent that many of my comments were of a negative nature. I have to be constantly on guard when it comes to these areas of weakness.

As spiritual growth occurred as the result of Bible study, prayer and putting the 12 steps into practice, I realized that the sleepless nights and the inability to focus on my daily tasks had greatly diminished. I was not as concerned about avoiding places that brought on claustrophobia. Anxiety was loosening its grip and what had been overwhelming was reduced to a manageable problem. This was not a benefit I expected to receive when joining the Al-Anon group hoping to find a way to help Kyle.

Anxiety and worry still hits me forcefully on occasion, such as when we learned our new grandson was developmentally delayed and the doctors really didn't know why he couldn't stand, hold a toy or make sounds. All the children in our family had been born healthy and normal. I immediately started projecting ahead.

What if he was confined to a wheelchair? What if he could never walk, talk or play? How would his parents cope with this extra responsibility? The list went on. This was normally something about which I would have worried incessantly, but my Al-Anon program kicked in quickly. I was able to gain control by focusing on the Serenity Prayer—accepting that I couldn't change the nature of his disabilities, but I could do everything possible to make his life enjoyable and assist his parents.

"One day at a time" proved invaluable as it does in any overwhelming situation.

He is now 14 with intellectual disabilities, autistic behavior and is mostly non-verbal. He is able to walk, dress himself, express his needs in one way or another and can even do simple computer tasks. He will never be able to hold a job, drive a car, get married or perform usual adult tasks. I try not to project ahead as to what the future holds for him. But I do try to assist his parents by giving them a break from caring for him or even an occasional vacation without him.

If not for the Al-Anon program, I would have probably obsessed years into the future, trying to figure out who would care for him when his grandparents and parents are deceased.

These defects of worry and anxiety tend to reappear as new situations emerge and changes and adjustments occur that are a normal part of aging.

The more I am able to pray and trust God with the outcome, the more He is faithful to provide strength and courage to face these challenges, and the less they interrupt my peace of mind. God may simply help me get through a difficulty and at times may bless me "…far more abundantly beyond all that we ask or think, according to the power that works within us…" (Ephesians 3:20, p. 268).

Marriage Improvements

I had tried for some time to detach from what I perceived as criticism or negativity coming from Flynn and stop reacting and responding in kind. I almost had to put duct tape over my mouth at first, but it got easier with practice. It alleviated the tension and made for a more peaceful atmosphere. Trading insult for insult had never done anything to improve the situation.

I was eventually able to take it to the next level and offer praise where it was due from time to time. Flynn was always a hard worker and never signed a paycheck. He just handed it to me on pay day. I signed his name and deposited it in the bank to pay bills. He even did extra jobs for his own spending money.

Flynn kept things up around the house and took care of car maintenance. He always attended church and participated in the work of the church. We had many Christian friends and enjoyed spending time with their families. He took me out on a date night each week and bought me gifts and flowers. Though he might sometimes get angry, he had never been physically abusive. Yet I dared not praise him for the positive things he did for fear it would give him the idea that the negative behavior was okay. When I finally praised him for something, he practically glowed!

I also started to notice that he was a little less critical and praised me for cooking meals and other things he had taken for granted.

As usual, God's way was working better than mine. "Finally, brethren, whatever is true, whatever is honorable, whatever is right, whatever is pure, whatever is lovely, whatever is of good repute, if there is any excellence and if anything worthy of praise, dwell on these things" (Philippians 4:8, p. 274).

Facing Kyle's upcoming court date was the next hurdle to cross. It was painful to think of him possibly going to prison when he seemed ready to continue his education and get his life straightened out, but I did my best to take it one day at a time.

Biblical Questions for Self-Examination

HUMILITY/HUMILIATION

Use the *Journey to Recovery Through Christ: CASA's 12-Step Study Bible* or any other version of the *New American Standard Bible* © 1995 to fill in the blanks in biblical passages below.

1. a. In what way is humility the opposite of pride? _____

   _____

   _____

   b. **A man's _____ will bring him _____, but a _____ spirit will obtain _____** (Proverbs 29:23, p. 516).

   c. How did Janet demonstrate pride in her relationship with Flynn and how did this impact their marriage?____

   _____

   _____

   _____

   d. What accounted for the improvement in their marriage and how does this reflect humility? _____

   _____

   _____

e. Describe a time in your life when you humiliated yourself due to pride.

_____

_____

f. Do you believe it was God's will for you to feel humiliated? (circle one)   yes   or   no

g. Why or why not? _____

_____

_____

h. If you were going to relive that same circumstance that you described in 1.e., what would you do differently so that the outcome would reflect your humility rather than your humiliation?

_____

_____

2. a. **The _____ of the _____ is the instruction for _____,
   and before _____ comes _____** (Proverbs 15:33, p. 497).

   b. The definition of fear found in the verse above is "awe, reverence."[8] Thinking of "fear" in those terms, give a specific example from your own life of how you discovered the truth of Proverbs 15:33 (p. 497).

   _____

   _____

   c. **When _____ comes, then comes _____, but with the
   _____ is _____** (Proverbs 11:2, p. 490).

   d. Give a specific example from your own life of how you discovered the truth of the above passage.

   _____

   _____

AM I NUMBER ONE?

Following is an exchange between Jesus and His disciples.

3. a. **...He *began* to question them, "What were you discussing on the way?" But they kept silent, for on the way they had discussed with one another which of *them* was the _____.
   Sitting down, He called the twelve and said to them, "If anyone wants to be _____,
   he shall be _____ of all and _____ of all"** (Mark 9:33-35, p. 93).

b. Read Luke 14:7-11 (p. 130). How does that passage parallel Mark 9:33-35 (p. 93) which is quoted above?

_____

_____

_____

c. Give an example of how you have seen the truth of these scriptures in your life. _____

_____

_____

GLIMPSES OF GOD'S POWER

4. Read Psalm 33:1-22 (pp. 371-372). Then in the spaces below, list five things from these verses that stand out in your mind about the power of God.

1) _____

_____

2) _____

_____

3) _____

_____

4) _____

_____

5) _____

_____

5. Read Psalm 139:1-18 (pp. 467-468). Then in the spaces below, list five things that stand out in your mind from these verses that indicate God's power as it relates to you.

1) _____

_____

2) _____

_____

3) _____

_____

4) _____

_____

5) _____
_____

6. a. How has your perception of your knowledge, wisdom and power changed since you took Step One?
        Be specific. _____

        _____

        _____

    b. How has your perception of God's knowledge, wisdom and power changed since you took Step One? _____

        _____

        _____

        _____

    c. How has your understanding of God changed since you took Step Two? _____

        _____

        _____

        _____

SOME IMPORTANT KEYS

7. a. **"For we walk by _____, not by _____"** (2 Corinthians 5:7, p. 252).

    b. **And Jesus answered and said to them, "Truly I say to you, if you have _____ and
        do not _____, you will not only do what was done to the fig tree, but even if you say
        to this mountain, 'Be taken up and cast into the sea,' it will happen. And all things you ask in
        _____, believing, you will _____"** (Matthew 21:21-22, p. 68).

    c. **"_____, and it will be given to you; _____, and you will find; _____,
        and it will be opened to you. For everyone who _____ _____, and he
        who _____ finds, and to him who _____ it will be _____"**
        (Matthew 7:7-8, p. 47).

    d. How do the three passages above apply to Step Seven? _____

        _____

        _____

        _____

        _____

8. a. Read Mark 9:14-30 (p. 50-51). **And Jesus said to him, "'If you can?' 'All things are possible to him who _____.' Immediately the boy's father cried out and said, 'I do _____; help my _____'"** (Mark 9:23-24, p. 93).

   b. What can you learn from the father's statement above that will be helpful as you work Step Seven? _____

   _____

   _____

ASKING FOR THE WRONG THING

9. a. **"You _____ and do not _____, because you _____ with _____ _____, so that you may _____ *it* on your _____"**
   (James 4:3, p. 310).

   b. Give an example of when you asked God for the wrong thing? _____

   _____

   _____

   c. What did it take for you to discover that you were off base in your request to God? _____

   _____

   _____

THE TIMING OF GOD'S ANSWERS

10. a. **"_____ for the _____; be _____ and let your _____ take _____; yes, _____ for the Lord"** (Psalm 27:14, p. 367).

    b. **"Therefore humble yourselves under the mighty hand of God, that He may exalt you at _____ _____ _____, casting all your _____ on Him, because He _____ for you** (1 Peter 5:6-7, p. 315).

    c. Can you think of a time in your life when God's answer to your petition was not answered according to your timetable? (circle one)   yes   or   no

    d. If yes, tell why God's timing was better than your timing. _____

    _____

    _____

11. a. Read 2 Corinthians 12:1-10 (p. 257). Paul said he had approached God three times to remove what he described as "a thorn in the flesh." But God's answer to him was, **"My _____ is**

sufficient for you, for _____ is perfected in _____” (2 Corinthians 12:9, p. 257).

b. Paul concluded, **“Therefore I am _____ _____ with**

_____, with _____, with _____,

with _____, with _____, for Christ's sake; for

when I am _____, then I am _____” (2 Corinthians 12:10, p. 257).

c. How is it possible for a person to delight in the negative things Paul mentioned in the verse above and find that weakness makes one strong? _____

_____

_____

d. Have you ever earnestly prayed for something specific, but God's answer to you turned out to be "no." (circle one)   yes   or   no

e. If yes to the above, what did you think after realizing the answer was "no"? _____

_____

_____

_____

f. Were you able to see in the long-term that God knew your needs better than you? (circle one)   yes   or   no

g. Describe it here. _____

_____

_____

_____

AA'S SEVENTH STEP PRAYER

My Creator, I am now willing that you

should have all of me, good and bad.

I pray that you now remove from me

every single defect of character which

stands in the way of my usefulness to

you and my fellows. Grant me strength,

as I go out from here, to do your bidding. [9]

IN CONCLUSION

What a relief it is to gain some glimpses of humility by having a much more realistic picture of who we really are and who God really is. With this new insight, we approach our all-powerful Heavenly Father and petition Him through prayer about taking away our defects of character. We have faith and believe that God's actions—or seeming inactions—will enable us to walk closer with Him.

Through prayer, I have sought God in a humble manner and have asked Him to remove my shortcomings.

_____   _____

Your Signature   **Today's Date**

Write down some insights you've gained from this lesson. To gauge your spiritual progress, in the future look back on what you've written here.

_____

_____

_____

_____

_____

End Notes

1. *Webster's New World Dictionary*, Popular Library, New York, 1973, 281.

2. Ibid.

3. op. cit., 452.

4. Dr. Robert Hemfelt and Dr. Richard Fowler, *Serenity—A Companion for Twelve Step Recovery, (complete with New Testament, Psalms and Proverbs)*, Thomas Nelson, Nashville, 1990, 54-55.

5. Don Umphrey, *12 Steps to a Closer Walk with God: A Guide for Small Groups*, Quarry Press, Dallas, 2004, 85.

6. *Courage to Change*, Al-Anon Family Group Headquarters, Inc., Virginia Beach, 126.

7. Joyce Meyer, *21 Ways to Finding Peace and Happiness: Overcoming Anxiety, Fear and Discontentment Every Day*, Faith Words, Brentwood, 2007.

8. *Webster's New World Dictionary*, Popular Library, New York, 1973, 214.

9. *Alcoholics Anonymous, Third Edition*, Alcoholics Anonymous World Services, Inc. New York, 1976, 76.

Assessing Harm Done to Others

Within a few days Kyle had to appear in court to plead to the charge of selling marijuana to an undercover officer. Since he could no longer afford the prominent attorney he had used previously, the judge would appoint an attorney to work on Kyle's behalf. Flynn and I assumed that he was facing at least two years in prison because he was already on probation. A year or so earlier, he had received a two-year suspended sentence after being convicted of attempting to purchase marijuana.

The good news was that the two-year sentence did not apply due to a legal technicality. The bad news was that the current charge carried a mandatory three-year sentence.

Since he was 19, Kyle could still apply for "youthful offender status." If approved, it would mean that Kyle would appear in juvenile court and information about the trial would not be disclosed to the general public. Young people may receive treatment methods that are aimed at rehabilitation rather than prison time for the purpose of punishment. Youthful offender status would also mean that a felony conviction would not be on his record for years to come, which was another one of my many prayer requests.

On the downside Kyle had already received this status once. Certainly, a judge would take this into consideration.

We had concerns about how well Kyle's court-appointed lawyer would defend him. He also represented the policemen in our city who, rightfully, had a particular disdain for Kyle and his drug-dealing buddies. They had declared on several occasions they would "put him away" as soon as he was old enough to be tried as an adult.

Until the trial, if there was a possibility that Kyle was going to live at home, I knew I had to make every effort to make our home as peaceful as possible. Through the previous steps, I had uncovered my own defects that had contributed to the problems in my marriage. I wanted to press on and continue to make adjustments in my relationship with Flynn, Kyle and others.

STEP EIGHT ▶ Made a list of all persons we had harmed and became willing to make amends to them all. (For additional information on Step Eight and a listing of Step Eight Reflections related to specific verses, see *Journey to Recovery Through Christ: CASA's 12-Step Study Bible*, pp. 27-28.)

In Step Eight we have two major concerns: 1) recognizing the people to whom we owe amends; and 2) becoming willing to make amends to them all.

This step can prove to be a challenge for codependents. As family members and friends of alcoholics and addicts, we have often been lied to, stolen from, manipulated and suffered a tremendous amount of worry, anxiety and financial hardship as a result of their self-centered behaviors. We usually feel that the harm we have done is quite miniscule compared to the harm done to us.

Of course, codependents are just as prone to live in denial as addicts.

The harm I had done to others became increasingly obvious through Steps Four and Five. If people coming out of addiction and codependency are truly ready to let God remove their defects of character in Step Six and ask Him to remove these things in Step Seven, the harm created through self-centered behavior becomes glaringly obvious. Self-justifications are stripped away.

A Sure Sign of Repentance

The principle of making amends has been around for thousands of years. Jesus encountered Zacchaeus, a dishonest tax collector who was entirely ready to give up whatever was standing between himself and God (See Luke 19:1-10, p. 138). Zacchaeus responded to Jesus by saying, "Behold, Lord, half of my possessions I will give to the poor, and if I have defrauded anyone of anything, I will give back four times as much" (Luke 19:8, p. 138).

The Law of Moses required that a person make full restitution for a wrong committed and add one-fifth to it (See Numbers 5:5-10). Rather than 20 percent interest added to the original debt, Zacchaeus was willing to pay 400 percent.

Step Eight does not involve actually making amends. Rather, the purpose of this step is to identify who may have been harmed by one's words and actions. It is not necessary at this stage to plan how to make any amends, which is a function of Step Nine, or to mentally rehearse actual amends.

It is beneficial to list even those who may be deceased or with whom we have lost contact and don't know their present whereabouts. There also may be people on our list whose names we either never knew or don't now recall.

Even if we have suffered harm by the self-centeredness of someone else, the words and example of Jesus serve to convince us that we are responsible for our wrongdoing whether or not the other party owns up to his or her part of it.

"...Love your enemies, do good to those who hate you, bless those who curse you, pray for those who mistreat you" (Luke 6:27-28, p. 115).

Jesus endured pain beyond our understanding at the hands of men who not only rejected His message but also despised Him. Yet He uttered the following words in response: "Father, forgive them; for they do not know what they are doing" (Luke 23:34, p. 146).

Forgiving others plays a large role in becoming willing to make all needed amends. A Christian author summed up the importance of this:

> The blame game is behind us; our goal is to be tough on self and easy on others. You can see, then, that Step Eight includes forgiving others—whether or not they have asked for forgiveness—and then becoming willing to ask their forgiveness for the harm that we have done to them. We forgive all others, not because they have apologized to us but rather to set us free from bitterness, resentments and the need for revenge.[1]

When taking Step Eight, it is helpful to review one's written Step Four inventory, particularly the resentment list.

My contributions to the problems in my marriage became clearer. I knew I needed to acknowledge them and become willing to make amends to Flynn. We had each brought our own baggage into the marriage.

Though I had read many books on improving marital relations, I had never taken seriously the advice that concerned me and often seethed in anger and resentments.

I had been less effective as a mother by not being proactive in ending the tension and anger in our home, so I owed amends to my children. By acting on my character defects I was partially responsible for their emotional wounds. Rather than blaming Flynn, I should have turned to God, studied His Word, and sought counseling on my own. Had I done so, I might have even discovered the Al-Anon group sooner.

Who Owes the Amend?

I also knew I owed amends to Kyle, even though he had caused me a tremendous amount of worry and distress. Resentment sometimes flared up because he could have been an asset to me, especially helping with his younger brother during my mother's illness. I had to own the fact that our family dysfunction had contributed to his emotional issues, even though it was his choice to turn to drug use to cope with it.

As a codependent, I also had to realize that though I meant well, a tremendous amount of harm may have been done by "enabling" the addict. Without someone cushioning their fall, providing financial support, making excuses for them, and picking up the pieces after a crisis, addicts may "hit bottom" sooner rather than later. One example of enabling Kyle had been buying him a car when he had not proven he was capable of handling that responsibility.

Despite my program, I continued to struggle with whether to shield him from the consequences of his actions, such as hiring him a good attorney now that he seemed serious about staying drug free. Still I felt this would be enabling.

I could definitely look back and see how I had enabled my mother and others so that they were never compelled to seek help for their problems. I had tried to control their surroundings and walk on eggshells to make sure they did not have cause to get angry, upset or anxious. I constantly tried to be the peacemaker rather than letting others deal with their own relationships and find solutions.

Most codependents who are working a recovery program readily admit to being controlling. We spend a lot of time and effort trying to manipulate and persuade others to act the way we think they should. Al-Anon members admit to hunting for hidden bottles of liquor and pouring them down the drain, hiding bottles of medication, warning the addict's physician of the problem, driving around town trying to locate the addict, and constantly reminding them of their responsibilities.

In our efforts to control, usually with constant nagging and criticism, we contribute to the addict's feelings of worthlessness, shame and guilt.

Though Flynn was not addicted to drugs or alcohol, I had been guilty of the same conduct of those dealing with active addiction by constantly trying to make him aware of his character defects and pointing out ways he could improve rather than working on my own problems.

My Willingness Would Have to Suffice

There were instances in my past where other people were wronged in some manner but making a true amend would have been impossible. While we were on vacation years earlier, for example, I had lied by asking for the "child discount" at a restaurant when actually the child was above the age limit to receive it. Looking back, I couldn't remember where it had occurred.

I had also received money on a couple of occasions that was due to a mistake and made only minimal effort to correct the error.

In those instances confession to God and "willingness" to make amends if the opportunity arose would have to suffice.

I would have loved the opportunity to make amends to some who were deceased—my father and my grandparents for not easing their burdens, spending enough time with them or demonstrating affection. There were many times I regretted just not giving someone a hug when they needed it.

Studying the Bible with fresh eyes confirmed the focus of Al-Anon. God's will for me is to discard the toxic traits of the flesh that keep me enslaved to the cycle of dysfunction while also embracing the fruit of the Spirit: love, joy, peace, patience, kindness, goodness, faithfulness, gentleness and self-control. (See Galatians 5:22-23, p. 264.) Making amends is a huge step in the right direction.

Though I was satisfied that Kyle seemed to be getting on the right track and I had forgiven him for all the worry, stress and sleepless nights he had caused me, even an apology would have meant a lot to me. But I knew that this would only come with time and if he immersed himself into a recovery program, which had not happened.

Kyle had made some positive changes in the months before he went to court such as getting his GED and enrolling in the local community college. However, he had moved out of the house and was staying with Shelley's family a few miles away. I had hoped he would proceed slowly with a romantic relationship and focus on his recovery.

It was of some relief that the move had at least put some distance between him and his drug-using cohorts. It was a bit disconcerting, though, when he told me he had met up with them at a restaurant for a birthday celebration. He admitted that he missed his friends and just wanted to see them occasionally yet not get involved with drugs again. This seemed like a dangerous compromise.

But I knew I needed to stay detached and let him make his own decisions without trying to control the situation and give him unwanted advice.

I started to wonder if it was in his overall best interest for the judge to be lenient, as per my prayers. Where previously I had made specific requests to God, I was finally truly submitting to His will. I knew God could see the "big picture" and I certainly could not predict or control Kyle's choices. Though he was almost 20 years old, his reasoning ability seemed more on the level of a young teen, which is typical for someone who has used mind-altering substances during developmental years.

The night before Kyle appeared in court, I was anxious, but ready to get it over with and begin the process of getting through whatever occurred. His attorney did not appear to have his best interests at heart, and I warned Kyle that he better be willing to speak up for himself and try to convince the judge he had truly changed. But Kyle still seemed to think he had it under control. He reasoned that it was only a small amount of marijuana involved rather than "hard drugs," the jails and prisons were overcrowded, and his friends had gotten off time and again.

I wasn't so sure that his reasoning was correct but held my peace.

Biblical Questions for Self-Examination

THIS STARTS WITH FORGIVENESS

Use the *Journey to Recovery Through Christ: CASA's 12-Step Study Bible* or any other version of the *New American Standard Bible* © 1995 to fill in the blanks in biblical passages below.

1. a. **To sum up, all of you be** _____, _____,
   _____, **kindhearted, and humble in** _____; **not returning**
   _____ **for** _____ **or insult for insult, but giving a**
   _____ **instead; for you were** _____ **for the very**
   _____ **that you might inherit a** _____ (1 Peter 3:8-9, p. 314).

   b. **"You have heard that it was said, 'YOU SHALL** _____ **YOUR**
   _____ **and** _____ **your enemy.' But I say to you,** _____ **your**
   _____ **and** _____ **for those who persecute you"** (Matthew 5:43-44, p. 44).

   c. Based on the two passages above, what two things do we need to do for people who we believed caused
   us harm?
   1) _____

   2) _____

2. a. **Never pay back** _____ **for** _____ **to anyone. Respect what is** _____
   in the _____ **of all men. If possible, so far as it depends on you, be at** _____
   with all men. Never take your own _____, **beloved, but leave room for the wrath of**
   _____, **for it is written, "**_____ **IS MINE, I WILL** _____ **" says the**
   Lord (Romans 12:17-19, p. 228).

   b. Whose job is it to punish people who have harmed you? _____

ETERNAL RELATIONSHIPS

3. a. **"Therefore if you are presenting your offering at the altar, and there remember that your**
   brother has something _____ **you, leave your** _____ **there**
   before the altar and go; first be _____ **to your brother, and then come and**
   _____ **your offering"** (Matthew 5:23-24, p. 43).

   b. **Beloved, if God so** _____ **us, we also ought to** _____ **one another. No one has**

_____ **God at any time; if we _____ one another,**

God _____ in us, and His love is _____ in us

(1 John 4:11-12, p. 322).

c. Go back and review what you wrote in 14.b. – 14.i. in the Step Four chapter. From that and from 3.a. and 3.b. above, what do you conclude about the way one's relationship with other people affects his or her relationship with God? _____

_____

_____

A DARKENED PATH

4. a. **The one who says he is in the _____ and yet _____ his brother**

is in the darkness until now. The one who _____ his brother abides in the

_____ and there is no cause for _____ in him. But the

one who _____ his brother is in the _____ and

walks in the _____, and does not know where he is going because the

_____ has _____ his eyes (1 John 2:9-11, p. 320).

b. What is the effect on one's walk with God when someone hates another person? _____

_____

_____

c. Have you found this principle to be true in your own life? (circle one)   yes   or   no

d. If yes, give an example.

_____

_____

WHY SHOULD WE FORGIVE?

5. a. **"For if you _____ others for their _____, your**

_____ Father will also _____ you. But if you do not forgive

_____ , then your Father will _____ forgive your transgressions"

(Matthew 6:14-15, p. 45).

b. **"Whenever you stand _____, forgive, if you have anything against**

_____, so that your _____ who is in _____

will also _____ you your transgressions" (Mark 11:25, p. 96).

c. What does Jesus tell us we gain by forgiving others? _____

_____

6.   Read Matthew 18:23-35 (p. 65).

a. In this parable who does the king represent? (circle one)

1) King Nebuchadnezzar

2) The President of the U.S.

3) God

4) A banker

b. Who does the man who owed the king ten thousand talents represent? (Note: One talent was more than fifteen year's wages for a laborer.) (circle one)

1) A man who charged too much on his credit card

2) Zacchaeus

3) The rich young ruler

4) You (No, not me, the author. You, the reader.)

c. Who does the fellow servant who owed the other man a hundred denarii represent?
(Note: A denarius was one day's wages.) (circle one)

1) A boy who spit on you in the fifth grade

2) A parent who abused you

3) A woman who cut you off in traffic this morning and gave you an obscene gesture

4) Your worst enemy (besides yourself)

5) Everyone else you have resentments against

6) All of the above

d. What did Jesus want you to understand when He compared a debt of ten thousand talents to a debt of a hundred denarii? _____

_____

_____

_____

7.   a. **Then Peter came and said to Him, "Lord, how often shall my brother sin against me and I _____ him? Up to seven times?" Jesus said to him, "I do not say to you, up to seven times, but up to _____ times _____"** (Matthew 18:21-22, p.65).

b. In the passage above was Jesus advocating that people keep a running total of the harm done to them? (circle one)   yes   or   no

c. If yes to 7.b., return to Go and do not collect $200.

d. If no to 7.b., what was the Lord's intent? _____

_____

e. How can you put this into practice in your life? _____

_____

_____

FINGER-POINTING PROBLEMS

8. a. Go back and re-read what you wrote in 11.a. – 11.c. in the Step Four chapter. According to the passage in 11.a., Step Four, we have a tendency to focus on other people's faults while at the same time overlooking our own, greater faults. Give three examples of when you have done this.

1) _____

_____

2) _____

_____

3) _____

_____

b. Why is it important for us to recognize our tendency toward finger-pointing as we approach Step Eight? ____

_____

_____

_____

_____

9. Read Romans 1:18-32 (p. 216).

a. What kind of activities are described there and what is the mindset of the people involved? _____

_____

_____

_____

b. **Therefore you have no excuse, every one of you who passes _____, for in that which you _____ another, you _____ yourself; for you who _____ practice the same things** (Romans 2:1, p. 217).

c. **"Do not** _____ **, and you will not be** _____ **; and do not**
_____ **, and you will not be** _____ **; pardon, and**
you will be _____ **"** (Luke 6:37, p. 116).

d. How is finger-pointing tied to judging others? _____

_____

_____

e. How is judging others related to forgiveness? _____

_____

_____

A NEW PERSPECTIVE

10. a. **Do nothing from** _____ **or** _____ _____ **, but**
    with _____ **of mind regard one another as more** _____
    than yourselves; do not *merely* **look out for your own personal** _____ **, but**
    also for the interests of others. Have this _____ **in yourselves which was also**
    in _____ _____ **...** (Philippians 2:3-5, p. 272).

b. After working Step Seven and possibly getting some new ideas about humility, the passage above may take
   on a new meaning for you. What do you now get out of this Scripture? _____

_____

_____

c. How does this insight help you in determining those to whom you need to make amends? _____

_____

_____

AMENDS NEEDED

11. a. Think of a person to whom you owe amends but have only recently recognized the need to make this amend.
    What prompted you to come to the realization that amends are now necessary? _____

_____

_____

_____

b. What is different in your life now that allowed you to see that amends are needed? _____

_____

_____

c. What do you gain by realizing there are people to whom you owe amends? _____

_____

_____

d. After recognizing the individuals to whom you need to make amends, what would prevent you from becoming willing to make the needed amends? _____

_____

_____

12. a. **All the ways of a man are _____ in his own sight, but the _____ weighs the _____** (Proverbs 16:2, p. 497)

b. How does the above passage relate to being in denial? _____

_____

_____

c. How could denial prevent a person from working Step Eight successfully? _____

_____

_____

13. Janet wrote the following in regard to Step Eight: "This step can prove to be a challenge for codependents. As family members and friends of alcoholics and addicts, we have often been lied to, stolen from, manipulated and suffered a tremendous amount of worry, anxiety and financial hardship as a result of their self-centered behavior. We usually feel that the harm we have done is quite miniscule compared to the harm done to us."

a. Does it make sense to you that some codependents feel this way? (circle one)   yes   or   no

b. To what extent do you feel this way? _____

_____

c. What did Janet finally conclude about making amends to Kyle? _____

_____

_____

_____

d. Why did she think it was important to make amends to Kyle? _____

_____

_____

_____

e. How does a codependent individual become willing to make amends to an addicted loved one who may never make any amends to them? _____

_____

_____

MAKING OUR LIST

Having completed this lesson, you are now ready to go to work on Step Eight. Pray for God's guidance in this process. Using separate sheets of paper, write down the names of the people you have harmed and ways in which you have harmed them. This may take place over a period of time as you will probably think about names that need to be included as you go about your daily routine. There is a good chance that you will want the help of a minister, spiritual advisor or sponsor. When you have completed the list, confess these names to God and ask Him to give you the willingness to make things right with these people.

IN CONCLUSION

If it were just God and us, we probably wouldn't need Step Eight. But since we do live in a world filled with other people who also are created in the image of God, our relationship with Him is tied to our relationship with them. We've hurt some people in our self-centered pasts, and it is now time to recognize these individuals. Once we do, we become willing to make amends to them. This is even the case when the harm went both ways. Our willingness to make amends will often be tied with our willingness to forgive. As we go to work on this step, we need to remember how much God has forgiven us.

I have now completed my Step Eight list and have become willing to make amends to each person on it.
(circle one)   yes   or   no

_____   _____

Your Signature   **Today's Date**

Write down some insights you've gained from this lesson. To gauge your spiritual progress, in the future look back on what you've written here.

_____

_____

End Notes

1. Don Umphrey, *Journey to Recovery through Christ, CASA's 12 Step Study Bible*, Quarry Press, Dallas, 2015, 27-28.

Making Amends

Kyle's long-anticipated court date finally arrived after nine months of waiting. Kyle took with him proof that he had finished a semester of college and references from people for whom he had done yard work and from his current job as a farmhand.

Surely these things would help to show the judge that Kyle was serious about making positive change in his life. But there was really no question of his guilt. We were only hoping for mercy.

Prior to going before the judge, Flynn, Kyle and I briefly met with his attorney and presented him with Kyle's information. This was only the second time Kyle had spoken to him in the several months since he was appointed by the court.

Just as we had feared, when they went before the judge, the only information his attorney offered was that Kyle had finished rehab in the past. He mentioned nothing about his attending college, his employment or anything else. The judge gave Kyle a chance to speak, and Kyle told about his incarceration in Colorado, the trip home on the prison van and how it had resulted in him hitting "rock bottom."

Asking the judge for another chance, Kyle testified that he was through with drugs and a life of crime.

I wanted to scream at Kyle to speak up about what he had accomplished since then but knew it wasn't my place to do so. The judge reminded him that the mandatory sentence for this charge was three years in prison. His lawyer said nothing, and neither did Kyle.

My heart sank.

In a sudden case of role reversal, the district attorney spoke up and recommended that Kyle be sent to a military style boot camp facility, which could be completed in six months if he did well. Otherwise, his sentence would be carried out.

While this was a big relief in contrast to three years in prison, the boot camp would be no walk in the park. An acquaintance's son had been there, and she had shared some experiences that were quite disturbing. If one person broke the rules, they were all punished with excessive exercise, withholding some of their food, and not allowing them to make their weekly phone calls. She also said the inmates were not given prompt medical care and parents were not allowed to call the facility about any concerns or send anything that might be needed. If a parent did send something, the inmate was punished for it.

Would Kyle survive there with his stomach problems? Could I survive his six-month sentence?

I had already grown tremendously through this very turbulent time in my life. Looking back, I could see that each step I had taken in the Al-Anon program had been of great benefit and had both strengthened and prepared me for whatever we might face. I could only hope that with continued spiritual growth, I could survive what I earlier believed would have put me completely over the edge.

Though the boot camp would be difficult for Kyle, I knew it was possible for him to turn it into an experience for positive spiritual growth. All I could do was press on with my program.

STEP NINE ▶ Made direct amends to such people wherever possible, except when to do so would injure them or others. (For additional information on Step Nine and a listing of Step Nine Reflections related to specific verses, see *Journey to Recovery Through Christ: CASA's 12-Step Study Bible*, pp. 29-30.)

Having done my best to name the people I had harmed and become willing to make amends to them in Step Eight, I was ready to turn that willingness into action in Step Nine.

First, it was necessary to determine if further harm could be done by making amends. An example would be a case of marital infidelity where spouse and children on both sides of the equation could be harmed by attempting to ease the guilt of an adulterer. In a case like this one's willingness must suffice. This also holds true for people on a Step Eight list who are either deceased or those of whom we have lost contact.

A sponsor can help to sort out where further harm might be done by attempting to make amends.

Why are we well-grounded in recovery before making amends? A Christian author explains:

> There are good reasons for the restitution steps to be numbers eight and nine rather than two or three. At the beginning of our journey through the steps, we would have a difficult time recognizing when our actions may have harmed others. Having now gained some humility, we are in a much better position to recognize not only who belongs on our list, but also why someone might be harmed by our making amends.[1]

Amends may be made by phone, letter, or e-mail, but a personal meeting is best if at all possible. According to author Pinchas Lapide:

> How much more difficult it is to face an offended person, to swallow one's pride, and offer an apology than to go into the synagogue (or church) and confess one's sins together with the congregation! Yet it is precisely in this personal sacrifice that we must wring from our egos proof of the seriousness of our aspirations to reconciliation… Only the self-transcendence of asking for forgiveness and the personal courage of extending one's hand (with all the danger of being rebuffed) can bring the forgiveness that comes from above.[2]

There should be no expectations of how any person will respond to someone making amends. Some may have forgotten the incident that still bothered us, others will gladly accept our entreaty, but there may be some who continue to hold us in contempt. Regardless, we will no longer have to avoid people or assume they are carrying a grievance. We have done our part and can move on without shame and guilt.

What if individuals are not willing to make amends for the harm they have done to us? Then that is their problem. The only person over whom we have any control is ourselves. If we have been earnest in making amends and/or restitution, then we don't have to worry about the actions or inactions of others. Besides, we're the ones who are emotionally and spiritually crippled because of the resentments and guilt from our pasts.

As mentioned above, restitution may be included in making amends. Restitution is a part of the Old Testament Law (See Exodus 22:1-15).

"Blessed are the peacemakers, for they shall be called sons of God" (Matthew 5:9, p. 43).

A friend once told me of a family member whose life had been devastated by his use of alcohol. He had lost both his family and his business. Having turned his life over to God, he spent several years repairing the emotional damage he had caused and rebuilding his business. One day he called a business associate he had wronged years earlier and asked him if he could meet with him. Still resentful, this man told him something to the effect that he had no use for him and no desire to meet with him. The caller then informed his former partner that he had the $25,000 that he owed him and wanted to repay it. Needless to say, the man agreed to meet with him.

Gravesite Amends

When the offended party is deceased, there might be a way to secure peace in other ways such as by visiting the gravesite. I would have loved to have been able to make amends to my dad for not doing enough to relieve his burdens and not telling him how much I loved him. There was nothing that made my dad happier than doing a good turn for someone else. My amends could be made by filling a need for someone else. The first few years I tried to make a point to reach out to someone else on his birthday or Father's Day.

The amends with which I struggled the most were those to Flynn. Finally, one night as we were sharing a conversation about our past regrets, I acknowledged my part in our marital relations and apologized for my lack of forgiveness, resentment, sarcasm and criticism. He was overly gracious by replying that none of it was my fault and that he bore all the responsibility. I knew that wasn't true, but my amends to him lifted a big burden from me.

An Al-Anon devotional writer recounts her willingness to make amends to her mother in an upcoming visit.

> After my mother arrived, I had the feeling that this was "the time." I prayed for courage and asked my Higher Power to help me find the words. My mother sat down with me in a quiet moment and, to my amazement, brought up every subject I had wanted to discuss. I realized that the opportunity to be close to her had always existed, but I hadn't been willing, until then, to take part in it.[3]

Over a period of time, I acknowledged my role in the family drama to our sons. The only way I could truly make amends to them or to Flynn was to change my behavior and allow them to grow and mature by making their own choices even if it involved "trial and error."

Kyle was taking responsibility for his choices and refused to blame us for the consequence he was facing, so I felt he was maturing and growing. I regretted that he had to attend boot camp, but he and I both knew he deserved more than the sentence he received. It would have been easier if they would have taken him into custody immediately, but instead we were informed there was a waiting list for that facility. We had no idea when he would leave.

Biblical Questions for Self-Examination

Use the *Journey to Recovery Through Christ: CASA's 12-Step Study Bible* or any other version of the *New American Standard Bible* © 1995 to fill in the blanks in biblical passages below.

PEACE, BROTHER OR SISTER

1. a. **See that no one _____ another with _____ for _____, but always seek after that which is _____ for one another and for all _____** (1 Thessalonians 5:15, p. 281).

   b. **Pursue _____ with all men, and the _____ without which no one will see the _____. See to it that no one comes short of the grace of God; that no _____ _____ _____ springing up causes trouble, and by it many be defiled** (Hebrews 12:14-15, p. 305).

   c. Give an example of how such trouble could occur. _____

   _____

   _____

   d. **But the _____ from _____ is first _____, then _____, gentle, reasonable, full of _____ and good _____, unwavering, without hypocrisy. And the seed whose fruit is _____ is sown in peace by those who _____ _____** (James 3:17-18, p. 309).

   e. Peace-making is not confined to diplomats or the United Nations but also applies on a person-to-person basis. Thinking of peace in these terms, how does it fit your particular circumstance as you approach Step Nine?

   _____

   _____

   _____

   _____

GOD'S PLAN FOR MAKING THINGS RIGHT

2. a. Numbers 5:5-8 describes God's plan for His people to make restitution. It included confessing one's wrong and then making restitution by adding one-fifth to it. The passage then reads, **"But if the man has no relative to whom restitution may be made for the wrong, the restitution which is made for the wrong *must* go to the Lord for the priest..."** (Numbers 5:8).

b. Why do you think God wants His people to make the restitution to Him if neither the harmed person nor a close relative is available? _____

_____

_____

A TALE OF TWO SINNERS

3. Earlier we discussed the stories of both the Rich Young Ruler (Luke 18:18-25, p. 137) and Zacchaeus (Luke 19:1-10, p. 138). Before proceeding, please go back and re-read each story.

   a. Which of these two men do you think was more well-liked by the people around him?
   (circle one)   a) Rich Young Ruler;   b) Zacchaeus

   b. Why? _____

   _____

   _____

   c. Both sought out Jesus. What is the difference in their reasons for seeking the Lord?_____

   _____

   _____

   _____

   d. From strictly a monetary standpoint, how did each respond to Jesus? _____

   _____

   _____

   e. From strictly a spiritual standpoint, how did each respond to Jesus?_____

   _____

   _____

STEPPING UP TO THE PLATE

4. Read Hebrews 12:7-16, p. 305.

   a. How does the hardship of discipline discussed in this passage compare to the prospect of having to face someone you've been avoiding for a long time because of the harm you did him or her in the past?_____

   _____

   _____

   _____

b. **All** _____ **for the moment seems not to be** _____ **, but**

_____ **; yet to those who have been trained by it, afterwards it yields**

the _____ **fruit of righteousness** (Hebrews 12:11, p. 305).

c. Looking at the passage above, how is it possible that making amends and restitution would produce the positive things mentioned there? _____

_____

_____

5. a. Think of a time in your life when you had to apologize to someone and possibly make restitution for something you had done that was clearly wrong. How did you feel before making amends? _____

_____

_____

b. Why did you feel that way? _____

_____

c. How did you feel afterward? _____

_____

6. a. Benjamin Franklin wrote, "Never ruin an apology with an excuse." How does this apply to Step Nine? _____

_____

_____

7. a. Janet wrote that she faced her greatest challenge in making amends to whom? _____

_____

_____

b. What was the outcome of these amends? _____

_____

_____

8. a. In thinking about the amends you need to make, what are your major concerns?

_____

_____

b. Putting your concerns from 8.a. into the hands of God, how will you overcome your concerns? _____

_____

_____

_____

DISCERNING WHERE HARM COULD RESULT

9. a.. "In _____, therefore, _____ people the _____ way you want

them to _____ you, for this is the _____ and the _____ "

(Matthew 7:12, p. 47).

b. How do these words of Jesus apply to you when you are trying to determine how someone might be hurt by

your amend? _____

_____

_____

10. a. The _____ in _____ will be called _____, and

sweetness of _____ increases _____ (Proverbs 16:21, p. 498).

b. And this I pray, that your _____ may abound still more and more in real

_____ and all _____, so that you may _____

the things that are _____, in order to be _____ and

_____ until the day of Christ; having been filled with the fruit of

_____ which comes through Jesus Christ, to the glory and praise of God

(Philippians 1:9-11, p. 271).

c. How do the above two passages apply to you when trying to determine if amends would benefit or hurt

someone? _____

_____

_____

YOUR WILLINGNESS WILL BE ENOUGH FOR THESE

11. Of the people named on your list from Step Eight, which of those do you believe it would harm if you attempted

to make amends to them? You may wish to complete this and some of the other items below on separate sheets

of paper.

Name of Person	The Reason Amends Would Harm Him or Her
_____	_____
	_____
_____	_____
	_____
_____	_____
	_____
_____	_____
	_____
_____	_____
	_____

YOU'D MAKE AMENDS IF YOU KNEW THEIR WHEREABOUTS

12. List people to whom you owe amends but you don't know their whereabouts. This list could include anonymous individuals you've harmed. Write down names (where possible) and briefly describe what you will say to that person if the opportunity ever presents itself to make amends.

Name of Person	What You Would Say
_____	_____
	_____
_____	_____
	_____
_____	_____
	_____
_____	_____

_____   _____

_____   _____

                                 _____

THESE PEOPLE ARE NOT WITH US NOW

13.   List people to whom you owe amends who are now deceased. Write down the names and briefly describe what you would say to that person if you had the opportunity.

Name of Person   **What You Would Say**

_____   _____

                                 _____

_____   _____

                                 _____

_____   _____

                                 _____

_____   _____

                                 _____

_____   _____

                                 _____

_____   _____

                                 _____

WE OWE MORE THAN AMENDS TO THESE

14.   List people to whom you also owe restitution. Tell what you owe that person and what kind of plan you have for making that restitution.

                                                  What You Owe and
Name of Person   **Your Plan for Restitution**

_____   _____

                                 _____

_____ _____

_____ _____

_____ _____

_____ _____

_____ _____

_____ _____

 _____

APPROACHING THOSE WE HARMED

15. Start making amends to individuals on your Step Eight list whose whereabouts are known and who are not on your list of individuals who would be harmed by the amends. Write down the names of these people and tell the outcome of each amends.

Name of Person   **Outcome of the Amends**

_____ _____

 _____

_____ _____

 _____

_____ _____

 _____

_____ _____

 _____

_____ _____

 _____

16. **Do not withhold _____ from those to whom it is due, when it is in your _____ to _____** (Proverbs 3:27).

17. **Fools _____ at _____, but among the _____ there is _____ will** (Proverbs 14:9).

IN CONCLUSION

As we continue through the steps, we learn more about false pride; with Step Nine we see that it would prevent us from making amends to people we have harmed. Discernment from God will also provide insight as to when amends would cause harm. After we have done our very best with this step, we will no longer feel the need to cringe at the thought of certain people or hide at the sight of them. Again remembering that our relationship with other people is tied to our relationship with God, we grow even closer to Him as we mend our fences with others and make restitution where needed.

I have now completed Step Nine to the best of my ability by recognizing those who would be harmed by amends and making both amends and/or restitution when and where they were needed. (circle one)   yes   or   no

_____   _____

Your Signature   **Today's Date**

Write down some insights you've gained from this lesson. To gauge your spiritual progress, in the future look back on what you've written here.

_____

_____

_____

_____

_____

Endnotes

1. Don Umphrey, *Journey to Recovery Through Christ: CASA's 12-Step Study Bible*, Quarry Press, Dallas, 2015, 29-30.

2. Pinchas Lapide, *The Sermon on the Mount—Utopia or Program for Action?* Orbis Books, Maryknoll, 1986, 53-54.

3. *Courage to Change*, Al-Anon Family Group Headquarters, Virginia Beach, 1992, 163.

Ongoing Self-Examination

The night after Kyle received his sentence, I despaired over the fact that he was going to be incarcerated for several months or possibly longer. Had I been correct in my refusal to hire him a good attorney? Would he regress as a result of his being locked up with criminals? Or would this be the extra boost he needed to steer clear of drugs and stay on a spiritual path?

I prayed for peace and went to an Al-Anon meeting. Upon arrival, I noticed two guys who'd not been there previously. On the basis of their unkempt appearance, I wondered if they belonged. Perhaps they had mistaken our meeting for AA which met in the same building on a different night.

When it was my turn, I shared my misgivings about the attorney and my conflicting emotions about Kyle being incarcerated and whether he would be able to survive in that environment. I also wondered about my own ability to survive his imprisonment.

When it was their turn, it was these two men who provided the words of hope and peace that I needed. One admitted to having hated his father for allowing him to go to prison. It was there, however, that this man had turned his life over to God; his resentment had turned to gratitude because his father stood firm and demonstrated "tough love." The other man offered similar encouragement.

Shame on my judgmental attitude!

While waiting for the call to start serving his sentence, Kyle earned money to clear up fines, get his drivers license reinstated and put away some money for car insurance in anticipation of buying one later. He had a lot of clutter to clean up. Through God's grace I had cleaned up some of my own, but knew it was important to not regress and stay on track toward ongoing spiritual improvement.

STEP TEN ▶ Continued to take personal inventory and when we were wrong promptly admitted it. (For additional information on Step Ten and a listing of Step Ten Reflections related to specific verses, see *Journey to Recovery Through Christ: CASA's 12-Step Study Bible*, pp. 31-32.)

"But there is nothing covered up that will not be revealed, and hidden that will not be known. Accordingly, whatever you have said in the dark will be heard in the light, and what you have whispered in the inner rooms will be proclaimed upon the housetops" (Luke 12:2-3, p. 126).

This step brings to mind some acquaintances who were hoarders. Their living space dwindled as clutter piled up over the years. Their solution was to finally move out, abandon the avalanche of "stuff" and start over in a different house. I guessed that without some mindset changes, the clutter would pile up again in the new home. This turned out to be true.

Like the hoarders, my old thinking, old behaviors and destructive emotions would undoubtedly start accumulating again, and I could find myself in a worse situation than before if I didn't continue to work my spiritual program.

Such a plight is described below in Matthew 12:43-45 (pp. 55-56).

"Now when the unclean spirit goes out of a man, it passes through waterless places seeking rest, and does not find *it*. Then it says, 'I will return to my house from which I came'; and when it comes, it finds *it* unoccupied, swept, and put in order. Then it goes and takes along with it seven other spirits more wicked than itself, and they go in and live there; and the last state of that man becomes worse than the first..."

The book, *Narcotics Anonymous—It Works—How and Why*, describes the need for Step Ten.

The importance of keeping in touch with our thoughts, attitudes, feelings, and behavior cannot be overemphasized. Every day, life presents us with new challenges. Our recovery depends on our willingness to meet those challenges. Our experience tells us that some members relapse, even after long periods of clean time, because they have become complacent in recovery, allowing their resentments to build and refusing to acknowledge their wrongs. Little by little, those small hurts, half-truths, and "justified" grudges turn into deep disappointments, serious self-deceptions, and full-blown resentments. We can't allow these threats to compromise our recovery. We have to deal with situations such as these as soon as they arise.[1]

Just as addicts relapse and return to their addictive behavior even after years of abstinence, codependents can easily fall back into resentment, enabling, controlling and self-deception.

The idea of self-examination is not a new one for Christians. Paul wrote that it needs to occur when individuals take communion. "But a man must examine himself, and in so doing he is to eat of the bread and drink of the cup" (1 Corinthians 11:28, p. 242). This passage deals with divisions in the church based on economic status, but the self-examination mentioned in this passage reminds me of why Jesus died for my sins while giving me an opportunity to confess my wrongs to God in prayer.

Spiritual and Physical Health

This admonition from Paul continues as he makes a direct link between spiritual health and physical health, "For he who eats and drinks, eats and drinks judgment to himself if he does not judge the body rightly. For this reason many among you are weak and sick, and a number sleep" (1 Corinthians 11:29-30, p. 242).

Spiritual problems that I neglected to deal with had impacted me physically. When I allowed resentment to fester toward another person, I was allowing that person to become a literal "pain in the neck." When I finally realized my powerlessness over someone else's actions, I prayed and released her to God, and the pain in the neck began to subside.

Peace is powerful medicine!

In his book, *None of These Diseases*, S. I. McMillan, M.D. tied together a lack of forgiveness with physical diseases. "When Jesus said, 'Forgive seventy-times seven times,'[2] He was thinking not only of our souls, but saving our bodies from ulcerative colitis, toxic goiters, high blood pressure, and scores of other diseases.[3]

As an example from my own life, I was angry at a couple from church because I felt that they had taken advantage of my mother's declining mental state and lack of business expertise to make a deal with her on the sale of some property without one of her children present. They had apologized, denied any ulterior motives and we had worked out a compromise. I accepted their apology but struggled with forgiving them because the loss we incurred involved money that was needed for my mother's care. But especially when taking communion, I knew that I couldn't afford to nurse a grudge. I finally prayed about it and was able to truly forgive them.

I can eventually forgive but forgetting is sometimes another story. However, in this case, a few years later someone mentioned this disagreement and I realized I had actually forgotten it. I had not thought about it in a long time, even when I was in the company of the people I felt had wronged me.

I'm not sure that this saved me from having a toxic goiter, but I sure felt a lot of peace about it.

It has been tough for me to promptly admit wrongdoing as Step Ten requires. I didn't realize how hard it was for me to say "I was wrong" or "What I said sounded harsh; I didn't mean to hurt your feelings" until trying to practice it on a regular basis. In the past I may have realized that I had hurt someone or made them angry (usually by the look on their face or body language), but I kept trying to find a way to justify it, deny or ignore it, or wait and hope it would blow over. Sometimes I tried to gather my courage to make amends but would never get around to it.

Three Methods

The Alcoholics Anonymous book *Twelve Steps and Twelve Traditions* recommends three ways of utilizing the Step Ten inventory. They are: 1) a spot check; 2) an inventory of the day's activities at the end of each day; and, 3) a periodic inventory that may occur every six months or one year. [4]

With a "spot check" we may recognize immediately that we have said or done something offensive. If yes, we make immediate amends.

To give credit where it is due, Flynn was actually the one who began to make amends immediately after a display of anger. His example prompted me to "just do it!" when it came to making amends quickly to both him and others. Even better, I've become more prone to "stifle" what was about to proceed from my mouth, rather than saying it and then owing amends.

If I practice the first part of Step Ten regularly, the second part will rarely be necessary.

The second method, a day's end inventory, comes into play when I fail to recognize that I have said or done something that harmed another person and did not recognize it immediately. Sometimes, it may take several days, a week or longer before the need for making amends finally dawns on me.

Once, at a birthday party, Flynn and I gave a "gag gift" to a fellow Christian. The guy just looked shocked when he opened it and put it back in the box. As I thought about it later, I decided that though it was funny, it was probably inappropriate to give to someone with whom we weren't on a close personal basis. My conscience had bothered me for a few days, so at the next opportunity I decided to go and admit my poor judgment.

Another time, a close friend at church whom I had often taken places because she was no longer able to drive began to avoid my calls and my attempts for us to get together. Though I asked her if something was wrong, she made excuses that didn't seem legitimate. I had to think and pray about it for a period of time before I finally realized what might have happened. So I approached her in an attempt to make amends. Sure enough, something I had said to someone else had been repeated and taken out of context. My friend thought I was complaining about having to take her places. I apologized for mentioning her name in the conversation, even though I didn't mean it the way it was taken. The air was cleared, and we resumed our friendship.

In the past, I may have reasoned, "If she doesn't want to tell me what's wrong, let her sit at home!" Thanks to the program, I knew it was important to get to the bottom of it.

The third way to work Step Ten is a semi-annual or annual inventory. This would be similar to a fourth step except that it would cover only the period of time since actually taking the fourth step or the last tenth step. Like Step Four, it is beneficial to put this in writing and then share it with a sponsor or mentor.

Eventually an updated version of the inventory booklet—"Blueprint for Progress," that I used in Step Four—became available. I used it as a guide for Step Ten. Rather than "yes and no" questions and a short summary, the new version had questions that had to be answered in detail, which required deeper thinking, especially into how my family history had influenced me. I used the results to type out a summary of what I had learned about myself, which required several pages.

Making Progress

I could see improvement in areas such as detaching from the problems of others and could recognize enabling rather than helping. Ongoing character defects included getting caught up in resentments, being too critical and procrastination.

Practicing Step Ten has gone a long way in helping me to live in harmony with our family, friends and neighbors, and, of course, my relationships with others are tied to my relationship with God.

A member of Adult Children of Alcoholics describes her experience with Step Ten:

> Learning to promptly admit when I'm wrong has paid big dividends for me in peace of mind. Learning that the response from others is almost always positive has also made it easier. When I admit I am wrong quickly, I prevent possible grudges from building up. I don't have to expend huge amounts of energy blaming, rationalizing, and covering up. I don't get bogged down with guilt or shame. Being able to admit that I'm wrong when I am wrong makes me feel free. I am very grateful for this wonderful sense of freedom.[5]

By putting God's Word into action through these steps, rather than staying on the merry-go-round of self-will, I continued moving forward on my journey toward closeness with God and on the path to spiritual freedom. Yet in one way, I was at a standstill where Kyle was concerned as his incarceration continued to loom in the future. I had to balance my frustration with the timetable of the authorities by focusing on living one day at a time while depending entirely on God.

A year passed before we received the call that he was to report to the sheriff's office the following week. He had been living with and working for his girlfriend's father, as well as doing some other odd jobs. He had mentioned having some contact with his old drug-using friends by phone, but he seemed to be mostly staying away from them. I hoped the six months away might be the clincher in him breaking ties with them for good.

Relief that the end was in sight almost overpowered my apprehension. Once he left, we could finally start the countdown.

Biblical Questions for Self-Examination

STAYING ON COURSE

Use the *Journey to Recovery Through Christ: CASA's 12-Step Study Bible* or any other version of the *New American Standard Bible* © 1995 to fill in the blanks in biblical passages below.

1. a. **...In reference to your _____ _____ of _____, you lay aside the _____ _____, which is being corrupted in accordance with the _____ of _____, and that you be renewed in the spirit of your _____, and put on the _____ _____, which in *the likeness of* _____has been _____ in _____ and _____ of the truth** (Ephesians 4:22-24, p. 268).

   b. **I will _____ what God the Lord will say; For He will speak _____ to His people, to His godly ones; but let them not turn back to _____** (Psalm 85:8, p. 420).

   c. **For if _____ is a _____ of the word and not a _____, he is like a man who looks at his natural face in a mirror; for *once* he has looked at himself and gone away, he has immediately _____ what kind of person he was. But one who looks intently at the perfect _____, the law of _____, and abides by it, not having become a forgetful _____ but an effectual _____, this man will be blessed in what he does** (James 1:23-25, p. 308).

   d. Relate the above passages to your spiritual walk as you approach Step Ten. _____

   _____

   _____

   _____

2. Janet quoted Matthew 12:43-45 (p. 55-56) earlier in this chapter. How does that passage apply to a person who has diligently worked the first nine steps but lets up on his or her spiritual program of action and does not proceed to Step Ten? (Think of the evil spirit as sin/your codependency/addictive substance, character defects and the unoccupied house as a person who loses contact with God.) _____

   _____

   _____

   _____

a. Has there ever been a time in your life when you let up on your spiritual program of action? (circle one) yes or no   (If "yes," go to 2.c.; if "no," go to 2.b.)

b. If you answered no to the above, would you like to rethink your answer? (circle one)   yes or no

c. If yes to 2.a. how did you discover that you were avoiding God's will in your life? _____

_____

_____

d. What was the result in your life when you let up on your spiritual program of action? _____

_____

_____

KEEPING THINGS RIGHT WITH OTHERS

3. a. A man once wrote this about Step Ten: "There are also times when my addict brain creates scenarios that seem logical to me but in the cold light of day are actually nuts."[6] List three of your own thoughts that seemed logical in the cold light of day that were actually nuts.

1) _____

2) _____

3) _____

b. List two ways to help you discern the difference between healthy God-centered thoughts or nutty self-centered thoughts?

1) _____

2) _____

4. a. Janet wrote: "A close friend at church whom I had often taken places because she was no longer able to drive began to avoid my calls and my attempts for us to get together. Though I asked her if something was wrong, she made excuses that didn't seem legitimate." What did Janet do then? _____

_____

_____

b. Janet continued: "In the past, I may have reasoned, 'If she doesn't want to tell me what's wrong, let her sit at home!'" Why do you think the woman did not respond to Janet's initial efforts?_____

_____

_____

_____

c. What are three ways that people may communicate to us that we have hurt their feelings or perceived that we harmed them in some other way, even though they haven't yet told us about it verbally?

1) _____

2) _____

3) _____

AVOIDING INTEREST PAYMENTS

5. Read Matthew 5:21-26 (p. 43).

   a. **"Make friends quickly with your _____ at law while you are with him on the way, so that your _____ may not _____ _____ _____ to the judge, and the judge to the officer, and you be _____ into _____"** (Matthew 5:25, p. 43).

   b. In this passage who is the person who has apparently done wrong? (circle one)   a. you;   b. your opponent.

   c. This passage notes an escalation in consequences, almost as if the "debts" we owe gather "interest" until they are paid. Briefly tell about a situation in your life when you failed to make things right with another person and the problem continued to escalate.

   _____

   _____

   d. What finally happens to the person who fails to make friends with his opponent on the way to court?_____

   _____

   _____

6. Read Ephesians 4:17-32 (pp. 268-269).

   a. **"Therefore, laying aside _____, SPEAK _____ EACH ONE of you WITH HIS _____, for we are members of one another. BE _____, AND yet DO NOT _____; do not let the sun go down on your _____..."** (Ephesians 4:25-26, p. 268).

   b. How is it possible to be angry but yet not sin? _____

   _____

   c. How does this passage apply to the day's-end inventory that is recommended to be utilized with Step Ten?

   _____

   _____

d. What is the parallel between the reading from Ephesians 4:25-26 (p. 268) and Jesus' admonition from Matthew 5:25 (p. 43) to settle matters quickly? _____

_____

_____

e. When was the last time you went to bed angry over something that had occurred in your life and what were you angry about? _____

_____

f. How did this affect you? _____

g. Following the principles of Step Ten, what could you have done to improve this situation?_____

_____

_____

SURVEYING OUR RECENT PASTS

7. Cited below are Bible passages that focus on various difficulties we may encounter in our day-to-day routines. Sometimes we fall short of our ideal behavior because our egos take over. Sometimes we make wrong decisions in a split second. Think about these passages in relation to your life during the past 12 months or since you worked Steps Four through Nine, whichever is more recent.

a. **But refuse _____ and _____ speculations, knowing that they produce _____** (2 Timothy 2:23, p. 290).

b. Can you think of a time when you fell short? (circle one) yes or no

c. If yes, briefly relate the incident here. _____

_____

_____

d. Have you confessed this to God and repented? (circle one) yes or no   (If no, it's not too late.)

e. Is an amend needed? (circle one) yes or no

f. Why or why not? _____

_____

8. a. **He who is slow to _____ has great _____, but he who is _____-_____ exalts folly** (Proverbs 14:29, p. 495).

b. Can you think of a time when you fell short? (circle one) yes or no

c. If yes, briefly relate the incident here. _____

_____

_____

d. Have you confessed this to God and repented? (circle one) yes or no (If no, that opportunity still awaits.)

e. Is an amend needed? (circle one) yes or no

f. Why or why not? _____

_____

9. a. **When there are many** _____, _____ **is unavoidable,**

   but he who _____ **his lips is** _____ (Proverbs 10:19, p. 490).

b. Can you think of a time when you fell short? (circle one) yes or no

c. If yes, briefly relate the incident here. _____

_____

_____

d. Have you confessed this to God and repented? (circle one) yes or no

   (If no, the Lord would still like to hear from you.)

e. Is an amend needed? (circle one) yes or no

f. Why or why not? _____

_____

10. a. **But no one can tame the** _____; *it is* **a** _____ _____ _____

   and full of _____ _____. **With it we** _____

   our **Lord and Father, and with it we** _____ **men, who have been made**

   in the _____ **of** _____; **from the same mouth come** *both*

   _____ **and** _____. **My brethren, these things**

   ought not to be this way (James 3:8-10, p. 309).

b. Can you think of a time when you fell short? (circle one) yes or no

c. If yes, briefly relate the incident here. _____

_____

d. Have you confessed this to God and repented? (circle one) yes or no

   (If no, there's no time like the present.)

e. Is an amend needed? (circle one)   yes   or   no

f. Why or why not? _____

_____

11.   a. **He who goes about as a** _____ **reveals** _____,

but he who is _____ **conceals a matter** (Proverbs 11:13, p. 491).

b. Can you think of a time when you fell short? (circle one)   yes   or   no

c. If yes, briefly relate the incident here. _____

_____

d. Have you confessed this to God and repented? (circle one)   yes   or   no
(If no, recall that God is patient and would be pleased to hear from you.)

e. Is an amend needed? (circle one)   yes   or   no

f. Why or why not? _____

_____

12.   a. **Lying** _____ **are an** _____ **to the Lord, but those who deal**
_____ **are His delight** (Proverbs 12:22, p. 492).

b. Can you think of a time when you fell short? (circle one)   yes   or   no

c. If yes, briefly relate the incident here. _____

_____

_____

d. Have you confessed this to God and repented? (circle one)   yes   or   no
(If no, don't you think it is about time that you did?)

e. Is an amend needed? (circle one)   yes   or   no

f. Why or why not? _____

_____

13.   a. **He who gives an** _____ **before he** _____, **it is folly and shame
to him** (Proverbs 18:13, p. 501).

b. Can you think of a time when you fell short? (circle one)   yes   or   no

c. If yes, briefly relate the incident here. _____

_____

_____

d. Have you confessed this to God and repented? (circle one)   yes   or   no

   (If no, don't wait 'til the Second Coming to take care of this.)

e. Is an amend needed? (circle one)   yes   or   no

f. Why or why not? _____

_____

14. a. **Keeping away from** _____ **is an** _____ **for a man, but any**

   _____ **will** _____ (Proverbs 20:3, p. 503).

b. Can you think of a time when you fell short? (circle one)   yes   or   no

c. If yes, briefly relate the incident here. _____

_____

_____

d. Have you confessed this to God and repented? (circle one)   yes   or   no

   (If no, why not? Is pride holding you back?)

e. Is an amend needed? (circle one)   yes   or   no

f. Why or why not? _____

_____

15. a. **Let another** _____ **you, and not your own** _____ **; a stranger,**

   and not your own _____ (Proverbs 27:2, p. 513).

b. Can you think of a time when you fell short? (circle one)   yes   or   no

c. If yes, briefly relate the incident here. _____

_____

_____

d. Have you confessed this to God and repented? (circle one)   yes   or   no

   (If no, are you trying to test God's patience?)

e. Is an amend needed? (circle one)   yes   or   no

f. Why or why not? _____

_____

16. a. **A _____ always loses his _____, but a _____ man holds it back**
     (Proverbs 29:11, p. 516).

     b. Can you think of a time when you fell short? (circle one)   yes   or   no

     c. If yes, briefly relate the incident here. _____

     _____

     _____

     d. Have you confessed this to God and repented? (circle one)   yes   or   no
     (If no, do we need to send you back to Step Three?)

     e. Is an amend needed? (circle one)   yes   or   no

     f. Why or why not? _____

     _____

17. a. **Why do you look at the _____ that is in your _____ eye,
     but do not notice the _____ that is in your own eye?** (Luke 6:41, p. 116).

     b. Can you think of a time when you fell short? (circle one)   yes   or   no

     c. If yes, briefly relate the incident here. _____

     _____

     _____

     d. Have you confessed this to God and repented? (circle one)   yes   or   no
     (If no, did you not understand this concept when we covered it in Step Four? Why not talk to the Lord today.)

     e. Is an amend needed? (circle one)   yes   or   no

     f. Why or why not? _____

     _____

18. a. **Never pay back _____ for _____ to anyone. _____ what is
     _____ in the sight of all men** (Romans 12:17, p. 228).

     b. Can you think of a time when you fell short? (circle one)   yes   or   no

c. If yes, briefly relate the incident here. _____

_____

_____

d. Have you confessed this to God and repented? (circle one)   yes   or   no

(If no, are you getting tired of kicking this can down the road? Why don't you do something about it?)

e. Is an amend needed? (circle one)   yes   or   no

f. Why or why not? _____

_____

19. a. **Be of the same _____ toward one another; do not be _____**

in mind, but _____ with the lowly. Do not be _____

in your own estimation (Romans 12:16, p. 228).

b. Can you think of a time when you fell short? (circle one)   yes   or   no

c. If yes, briefly relate the incident here. _____

_____

_____

d. Have you confessed this to God and repented? (circle one)   yes   or   no

(If no, why don't you, put your knees on the floor and talk to your heavenly Father about this?)

e. Is an amend needed? (circle one)   yes   or   no

f. Why or why not? _____

_____

YOUR TURN

20. Find other Bible passages that remind you of an incident in your life where you suddenly recognize that you have fallen short. Write specific verses immediately below and then use separate pieces of paper for other examples.

a. Bible verse or verses. _____

_____

_____

b. Relate the incident here. _____

_____

_____

c. Have you confessed this to God and repented? (circle one)   yes   or   no

   (If no, please do that now.)

d. Is an amend needed? (circle one)   yes   or   no

e. Why or why not? _____

ARE THERE OTHERS?

21.   a. As you've been working this lesson, did you think of other people to whom you owe an amend for things not covered above? (circle one)   yes   or   no

   b. If yes, list them here.

Amend Needed to This Person	**The Reason It Is Needed**

c. What has kept you from making these amends? _____

_____

_____

_____

FINDING THE HAPPY MEDIUM

22. a. Why do some people never apologize, even when they know they have been in the wrong?_____

_____

_____

b. Why do you think some people constantly apologize, even for things that are not their fault?_____

_____

_____

c. Tell why you think constantly apologizing is or isn't consistent with the principles of Step Ten?_____

_____

_____

d. Thinking of the two extremes of never apologizing or always apologizing, describe how you will find the middle ground between them? Or in other words, what guidelines will you use in your life to know when it is appropriate to make an amend and when it is not?_____

_____

_____

_____

FROM THEORY TO PRACTICE

23. As you've filled in responses above in numbers 7 through 21, you may have uncovered several instances where you need to make amends or set things right with other people. Make amends to three of these people and record the outcomes here.

**Person to Whom
You Made an Amend**   **The Outcome**

_____   _____

_____

_____   _____

_____

_____   _____

_____

_____   _____

_____

_____   _____

                                            _____

_____   _____

                                            _____

IN CONCLUSION

We used to think we were nearly always right. Reflecting on that erroneous notion, we know that only God is always right. Praise the Lord for removing from us the burden of not only thinking we were always right but also trying to prove it to others. We've learned that our relationship with the Lord is tied to our relationship with other people. Step Ten provides us with an ongoing means of keeping right with our fellow human beings while at the same time walking closer with God.

Write down some insights you've gained from this lesson. To gauge your spiritual progress, several months from now look back on what you've written here.

_____

_____

_____

_____

_____

End Notes

1. *Narcotics Anonymous—It Works—How and Why,* World Service Office, 1988, Van Nuys, 97.
2. Quotation taken from *The King James Bible.*
3. S.I. McMillan, M.D., *None of These Diseases,* Fleming H. Revell Company, Old, Tappan New Jersey, 1977, 69.
4. *Twelve Steps and Twelve Traditions,* Alcoholics Anonymous World Services, Inc., New York, 1986, 89.
5. *Adult Children of Alcoholics/Dysfunctional Families,* Adult Children of Alcoholics World Service Organization, Torrance, CA, 2006, 250.
6. *12 Steps to a Closer Walk with God: The Workbook, Second Edition,* Quarry Press, Dallas, 2015, 142.

Prayer and Meditation

Kyle was nervous, nauseated and had been vomiting the morning he had to go to boot camp. He had been taking prescription drugs for his stomach issues. But he was not allowed to take them into the boot camp; they had to be filled at the facility. Though these arrangements had been made, we had been told it would take some time for this to occur.

I knew God had lessons for us all to learn through this. If Kyle could not endure the rigorous discipline and exercise, he would serve a longer sentence in prison. My main concern was that his stomach problems might interfere with what was required of him.

Flynn hugged Kyle, wished him the very best and told him goodbye. Then Shelley and I went to drop him off at the sheriff's office. On the way Kyle was still nauseated and though he wanted to get it over with so he could move on with his life, his main thought was, "I'm just hoping I will wake up soon and find out this is not happening."

A deputy was waiting with a sheriff's car to take him 158 miles to the correctional facility located in Childersburg, Alabama. Before leaving, Kyle had to check into the sheriff's office. I was numb, just trying to put one foot in front of the other and trying to keep my emotions in check.

We all got out of the car. Shelley and I each hugged him briefly, told him we loved him and then watched him approach the door. He looked back at us briefly and then entered. We got back in the car and drove away. If they were going to handcuff him for the three-hour drive, I preferred not to witness it or see them drive away.

When I returned home, I opened my Bible and sought God in prayer. Reading from Hebrews, two verses immediately registered. "For we do not have a high priest who cannot sympathize with our weaknesses, but One who has been tempted in all things as we are, yet without sin. Therefore let us draw near with confidence to the throne of grace, so that we may receive mercy and find grace to help in time of need" (Hebrews 4:15-16, pp. 298-299).

This passage had been the theme of an area-wide weekend youth conference that Flynn, Casey and I attended with our church youth group a year or so before. The speaker, Lonnie Jones, drew upon his mountain-climbing experience and used his equipment to illustrate. He said that God would not just lift us up on the top of the mountain but would provide the ropes, spikes and other gear to assist us.

Clinging to this idea and knowing that neither Flynn nor I had any control over how Kyle would be treated, I went boldly to God as the scripture instructed, pleading with Him about every detail of every day. Kyle had his journey to travel, and I could pray for him each step of the way. At the same time I had my own journey to draw closer to God and seek His will for me.

A New Identity

In the past my life had been so intertwined with the dysfunctional behavior of other people, I'm not sure I even saw myself as a separate entity. I had been caught up in trying to fix, control and find ways to convince other family members to "shape up" and realize their talents and potential. Perfecting the environment around me seemed like the only way for me find to peace and happiness. It seems strange that it never occurred to me before attending Al-Anon that my method for achieving happiness *never worked*. All I did was create a bigger void inside of me.

I gradually got the idea that rather than trying to fix everyone around me, I had to undertake my own assessment, consider my own thoughts and feelings and discover my own potential.

"People-pleasing" was often mentioned in Al-Anon meetings. I thought it was a noble trait to try hard to get along with everyone and not offend or annoy anyone. The following definition of "people pleasers" described me quite accurately:

> People who have a disproportionate and unhealthy need in their personality to give in to the wants, whims and desires of others around them, to the point of sacrificing their own wants or needs. People pleasers, pushovers and doormats lack assertiveness skills and hold back from speaking up and saying what they really think or feel, and they hold back from asking for what they need or want because they're worried someone will get upset about it.

> People pleasing personality types find it virtually impossible to deny any or all requests made upon them even when doing so creates stress, chaos, financial burden, anxiety attacks, depression and even bankruptcy. The need for the approval and acceptance of others becomes debilitating for people pleasers, where fear of saying no and the intense aversion to confrontations or angry reprisals causes people pleasers to give in time after time after time.[1]

The Apostle Paul addressed the problem with people-pleasing in this passage: "For am I now seeking the favor of men, or of God? Or am I striving to please men? If I were still trying to please men, I would not be a bond-servant of Christ" (Galatians 1:10, p. 260).

I came to see that my attempts at people-pleasing were aimed more at filling my own needs for approval rather than serving God. As I continued to recognize destructive traits in myself, I could picture myself as walking away from the merry-go-round of frustration and defeat.

I was coming to accept that God had a plan for me as an individual regardless of what others chose to do with their lives. God had blessed me with the gift of life, a healthy body and a normal functioning mind. My primary responsibility was to use these blessings to His glory. The next step of the recovery program guided me in spiritual growth even when my son was incarcerated.

STEP ELEVEN ▶ Sought through prayer and meditation to improve our conscious contact with God as we understood Him, praying only for knowledge of His will for us and the power to carry that out. (For additional information on Step Eleven and a listing of Step Eleven Reflections related to specific verses, see *Journey to Recovery Through Christ: CASA's 12-Step Study Bible*, pp. 33-35.)

In Step Three I made a decision to turn my life over to the care of God as I then understood Him. Steps Four through Ten guided me toward a better understanding of God's will in my life and my thoughts and attitudes of the people around me.

Improving my conscious contact with God through prayer is the first part of Step Eleven.

My dad always said, "If you want to get something done, ask a busy man." There is some truth in that saying, but it is easy to fall into the trap of filling one's life with activity while the optimal response may be just the opposite. Look at the Lord's example. "…large crowds were gathering to hear *Him* and to be healed of their sicknesses. But Jesus Himself would *often* slip away to the wilderness and pray" (Luke 5:15-16, p. 113).

The loveseat in my den was where I went to pray and meditate on the scriptures early each morning.

Before entering into the program, I prayed wherever and whenever I perceived there was a need or if I had the time. Thankfully, this changed. When facing an extremely busy day, rather than skipping prayer to save time as I had done in the past, I found how important it was to take time for my morning devotional. It helped me to focus on God, set my priorities and to start the day in the right frame of mind.

Jesus taught his disciples to pray by what we know today as "The Lord's Prayer" found in Matthew 6:9-13 (p. 45). At the end of their meetings, people in many recovery groups join hands and say this prayer in unison. An examination of this model prayer will show why it is embraced by 12-step groups. I have used the wording usually cited by recovery groups.[2]

Our Father who art in heaven, hallowed be Thy Name,

As we consider the order of Jesus' words to His Father, it begins by recognizing God's power and omniscience as the Creator of the universe.

I can now see that I put myself at the center of the universe rather than seeking His will for me and allowing others the same privilege. I thought I had all the answers when actually I possessed only minimal Bible knowledge and knew little about addiction and the far-reaching effects of family dysfunction.

I had continually thought of new ways to reason with Flynn and convince him to stop getting angry over minor incidents and common mistakes. I almost never thought about my part of the discord or my ongoing obsession with worry.

Thy kingdom come. Thy will be done on earth as it is in heaven.

As I continued to pray, "Thy will be done," I was admitting that though I thought I could see a few miles up the road and map out my own course, God can see around the curves and over the hills to infinity. His knowledge and wisdom are complete; therefore, I did my best to become willing to allow Him to direct my life.

In my "pre-Al-Anon" existence, not only did I want to live my life according to my own blueprint, I wanted to draw up the blueprint for others. I came to the realization that some of my loved ones might have to sink low enough and go through enough hardship that they would choose to seek God.

I could see that Kyle being at boot camp could be positive for him. The time away from home might give him some spiritual perspectives that he wouldn't gain otherwise. He needed to seek and find God for himself, not as I directed him.

Give us this day our daily bread

In this part of The Lord's Prayer, Jesus makes reference to God providing manna on a daily basis to the children of Israel after their departure from the land of slavery (see Exodus 16:11-31.) This one-day-at-a-time principal is embraced by recovery groups. Newcomers to such groups might ask, "Do you mean I have to go the rest of my life without _____?" A veteran of the group would reply, "No, all you have to do is go without it today. Then when you get up tomorrow, do the same thing."

Jesus stressed the same concept when he stated, "So do not worry about tomorrow; for tomorrow will care for itself. Each day has enough trouble of its own" (Matthew 6:34, p. 46).

When Kyle was away, I would have liked to fast-forward six months into the future when this period of our lives would be over. Of course, that is a fantasy. Instead, I needed to make the most of the time, drawing strength from God each day, working on improving relationships and being of service to others.

Al-Anon slogans helped me to practice the Al-Anon program on a daily basis. "Live and let live" reminded me to stay out of the conflicts and business of other people as much as possible.

"Keep it Simple" kept me from going overboard and causing myself extra stress when I was entertaining company or planning family gatherings.

"Think!" helped remind me before I opened my mouth in haste: "Is it Thoughtful, Honest, Intelligent, Necessary, and Kind?"

When my mind began to work overtime in figuring out a way to reason with insane behavior, "Detach" was a simple way to remember, "Don't even think about changing him/her!"

and forgive us our trespasses as we forgive those who trespass against us;

I had to come to a realization of the truth of this. When I consider the grace of God to forgive all my past sins, the sins others have committed against me are very insignificant. Bitterness, resentment and failure to forgive stand as a barrier between God and me.

Though it was not toward any one person in particular, I held resentment for some time toward the churches in which I had grown up, especially the church leaders. I felt that the message I had absorbed through the years was distorted on many levels. I refused to attend their services, even though invitations were often extended to me.

On further contemplation, however, I realized I was no different than them in having failed to study and challenge what was being taught and emphasized. Even now, I know it would be completely arrogant to say that I fully understood all the scriptures or even come close to it. I was eventually able to forgive and extend the same grace to them that had been demonstrated to me. I now occasionally attend their meetings and reconnect with old friends.

And lead us not into temptation but deliver us from evil.

Sometimes I got caught up in another manifestation of me-me-me without realizing it— the merry-go-round of denial, blaming others for all my problems, and doing the same thing over and over and expecting different results. God's help has been crucial in guiding me away from these problems.

I recognized sins of the heart and mind that occurred daily, but it was easier to recognize these problems than to live without them on a daily basis. For example, I might confess the sin of anger in my morning prayer and ask for God's help in handling whatever situation arose. Then something like this might occur at breakfast:

Flynn: We're out of milk for my cereal. Why didn't you pick some up when you were driving around town yesterday?

Me: I would have if I was Einstein and had the mind of a steel trap. But since I'm just a normal human being, I forgot. That's something you never do, right? You passed a few stores yourself yesterday. What prevented you from taking just a minute of your precious time and stopping to get some milk?

You can see how it might escalate from there. Instead, I try to follow a less inflammatory response.

Me: Sorry that we're out of milk. Why don't I fix you some eggs and bacon instead of cereal? Would you like them scrambled?

It was usually easy to maintain self-control as long as something unexpected didn't happen, but if someone said something critical to me, I could easily return insult for insult in the heat of the moment. As I contemplated the "fruit of the Spirit" (Galatians 5:22-23, p. 264), it dawned on me that gentleness and kindness were not much of a virtue when practiced only when others were gentle and kind with me.

For thine is the kingdom, the power and the glory, forever and ever. Amen.

In the last line of the model prayer, I acknowledge God's authority and ownership of my life starting at this very moment and going into eternity.

In the past, I treated God more like Santa Claus, making requests and pretending I had been a good girl. Though I always asked Him to forgive me of my sins, I felt no need to specify what they were. This resulted in me continuing in the same spiritual rut.

Since the desire to change is now a priority, I confess sin specifically and as honestly as possible. I share with Him my struggles and disappointments and admit my doubts and fears. There is no reason not to reveal everything. He knows anyway!

Rather than just asking God to fix the problems and people that I perceived had complicated my life, I began to pray for wisdom in understanding my contribution to the problems, for patience, for peace in the midst of chaos, and for grace in loving those who I sometimes perceive as being unlovable.

Though prayers for something of a physical nature were not always answered on my terms, when I asked for strength, courage, self-control, wisdom or anything of a spiritual nature, it seemed to arrive, even miraculously.

Philip Yancey compares human communication to communication with God:

> I know what happens in human relationships when I remain at a shallow level. With casual friends I discuss weather, sports, upcoming concerts and movies, all the while steering clear of what matters more: a suppressed hurt, hidden jealousy, resentment of their children's rude behavior, concern for their spiritual welfare. As a result, the relationship goes nowhere. On the other hand, relationships deepen as I trust my friends with secrets.

> Likewise, unless I level with God—about bitterness over an unanswered prayer, grief over loss, guilt over an unforgiving spirit, a baffling sense of God's absence—that relationship, too, will go

nowhere. I may continue going to church, singing hymns and praise choruses, even addressing God politely in formal prayers, but I will never break through the intimacy barrier.[3]

Throughout the five or six-year ordeal with Kyle, the enormous power of prayer had become much more obvious.

Step Eleven also stresses the importance of meditation. Quite simply, prayer is talking to God and meditation is listening to Him. "Cease *striving* and know that I am God…" (Psalm 46:10, p. 386) applies here.

Many people automatically associate the idea of meditation with transcendental meditation (TM), which, according to Christian authors Josh McDowell and Don Stewart, is based on Hindu philosophy. This involves sitting perfectly still while one's mind focuses on a mantra, a monosyllabic word with no meaning. The purpose of such practices for the Eastern religions is "a striving for nirvana, the extinction of individual existence and the absorption of the soul into the supreme spirit."[4]

This is not connected with the type of meditation in which a Christian would engage, and some today connect this practice with the New Age Movement.

Christian Meditation

McDowell and Stewart wrote this about transcendental meditation: "Although some degree of success in relaxation can be achieved by practicing TM, the dangers far outweigh the benefits. There is a Christian alternative to TM and that consists of meditation on God's Word, the only source of real peace."[5]

Christian meditation turns the focus to God's Word, which is described by Ben Campbell Johnson in this way:

> …active speculation about biblical texts, Christian symbols, and life experience… the disciplined act of reflecting on the meaning of a word, an idea, or an experience. For example, we may meditate on the idea that "God is love." Reflecting on the love of God involves asking questions of it, turning it over in our minds, letting it draw forth other ideas that connect with it, and seeing this truth in a new light.[6]

I began meditation by seeking answers from God and trusting in Him alone. The psalmist wrote of the blessed person: "But his delight is in the law of the Lord, and in His law he meditates day and night" (Psalm 1:2, p. 346).

In reading the scriptures each day I focused on a verse or principle, especially if it was one I didn't quite understand. Then I thought about it as I went about my housework and on my daily walks. As I connected it to other scriptures, often the meaning became clear. Sometimes, one scripture seemed to contradict another, but with continuing meditation the discrepancies began to harmonize. Some scriptures with which I was long familiar took on different meaning. My search may be compared to fitting together the pieces of a puzzle until it began to form a complete picture of a plan that could not be of human origin.

Meditation played a significant role in learning to pray more effectively. On my daily walks, I carried a small card with a "memory verse" on which to focus while I walked. Verses I memorized, such as "Let your speech always be with grace, *as though* seasoned with salt, so that you will know how you should respond to each person," (Colossians 4:6, p. 278) were incorporated into my prayers. This thought would pop in my mind when I might have normally reacted negatively to something someone said or did. I noticed in Acts

16:14 (p. 199) that when Paul preached to Lydia, "…the Lord opened her heart to respond to the things spoken by Paul."

This led me to pray that God would open the hearts of my family members and friends who were in need of His truth.

With other scriptures, words or phrases stood out that I hadn't noticed before. I often quoted Philippians 4:6-7 (p. 274) for help with my anxiety. "Be anxious for nothing, but in everything by prayer and supplication with thanksgiving let your requests be made known to God. And the peace of God, which surpasses all comprehension, will guard your hearts and your minds in Christ Jesus." As often as I quoted it, I still felt anxious.

One day the phrase "with thanksgiving" registered with me as the possible key to the peace that was promised. As I began to focus more on being thankful and actually listed my many blessings, my problems didn't seem quite as overwhelming. Recently, when I was becoming resentful and obsessed with some of Flynn's behavior, I decided to make a gratitude list. When I finished and looked back over it, it dawned on me that Flynn was a hard worker who had done a great job of providing for our family.

The more I meditated on the great stories and characters of the Bible, it seemed more plausible that a supernatural God who hung the moon and stars could surely communicate with us on a spiritual level and handle our simple requests. Prayer became more frequent and meaningful.

The daily Al-Anon meditation and other Al-Anon literature may furnish me with a special thought that helps me get through a trying situation. The "Thought for Today" in this morning's meditation was, "Worry is like a rocking chair. It gives me something to do, but it gets me nowhere." [7]

My morning devotional time became a time to recharge and renew my mind for the day ahead. Carrying around a lot of tension, especially in my neck and shoulders, had always been a huge problem for me. Though walking a few miles a day and water exercise had helped, the only other relief I found was to take an occasional Ativan, a prescribed drug for relief of anxiety.

Eventually, during my morning devotional as my mind centered on spiritual things, I felt the tense muscles begin to release even when I didn't realize they were in "knots." Rather than relying on a drug, I often take an extra devotional break and just relax and read something out of the Psalms when I'm especially stressed.

Perceptions of God

The next part of the step reads "God as we understood Him." My understanding of God had evolved from the mental picture of a wise old gentleman in physical form, to a Spirit being—the actual essence of truth, love and grace. This being the case, my conscious contact could only improve by facing the truth about myself and in every area of life.

In my continuing attempts to place God at the center of my life, and seek spiritual solutions, there were times when it seemed that I knew how to deal with situations that had bewildered me in the past. I realized that God was doing for me what I could not do for myself and speaking to me through my thoughts and conscience.

The last part of the step reads "praying only for knowledge of His will for us and the power to carry it out."

The thought of praying for God's will for my life was sometimes frightening. What if He wanted me to move to Uganda for mission work or do something beyond the scope of my imagination? Did I even have the courage to ask for His will concerning me?

According to Dr. David Jeremiah:

> Each of us has a unique role to play in reflecting the nature of God. That's why God created each of us with unique abilities. This means that within the "generic" will of God, He has a specific will for you. How you find that plan is simply to follow my father's advice. "Get the car moving." We fulfill God's will for every Christian by giving, studying, encouraging others, serving where needs exist, worshipping and keeping ourselves unstained by the world. And in the midst of that service, God will begin to reveal new, creative directions for you personally. Make the decision to do what you know of His will, and creative parts that apply to your particular life will begin to flow. [7]

Seeking His will for my life involved a deeper trust and what I needed to do was just "get the car moving!" I was both frightened and excited at what God might have in store for me. He eventually steered me in a direction I had never even considered.

As I prayed for His will for me in my personal relationships and the power to carry it out, I felt God whisper in my thoughts, "Just love them." Though I was still quite introverted and often didn't speak out or act when I felt the need to say something, I would find myself giving a hug or would hear the right words slipping from my lips which surprised even me.

When I prayed for God's help with self-control in eating healthier, I often found myself breezing through the day content with eating smaller portions or healthier foods, while in the past I had tried dieting for weeks on end and failed on a daily basis.

I felt God urging me to pray personally with people when they were sick or going through some type of hardship, as some of my charismatic friends did for me. As usual, I feared not knowing what to say because it wasn't something I could always rehearse or plan.

I remember visiting an elderly lady in my neighborhood who had broken her hip. Though we chatted sometimes briefly in the yard, I had never been inside her home or gotten close to her. She had a reputation for being an alcoholic, and had seemed drunk during some of our chats.

She seemed sincerely appreciative for my visit. She was very distraught over her health problems, so I found myself asking if she would like me to pray for her. She agreed, and the words of my prayer seemed to flow out from another source.

She cried and hugged me, and I promised to go back. After that when I passed by and she was sitting on her porch, though I had never known her to be religious, she always requested prayer. I was realizing more and more that God would supply the power when I was lacking.

I hoped he would do the same for Kyle in surviving the exercise regimen in which he would be forced to participate.

After he left for boot camp, I had prayed especially that his nervous stomach would be calmed until he received his prescriptions. No communication with him was allowed for a couple of weeks. When he was allowed to call, he had still not obtained his medication. He said it seemed strange, but he was doing fine without it.

Biblical Questions for Self-Examination

GOOD, ORDERLY DIRECTION

Use the *Journey to Recovery Through Christ: CASA's 12-Step Study Bible* or any other version of the *New American Standard Bible* © 1995 to fill in the blanks in biblical passages below.

1. a. **I will instruct you and teach you in the way which you should go; I will counsel you with My eye upon you. Do not be as the** _____ **or as the**_____ **which have no** _____**, whose trappings include bit and bridle to hold them in check,** *otherwise* **they will not come near to you. Many are the** _____ **of the** _____**, but he who** _____ **in the Lord,** _____ **shall surround him** (Psalm 32:8-10, p. 371).

    b. Why do the horse and mule need a bit or bridle? _____

    c. Describe the last time you were like a horse or mule.

    _____

    _____

    d. Which of the following would most aptly describe you at that time? (circle as many as are appropriate)

    1) stubborn as a mule

    2) the south end of a horse facing north

    3) in a photo finish for last place

    4) a real nag

    5) headed for the glue factory

    6) a first-class jackass

    7) other; fill in the blank _____

    e. How did Janet's problems with self-will impact her relationships with God and with other people?

    _____

    _____

    _____

    f. How did your "muleyness" or "horseyness" affect your relationships with God and other people?

    _____

    _____

    _____

g. What did it take for you to discover you needed a bit or bridle to get you going in the right direction?

_____

_____

_____

CHOOSING THE RIGHT SUSTENANCE

2. a. **My soul _____ for _____, for the living _____; When shall I _____ and _____ before God?** (Psalm 42:2, p. 382).

    b. **Jesus answered and said to her, "Everyone who _____ of this _____ will _____ again; but whoever _____ of the _____ that I will give him shall never _____; but the _____ that I will give him will become in him a _____ of _____ springing up to _____ _____"** (John 4:13-14, p. 153).

    c. **Jesus said to them, "I am the _____ of _____; he who comes to Me will not _____, and he who believes in Me will never _____"** (John 6:35, p. 157).

    d. **...Jesus stood and cried out, saying, "If anyone is _____, let him come to _____ and _____. He who believes in Me, as the Scripture said, 'From his _____ being will flow rivers of living _____"** (John 7:37-38, p. 159).

    e. **"_____ are those who _____ and _____ for righteousness, for they shall be _____"** (Matthew 5:6, p. 43).

    f. Thinking of Step Eleven, how do you put these verses to work in your life? _____

    _____

    _____

    _____

    _____

    _____

AN IMPOSSIBLE TASK?

3. a. **But his delight is in the law of the Lord, and in His _____ he _____ day and night** (Psalm 1:2, p. 346).

b. ..._____ **without** _____ (1Thessalonians 5:17, p. 281).

c. **Seek the** _____ **and His** _____; _____ **His face**
_____ (Psalm 105:4, p. 437).

d. To literally carry out these three passages, it would seem that one would never sleep, but of course that is not possible. In light of Step Eleven, describe how you could put these verses to work in your life.

_____

_____

_____

_____

TALKING TO GOD

4. a. _____ _____; **pray without ceasing; in everything give**
_____; **for this is God's** _____ **for you in Christ Jesus**
(1Thessalonians 5:16-18, p. 281).

b. The above verse was also found in StepThree, number 16.b. In what ways has your prayer life improved since you first took StepThree? _____

_____

_____

_____

5. a. **Be anxious for** _____, **but in everything by** _____ **and**
_____ **with thanksgiving let your** _____ **be made**
known to God. And the _____ **of God, which surpasses all** _____,
will guard your _____ **and your** _____ **in Christ Jesus**
(Philippians 4:6-7, p. 274).

b. This is another verse you saw in StepThree, 15.a. In what way are you more in tune with the peace of God since you first took StepThree? _____

_____

_____

6. a. **Oh give** _____ **to the** _____, _____ **upon His name; make**
_____ **His deeds among the peoples** (Psalm 105:1, p. 437).

b. The last time you prayed, for what things were you grateful? _____

_____

_____

_____

c. What other things could have been on this list? _____

_____

_____

_____

d. What did Janet say about the importance of gratitude in her life? _____

_____

_____

_____

e. Do you currently express gratitude in your prayer life? (circle one)   yes   or   no

f. If yes to 6.e., are you satisfied with your current level of expressing gratitude in your prayer life or could it stand improvement? _____

_____

_____

_____

g. If no to 6.e., what is preventing you from expressing your gratitude to God for the things He has given you?

_____

_____

_____

7. We recently heard from a friend that he and another person would sit down together and go through the alphabet finding words expressing gratitude with each letter. For example, for the letter "A," someone might say that he or she is grateful for acquaintances who are seeking God in their lives. Our friend was asked what he said when he arrived at the letter "Z," and all he could think of were zebras, zoo and Zorro. Maybe you can improve on this.

a. Z _____

POINTERS ON PRAYER

8. Just before He gave His followers what we know as The Lord's Prayer, Jesus spoke the words found in Matthew 6:1-8 (p. 45). Read these verses.

a. What do you conclude about prayer after reading Matthew 6:1-8 (p. 45)? _____

_____

_____

_____

_____

b. **"…for your Father _____ _____ you _____ _____**
   you ask Him" (Matthew 6:8, p. 45).

c. How do Jesus' words from Matthew 6:8 (p. 45) affect your prayer life? _____

_____

_____

_____

_____

9. a. **…the _____ also helps our _____; for we do not know how**
   to _____ as we should, but the _____ _____
   _____for *us* with groanings too deep for words; and He who searches the
   hearts knows what the mind of the _____ is, because _____ intercedes for the
   saints according to the *will of God*. And we know that God causes all things to _____
   together for _____ to those who _____ God, to those who are called
   according to *His* purpose (Romans 8:26-28, pp. 223-224).

   b. Who searches our hearts? _____

   c. The Spirit helps us in our _____.

   d. Describe an incident from your past involving your weaknesses that left you baffled about what to pray for?

   _____

   _____

   _____

   e. What was the outcome of this incident? _____

   _____

   _____

   f. No matter how it came out, can you now see that God knew what was best for you? (circle one)   yes   or   no

   g. Why or why not? _____

   _____

h. What does this have to do with Step Eleven? _____

_____

10. a. According to Step Eleven, for what two things are we to pray?

    1) _____

    2) _____

FOLLOWING JESUS

11. Read Mark 14:12-72 (pp. 99-100).

a. **And He was saying, "Abba! Father! All _____ are _____ for You; remove this cup from Me; yet not what _____ will, but what _____ will"** (Mark 14:36, p. 100).

b. To what cup was Jesus referring in Mark 14:36 (p. 100)? _____

_____

c. Thinking of Step Eleven and your Christian walk, how will you emulate what Jesus said to His heavenly Father in Mark 14:36 (p. 100)? _____

_____

_____

_____

d. What are the implications in your life of Jesus doing His Father's will and submitting Himself to the cross?

_____

_____

_____

_____

LISTENING TO GOD

12. a. **For since the creation of the world _____ _____**

_____, His eternal _____ and _____

_____, have been_____ _____, being

_____ through what has_____ _____... (Romans 1:20, p. 216).

b. The following passage is from a Psalm of David writing about God: **When I consider _____**

_____, the _____ of _____ _____, the

_____ and the _____, which _____ have ordained;
what is man that You take _____ of him, and the son of man that You
_____ for him? Yet You have made him a little lower than God, and You crown him with
_____ and _____! (Psalm 8:3-5, p. 351).

c. Describe some works of creation that have given you greater insight into your Creator.

_____

_____

_____

_____

d. As described by Janet, how is this a form of Christian meditation? _____

_____

_____

_____

SETTING ASIDE TIME

13. a. True   or   False   (circle one) — My daily schedule often becomes so cluttered that I have a difficult time focusing on God.

b. If true, gives some specific examples of why it is true. _____

_____

_____

_____

_____

_____

_____

14. a. **Cease _____ and know that _____ _____ _____; I will be
_____ among the nations, I will be _____ in the earth**
(Psalm 46:10, p. 386).

b. Describe how and when you can put the above passage to work in your life. Be specific.

_____

_____

_____

15. Read Luke 10:38-42 (p. 124).

    a. "...**Martha, Martha, you are** _____ **and** _____ **about** _____
       _____ _____ " (Luke 10:41, p. 124).

    b. Describe a time in your life when you had Martha-like attitudes that negatively impacted your spiritual focus,
       including your prayer life.

       _____

       _____

       _____

       _____

       _____

GROWING CLOSER

16. a. ...**If** _____ **is** _____ _____ **, who is** _____ _____ **?**
       (Romans 8:31, p. 224).

    b. **For I am convinced that neither** _____ **, nor** _____ **, nor** _____ **,**
       nor _____ **, nor things** _____ **, nor things to**
       _____ **, nor powers, nor** _____ **, nor** _____ **,**
       nor any other _____ **thing, will be able to** _____ **us from the**
       _____ **of** _____ **, which is in** _____ _____ **our**
       _____ " (Romans 8:38-39, p. 224).

    c. About how often do you wholeheartedly believe in the two Scriptures above and act as if you believe them?
       (check one)

       _____ 100% of the time (Unless your name is Jesus Christ, you need to rethink this.)

       _____ most of the time

       _____ quite a bit of the time

       _____ some of the time

       _____ not very often

       _____ never

    d. If you are not satisfied with your response to 16.c., how can Step Eleven and the word of God help you to
       improve? Be specific.

       _____

       _____

_____

_____

OUR FOUNDATION IN LIFE

17. a. Read Luke 6:46-49 (p. 116). Recall an incident from your past when the rains came and you had no foundation as in verse 49. What were the rains? What happened to you? _____

_____

_____

_____

_____

_____

_____

   b. Now tell about an incident that occurred when you did have a spiritual foundation as in verse 48. What were the rains? How did the rains affect you this time? _____

_____

_____

_____

_____

_____

_____

_____

KEEPING FIRST THINGS FIRST

18. a. **I said to the Lord, "You are _____ _____; I have no _____ besides You"**
(Psalm 16:2, p. 355).

   b. What does that passage have to do with your thoughts about putting Step Eleven to work in your life?

_____

_____

_____

IN CONCLUSION

We used to live as though we were at the center of the universe, and we were disappointed because everything didn't revolve around us. Of course, we were on a crash course with reality, and we were bound to be disappointed by unrealistic expectations. We now place God at the center of the universe and are in the process of moving to our rightful place somewhere in the periphery. Our goal is to seek only God's will in our lives, and we do this by both listening and talking to God. We gain our ultimate comfort by a knowledge of the fact that through the grace of Jesus, we will walk even closer to God, even when we fall short of our goal of seeking only God's will for us.

Through prayer and meditation, I am doing my very best to seek only God's will in my life and the power to carry that out. (circle one)   yes   or   no

_____   _____
Your Signature   **Today's Date**

Write down some insights you've gained from this lesson. To gauge your spiritual progress, in the future look back on what you've written here.

_____

_____

_____

_____

_____

End Notes

1. http//www.tellinitlikeitis.net/2010/01/people-pleasers-and-doormats-care-what-people-think-about-them.html.

2. http.//www.cyberrecovery.net/forums/showthread.php?t=16972.

3. Philip Yancey. *Prayer: Does it Make Any Difference?* Zondervan, Grand Rapids, 2006, 41.

4. Paul Hinnebusch (editor) *Contemplation and the Charismatic Renewal*, Paulist Press, New York, 1986, 12.

5. Josh McDowell and Don Stewart, *Understanding the Cults*, Here's Life Publishers, Inc., San Bernardino, 1982, 110.

6. Ben Campbell Johnson, *To Pray God's Will: Continuing the Journey*, The Westminster Press, Philadelphia, 1987, 15.

7. David Jeremiah, *I Never Thought I'd See the Day*. Faith Words, Hatchette Book Group, New York, 2011, 285.

8. *Hope for Today*, Al-Anon Family Group Headquarters, Virginia Beach, 2002, 98.

Summing It Up

Kyle's six months in boot camp would prove to be the ultimate test of how I would apply the spiritual principles of the program I'd been working for the past five years. This is where Step Twelve comes in.

Before joining the Al-Anon program, I often laid awake at night, worrying and projecting into the future. I often focused on Kyle having to pay the consequences for the lifestyle he had chosen. The thought of him being incarcerated was my worst nightmare. As a part of my spiritual growth, I began to accept the idea of him being imprisoned if that's what it took to get the real Kyle back.

Kyle's news after two weeks at the boot camp that his stomach was doing fine without the medication demonstrated to me that God was in control. Another evidence of this was his response to my asking about the three-hour trip in the back of the sheriff's car. I imagined the fear and anxiety he felt during that trip. I was shocked when he admitted he'd slept all the way there.

As a part of my spiritual awakening and claiming my own identity, it was sinking in that Kyle and I were totally different in the way our thinking processes worked. The same was true with other members of my family.

The bottom line was that I didn't know what other people were thinking or anything about their motivations. It was becoming easier to practice the principle of the program of "live and let live." I could allow others to make their own choices, learn from painful consequences and make different choices in the future (or not).

Though Kyle's situation was on my mind much of the time, the program had seeped into my thinking enough that I constantly brought myself back into the present moment and my own surroundings. I was enduring what I had thought would be impossible to bear by seeking God's guidance, returning continuously to the slogans and applying the Serenity Prayer, "God grant me the serenity to accept the things I cannot change, courage to change the things I can, and the wisdom to know the difference."

Al-Anon meetings were always uplifting and some tidbit of insight would always lift my spirits.

I looked back at my spiritual growth and maturation through adversity and realized this was Kyle's time to do the same. My awareness that the experience would likely have some value for him in the future helped me to detach. I did not "go off the deep end" as I always thought I would, but there were challenges.

For example, the chances to talk with Kyle were quite limited. We would be allowed only one face-to-face visit and that would come in the middle of his six-month sentence. Also, he was allowed only one call a week that could last no more than 15 minutes. He alternated between Shelley and us. Phone privileges would sometimes be taken away or occasionally the call was disconnected. Then Flynn and I might sit there for a couple of hours waiting and hoping and then wondering whether Kyle had done something wrong, although the whole group often lost privileges because of the behavior of a few.

I was aware that things could always grow worse. For example, a fight with another inmate or another infraction could still result in him being sent to an adult prison with a longer sentence.

I fought the urge to use controlling tactics such as giving unsolicited advice, lecturing or pleading with him to follow the rules. I had no more control over his behavior at the boot camp than I did while trying to control his choice to use drugs.

Our Boot Camp Visit

I was both excited and apprehensive as the "half-time visit" approached. What would our surroundings be like? Would I be able to control my emotions? Would Kyle?

For this one visit five of us—Shelley, her sister, a friend, Flynn and I—drove the three-hour trip. As we approached the gate to go inside the fenced-in area, we stood in a long line with others planning to visit. We were told to empty our pockets, and no one was allowed to take items inside. Anything such as keys, phones, or purses had to be left at the desk or returned to the car. I had brought some books and magazines for the library and surprisingly, they allowed me to take them in without even flipping through them.

We followed the crowd and were all directed to the cafeteria, and each group was seated at a round table. Though some facilities don't allow physical contact, when the inmates were brought in at this one, families and friends were allowed to embrace. Though the people there appeared to come from all walks of life and socio-economic levels, we all had something in common; all were overjoyed at seeing their loved ones again. There was plenty of crying and hugging intermingled with smiling and laughter for the next two or three minutes. Then we were instructed to sit down.

I was thrilled to see Kyle again. He looked a little different with his head shaved and dressed in an orange jumpsuit like all the other inmates, but otherwise he was the same old Kyle, smiling and upbeat. I wished there had been some way to prolong the two hours. I tried to savor every moment of it.

The noise level compared to that of a school cafeteria. Some of the family members at the other tables were emotional or even arguing, but our conversation was relaxed and mostly consisted of small talk and Kyle describing his daily routine. Though he complained about harsh treatment from the guards, small portions of horrible food and problems with the other inmates, he seemed to take it all in stride.

Since we were all together, it was a little awkward to say what we would want to say if he could have been alone with us. I imagine he and Shelley would have loved some time alone as well.

The visit was pleasant, and the two hours passed quickly. I wish I could have hugged him and not let go, but everyone wanted their turn. We said our goodbyes, knowing that Lord willing, the next time we saw him, we would be taking him home. I couldn't help but tear up but tried to stay strong for Kyle's sake.

God had gotten us through the first half; I knew we could get through the second half, one day at a time.

Kyle continued to write home about attending anger management, addiction recovery and Bible classes. He expressed gratitude for the men who came from various churches to teach the inmates, relating scriptures in his letters that held personal meaning for him.

While he worked his program and grew spiritually, I continued to try to apply both the program and the Bible to my life.

Near Mother's Day, I received from Kyle one of the most meaningful gifts of my life. He began his letter by saying, "I would love to give you a real Mother's Day gift, but I'm giving you the only thing I can…" He then proceeded to acknowledge the wrong he had done to me personally, expressing a sincere apology and thanked me for standing by him through his rebellious years. I had already forgiven him but was gratified that he had grown to the point where he could practice Step Nine.

STEP TWELVE ▶ Having had a spiritual awakening as the result of these steps, we tried to carry this message to others and to practice these principles in all our affairs. (For additional information on Step Twelve and a listing of Step Twelve Reflections related to specific verses, see *Journey to Recovery Through Christ: CASA's 12-Step Study Bible*, pp. 36-37.)

As you can see, there are three parts to this, the final step, that are connected and dependent on one another. We will consider them individually.

First, **"Having had a spiritual awakening…"**

How can someone tell if he or she has had a spiritual awakening?

During Kyle's incarceration I could see that I was in the midst of a spiritual awakening as a result of comparing the way I would have handled this previously in comparison to the present. I was growing closer to God after putting the steps to work in my life.

A neighbor related that he fell to his knees one day and begged for help from his drug and alcohol addiction. He claimed to have been instantly healed of his cravings. A preacher showed up unexpectedly at his doorstep that day and studied with him over the next few days. As a result, the addictive cravings stopped immediately. He has since matured into a sincere Christian who both teaches and preaches.

Saul's spiritual awakening was nearly instantaneous after seeing a flash of light from heaven and hearing the voice of Jesus Christ. Blinded for three days and then regaining his sight (both spiritually and physically), Saul became the Apostle Paul and preached the Lord's message to countless people while also becoming the most prolific New Testament author. (See Acts 9:1-30, pp. 190-191.)

With some other people, including me, the spiritual awakening has been a process that occurred over time. It started to become apparent when my involvement in Al-Anon opened my eyes to biblical principles that could guide me on a daily basis. I was also awakened to the fact that ordinary people could work as a group toward common solutions while helping each other to grow spiritually. What it took was opening my mind to new ideas, becoming willing to take an honest look at myself and sharing my experience, strength and hope with others.

Previously, Bible reading was difficult and tedious because I thought I knew the truth and read more from a sense of duty. Searching for the truth in God's Word is much more exciting and fascinating. It changed my thoughts and attitudes and filtered over into my behaviors.

It was wonderful to finally understand that grace is unmerited favor and God's gift given to his children, something that could not be achieved by following a set of rules.

I focused on Bible study exclusively for two years. Then, though I continued reading and studying various subjects in the Bible on a daily basis, I also sought out spiritual and inspirational books by other authors. I was learning quickly that even though I might not totally agree with the author, it didn't mean the whole book should be discarded. And it didn't mean that the author was a heretic. These books have given me tremendous insight on grace, the Holy Spirit, prayer, science and the Bible, and other topics.

The second phrase in Step Twelve, **"we tried to carry this message to others,"** is based on the concept that faith without works is dead. (See James 2:17, p. 308.) Members of 12-step programs say, "You can't keep it unless you give it away." They are referring to the program that delivered them from their obsession with the addict or addiction toward a God-centered life.

"Giving it away" may include speaking and sharing at meetings, sponsorship or one-on-one sharing, or visiting jails to talk to others with the same problems. It may also involve service work to the group in something as mundane as making coffee.

Since I was a good typist, I took on the responsibility of updating lists of members and their phone numbers and lists of area Al-Anon meetings. In addition to chairing meetings and serving as a sponsor (mentor) to others, I also volunteered to serve as treasurer when the previous one gave up that position.

Via what we know as "12-step work," an individual's Step One problem can become God's opportunity. Those who have suffered from a particular problem and found spiritual healing are in a unique position to help others in the same situation. (See 2 Corinthians 1:3-5, p. 249 and 12:5-10, p. 257.)

As a result of my involvement in Al-Anon, people often opened up to me about the addiction of a loved one.

Writing letters was the main form of communication between Kyle and me. Rather than giving advice, I had learned to share my own experience.

I wrote to him about how I had grown through the Al-Anon program and how reading the Bible from a fresh perspective had transformed my life. I also acknowledged mistakes from my past, such as blaming his dad for all our problems. I admitted my failure in disciplining effectively and being too permissive, which may have played a role in him trying drugs in the first place.

When I crossed paths with the parents of Kyle's former friends, I told them what the program was doing for me. I was often met with disinterest and skepticism and once, outright anger. Some people admitted they had tried the program once or twice but didn't find it helpful. They didn't think they were the problem— their son or daughter was. So far, my success in reaching this group of people has been minimal, but one never knows when a planted seed will grow.

Extending My Reach

Though I was involved in teaching classes for Christian women, I longed to carry Christ's message to unbelievers. I prayed about this and almost immediately, I was approached by a lady at church who was ministering to the female inmates at the local detention center. I was a little hesitant because I had never been inside a jail or prison except for the one visit with Kyle. It didn't take long for me to realize it was an answer to my prayer.

Another Christian lady and I were assigned to meet with 16 female inmates every Tuesday night. I developed several lessons on subjects that I thought would benefit them the most such as how the grace of God applies to each of our lives, how stronger faith can aid in overcoming temptation, and the ways of Satan.

One young woman was distraught over losing custody of her three children. She had grown up in a severely dysfunctional family and her lack of education and ignorance of anything biblical was evident. She came to know Christ and was baptized, but she and her husband were eventually sentenced to life in prison for exploiting their daughter in child pornography. I felt so sad for her because I wasn't sure she had even understood the seriousness or possible consequences of what they were doing. It impressed upon me the urgency of reaching people with the gospel before such tragedies occur.

I had learned from my father one form of serving others. As a youngster I was puzzled about why he bothered with an elderly widow who dipped snuff and had a speech impediment. Anytime she called, my dad left his store in the hands of the assistant manager to take her whatever item she requested.

When he died suddenly, I knew she missed him and decided to start visiting her.

Now I visit "the least of these" on a regular basis because I've learned from personal experience why daddy did it; he was incredibly blessed by serving others.

I can picture him smiling and saying, "Now you get it!"

Delightful relationships were developed not only between the elderly folks and me but also with their families, caregivers, roommates and others. In the midst of all this, I noticed that my self-worth had improved drastically. The law of "sowing and reaping" worked! It really is "more blessed to give than to receive" (Acts 20:35, p. 206).

According to the third part of this step, we are to continue to **"practice these principles in all our affairs,"** summed up in this way:

> They include unselfishness, serving, helping others, making amends, being more like Jesus, being a part of the solution rather than a part of the problem, responding instead of reacting, living God-centered lives.

> In "all our affairs" means we're not going to do this just at church or with our 12-step groups. It means with our families and strangers, at work, and play, at home and away...we will attempt to live God-centered lives in all circumstances, under all conditions.[1]

It is a worthwhile goal to have our spiritual transformation evident in every area of our lives, even though perfection is not possible while we live in the flesh. Neither the 12-step program nor any other method will enable us to earn our way to Heaven. God provided one way to attain true righteousness, according to Romans 3:21-24 (pp. 218-219):

> But now apart from the Law *the* righteousness of God has been manifested, being witnessed by the Law and the Prophets, even *the* righteousness of God through faith in Jesus Christ for all those who believe; for there is no distinction; for all have sinned and fall short of the glory of God, being justified as a gift by His grace through the redemption which is in Christ Jesus...

Upon starting to attend Al-Anon meetings, I never would have dreamed the impact the program would have on every aspect of my life.

Initially, it was a valuable tool in my responsibilities as the primary caregiver for my mother. I learned to delegate responsibility rather than playing the role of a victim or martyr by trying to do it all and then resenting those who didn't help. The often repeated phrase in Al-Anon—"there are no victims, only volunteers"—struck home.

One subject our group often discussed was "setting boundaries," which became essential to my well-being. I worked on finding a healthy balance between my own well-being, the needs of my family and the needs of others in the church or community.

Through learning the art of detachment, I could stay out of the middle of conflict. I was able to sit on the sidelines and read a book or engage in another activity while others argued. I could allow them to work it out for themselves rather than trying to constantly serve as peacemaker.

If someone else wanted my advice or help, I was happy to give it, as long as it didn't consist of enabling. If it was a problem that needing correction, the same sources and information were available to help them that had helped me and countless others. What a relief to relinquish such a heavy burden of misplaced responsibility and guilt.

Though kindness and gentleness did not always emanate from my lips as easily as sarcasm, insults and criticism, at least I had a program and plan in place. Previously, there had been a huge chasm between my perch on the merry-go-round and the spiritual goals and emotional balance I wanted to achieve.

One way I approached my marital conflicts was by accepting that I was first married to Christ. In so doing, my treatment of Flynn improved. I tried to find joy in each day and focus on the good, despite the fact that everything I perceived was not perfect.

This program has also helped me to face irrational fears and move forward in spite of them. Since my thought patterns and behaviors had formed over a 40-year period, I realized that immediate changes would not come overnight. The major thing was to strive for improvement.

I was also able to detach somewhat when it concerned Kyle's incarceration.

Kyle Comes Home

The day Kyle was released was a high point in my life. I could relate to the father's reaction in the parable of the prodigal son. He instructed his servants: "'Quickly bring out the best robe and put it on him, and put a ring on his hand and sandals on his feet; and bring the fattened calf, kill it, and let us eat and celebrate; for this son of mine was dead and has come to life again; he was lost and has been found.' And they began to celebrate" (Luke 15:22-24, p. 133).

For this father there was no longer an empty seat at the dinner table, no more concern about where his son was and what he might be going through, no more looking down the road and praying to see his boy walking home. The son was safe at home at last.

Of course, I couldn't predict what would happen in the future and whether Kyle would make the right choices but at least this portion was over; it was something I had dreaded and survived. For the moment, there were no more court appearances to face or jail/prison sentences that needed to be served. Several of our family members, along with Shelley and her family, went to pick him up.

We stopped for lunch on the way home. Like the father of the prodigal son, our family was in the mood to celebrate.

Since Kyle's absence had dampened each holiday he had missed, we tried to make up for it. At a family celebration that weekend, his brother, Brian, and Brian's wife made five small cakes, one for each holiday that we had celebrated in Kyle's absence (Thanksgiving, his birthday, Christmas, New Year's Day and Easter).

My experience with a wayward son spoke volumes to me about the love of God.

Even though my son's self-centered behavior had been traumatic and painful for me, my love for him never diminished and I desperately wanted him to reach his potential. Though people who didn't know him well may have viewed him as only a common criminal or possibly "drug dealing scum," I knew his intelligence, charismatic personality and compassion for people and animals could propel him to great heights if he channeled these admirable qualities in the right direction.

Even his knowledge of the criminal element of society could be directed toward some positive endeavors.

I believe God's love for His children is beyond human comprehension. He can't not love me because He is love. I have concluded that His greatest desire for me (and every one of His children) is to be the person He created us to be. He wants me to reach my full potential, just as I do with Kyle and my other children. I can do this by allowing His Spirit to work through me as I build on my positive qualities.

Biblical Questions for Self-Examination

OUR SPIRITUAL AWAKENING

Use the *Journey to Recovery Through Christ: CASA's 12-Step Study Bible* or any other version of the *New American Standard Bible* © 1995 to fill in the blanks in biblical passages below.

1. a. **"I am the Lord your God, who brought you out of the land of Egypt, out of the house of slavery. You shall have no other gods before Me"** (Exodus 20:2-3).

    b. The first of the 10 Commandments is quoted in 1.a. Note that it was God with a capital "G" who brought His people out of the land of slavery and gods with a lower case "g" that we are to avoid. What are some things other than God (lower case "g" gods) that you have put as number one in your life?

    _____

    _____

    _____

    _____

    _____

    _____

    _____

2. a. **...then watch yourself, that you do not forget the Lord who brought you from the land of Egypt, out of the house of slavery** (Deuteronomy 6:12).

    b. **He then answered, "Whether He is a sinner, I do not know; one thing I do know, that though I was _____, _____ I _____"** (John 9:25, p. 162).

    c. Read Acts 9:1-30 (pp. 190-191). As a part of his spiritual awakening, Saul (later known as Paul) was blinded (verses 8-9) but then regained his sight (verse 18). As a part of your spiritual awakening, you know that in your denial, you, too, were formerly blind—at least spiritually—but have since regained your sight. Describe your spiritual blindness and the spiritual awakening that has given you new and improved vision.

    _____

    _____

    _____

    _____

    _____

3. Thinking about your spiritual journey since taking Step One, read Psalm 116 (p. 448-449). In the left-hand

column list the verse numbers with which you personally identify and in the right-hand column briefly explain how your life corresponds with that verse. For example, someone might list verse 3 and then say that her codependency and/or addiction nearly killed her.

Verse Number   **Ways You Identify**

a. _____   _____

b. _____   _____

c. _____   _____

d. _____   _____

e. _____   _____

f. _____   _____

g. _____   _____

h. _____   _____

i. _____   _____

PASSING IT ALONG

4. a. **What use is it, my brethren, if someone says he has _____ but he has no _____? Can that faith save him? If a brother or sister is without clothing and in need of daily food, and one of you says to them, "Go in peace, be warmed and be filled," and yet you do not give them what is necessary for *their* body, what use is that? Even so _____, if it has no _____, is _____ being by itself** (James 2:14-17, p. 308).

    b. Why is faith dead without works? _____

        _____

        _____

5. a. **Blessed *be* the God and Father of our Lord Jesus Christ, the Father of mercies and God of all comfort, who _____ _____ in all our _____ so that we will be able to _____ those who are in any _____ with the _____ with which _____ ourselves are _____ by _____** (2 Corinthians 1:3-4, p. 249).

b. Recognizing the source of your ability to help others, relate an incident from your life when God helped you, and you were able to bless others because of it. _____

_____

_____

_____

_____

6. Re-read 2 Corinthians 12:1-10 (p. 257), which was earlier covered in Step Seven, 11.a. and 11.b.

a. **...for when I am _____, then I am _____** (2 Corinthians 12:10, p. 257).

b. Thinking of the sentence above in the context of the verses in which it appears, how does that sentence apply to Step Twelve in your life? _____

_____

_____

_____

_____

7. a. **Now He who supplies _____ to the _____ and _____ for food will supply and multiply your seed for _____ and _____ the harvest of your _____** (2 Corinthians 9:10, p. 254).

b. What is the "seed" and the "harvest of your righteousness" in the above sentence? How do these things apply to you putting Step Twelve to work in your life? _____

_____

_____

_____

_____

OUR ROLE IN LIFE

8. a. Janet referred to the story of the prodigal (or lost) son told by Jesus (Luke 15:11-32, p. 133-134) and we have referred to this story in earlier chapters. Let's return to it once more. When the son was still in the pigpen, he decided to return to his father and then determined what he would say:

"**...Father, I have sinned against heaven, and in your sight. I am _____ _____ _____ to be called your _____; make me as one of your _____ men**" (Luke 15:18-19, p. 133).

b. As the son was returning home, it was with the idea of having what role in his father's household?

_____

c. Going home to fulfill this role represents a dramatic change in attitude from when the son left home in the first place. What accounts for this change? _____

_____

_____

_____

_____

d. How do you identify with this change in attitude? _____

_____

_____

_____

_____

e. Thinking of the son's change in attitude concerning his role in his father's household, what is your major role in God's kingdom? _____

_____

9. a. Read Luke 14:12-14 (p. 131). Be specific in itemizing some ways that you could carry out this passage.

_____

_____

_____

_____

_____

10. a. **"If I then, the Lord and the Teacher, _____ your _____, you also ought to _____ _____ _____ _____. For I gave you an _____ that you also should do as I did to you"** (John 13:14-15, p. 168).

b. Put this foot-washing episode into its proper context by reading John 13:1-17 (p. 167-168). Also keeping in mind that this occurred the night before Jesus was crucified, how does the foot-washing apply to your understanding of Step Twelve? _____

_____

_____

_____

_____

_____

11. a. **For we are His** _____, **created in Christ Jesus for**

_____ **works, which God** _____ **beforehand so that we would**

walk in them (Ephesians 2:10, p. 266).

    b. **For we are** _____ **fellow workers; you are** _____ **field,** _____

building (1 Corinthians 3:9, p. 234).

    c. How do the two verses immediately above correspond with the foot-washing from John 13:1-7 (pp. 167-

168)? _____

_____

_____

PUTTING IT INTO PRACTICE

12. List the names of five people whom you have helped or to whom you have tried to carry the message in the past

few months. In the spaces provided, also tell what you did or attempted to do, the outcome in the life of the other

person, and the outcome of this in your own life (in other words, what you learned).

    a. Name _____ What you did _____

        Outcome in his/her life _____

        Outcome in your life _____

    b. Name _____ What you did _____

        Outcome in his/her life _____

        Outcome in your life _____

    c. Name _____ What you did _____

        Outcome in his/her life _____

        Outcome in your life _____

    d. Name _____ What you did _____

Outcome in his/her life _____

Outcome in your life _____

e. Name _____What you did _____

Outcome in his/her life _____

Outcome in your life _____

13. a. Suppose I tell you that I am an alcoholic who has been sober for a while. As a part of my 12-step work, I called on a man whose wife recently left him because he is drunk most of the time. I took the man to a 12-step meeting, and he didn't drink for two days thereafter. Then he bought some whiskey on the third day and has been drunk ever since. I called the man, but he hung up on me. I report to you that I have failed and that I am depressed over this situation. Recall that Janet encountered some disappointments in her attempts to carry the message to the parents of some of Kyle's former drug dealers. What would you tell me (the alcoholic described above) in regard to my seemingly failed attempt to help the man who was drinking?

_____

_____

_____

_____

b. Name an example from your own life when you tried to carry God's message to a person in need but felt you had failed. _____

_____

_____

_____

_____

c. What have you gained in the attempt to help another person listed in 13.b.?_____

_____

_____

_____

_____

_____

IN ALL OUR AFFAIRS

14. a. **"Let your _____ _____ before men in such a way that they may see your _____ _____, and glorify your Father who is in heaven"** (Matthew 5:16, p. 43).

     b. **Let us not lose _____ in doing _____, for in due time we will _____ if we do _____ grow _____** (Galatians 6:9, p. 264).

     c. **Brethren, even if anyone is caught in any trespass, _____ who are spiritual, restore such a one in a spirit of _____;** *each one* **looking to _____, so that you too will not be tempted. _____ one another's _____, and thereby fulfill the law of Christ** (Galatians 6:1-2, p. 264).

     d. **We urge you, brethren, admonish the unruly, encourage the _____, help the _____, be _____ with _____** (1 Thessalonians 5:14, p. 281).

     e. Step Twelve concludes with the statement, "and to practice these principles in all our affairs." How will you put this part of the step to work in your life? In your answer make sure to include what you have read from the four passages above. _____

_____

_____

_____

_____

_____

_____

OUR NEW REALITY

15. a. Jesus told some who believed in Him, "...and _____ will know the _____, and the _____ will _____ you _____" (John 8:32, p. 160).

     b. Read John 8:31 (p. 160). According to the words of Jesus in that verse, what does it take for a person to know the truth? _____

_____

_____

     c. When indulging yourself in your codependency and/or addiction, your thoughts and actions were based on a lie. How has the truth set you free? _____

_____

_____

_____

_____

d. What things can you do to help ensure that you will not return to believing that lie or other similar lies?

_____

_____

_____

_____

_____

_____

16. Read John 18:28-40 (p. 174).

a. At the trial of Jesus just prior to the crucifixion, **Pilate said to Him, "What is _____?"** (John 18:38, p. 174).

b. How do you answer Pilate? Feel free to use additional pages to complete your answer or if you are led by the Lord to do so, write a book about it. _____

_____

_____

_____

_____

_____

_____

c. How does Pilate's question apply to the world in which we live today? _____

_____

_____

_____

NO ONE PROMISED YOU A ROSE GARDEN

17. We're going to remind you of something you already know. We live in a fallen world, and this is not the Garden of Eden. No matter how much closer we grow to God, we will all encounter problems and tough times. In fact, we may encounter difficulties *because* we have grown closer to God. Read Matthew 5:11-12 (p. 43); Romans 8:18 (p. 223); 2 Corinthians 4:17-18 (p. 251); 1 Peter 4:12-19 (p. 315).

a. What are some problems you've encountered in the past? _____

_____

_____

_____

b. Besides pointing out that there will be tough times during your lifetime, itemize some very positive things that these verses reveal. _____

_____

_____

_____

18.   a. **No** _____ **has** _____ _____ **but such as is** _____ **to man; and God is faithful, who will not allow you to be** _____ **beyond what you are able, but with the temptation will** _____ **the** _____ **of** _____ **also, so that you will be able to** _____ **it** (1 Corinthians 10:13, p. 240).

b. Give some examples of how you have seen the truth of the verse above. _____

_____

_____

_____

_____

IN CONCLUSION

In Psalm 23:5 (p. 363) David wrote, "My cup overflows." Having had a spiritual awakening, we can now say the same thing. God has truly blessed us. What we now find is that the more we pour out of our cup in serving others, the more our cup overflows. This will be evident in every facet of our lives.

I have had a spiritual awakening as the result of these steps, and I plan to continue walking forward toward God while carrying the message to others and letting the light of Jesus shine in every aspect of my life. (circle one)   yes   or   no

_____   _____
Your Signature   **Today's Date**

Write down some insights you've gained from this lesson. To gauge your spiritual progress, several months from now look back on what you've written here.

_____

_____

_____

_____

_____

End Note

1. Don Umphrey, *Journey to Recovery Through Christ—CASA's 12 Step Study Bible,* Quarry Press, Dallas, 2015, 37.

Our Life Afterward

We had not taken a family vacation together in about five years, so it seemed like a great way to celebrate Kyle's return home. It had also been some time since he and his younger brother, Casey, now age 17, had a real brotherly relationship. Our two older sons were married, and Kyle's absence had been a huge loss for Casey. A vacation trip would give them a chance to reconnect.

I needed to get this trip going immediately before Kyle got involved in work or school, or God forbid, did not stay in recovery. He seemed as excited about it as the rest of us.

My sister suggested a cruise. I did some research and found we could embark on a trip to the Bahamas from Jacksonville, Florida, 617 miles away. We decided to drive to Atlanta, Georgia, spend some time with our son, Brian, who lived there, and then catch a flight from there to Jacksonville.

Fears Take a Backseat

This plan presented two major challenges to me.

My claustrophobia and irrational fear of crashing, getting hijacked and/or other unknown possibilities had prevented me from even considering flying in an airplane. I had always imagined the horror of those final minutes in an airplane, fully aware that we were going down and headed to a fiery crash with no way to escape.

In addition, to get on a ship with nothing in sight but water had also been out of the question for me. My fear of water was not as extreme as my mother's, because I could at least swim. But, I could imagine all sorts of possibilities—being adrift on a lifeboat for days, starving to death, sharks circling about looking for their next meal.

Though I knew death could occur at any time in countless ways, some forms of death had seemed too horrific to chance.

It seemed like an excellent time to face these two fears head on with God's guidance. After all, God had already guided me through one of my worst fears, having a child incarcerated. In addition, a short saying I read somewhere also had stuck with me: "If you're scared to do it, just do it scared."

I was sane enough by this time to realize I was not in control of my destiny. I could be killed just as easily in a car or suffer some painful chronic disability that might be worse than a plane crash. As for claustrophobia, if everyone else on the plane was breathing, surely I could too. A scripture I had memorized that helped immensely was 2 Timothy 1:7 (p. 289): "For God has not given us the spirit of timidity, but of power and love and discipline."

Since Flynn was the only one who had ever flown in an airplane—34 years prior when he was in the army—just getting through the airport checking baggage, obtaining our boarding passes and finding our terminal was the most stressful part.

After takeoff, I was pretty calm until we hit a little turbulence. The other passengers didn't appear to be disturbed, so I was able to relax. We were landing before I knew it. I was in the midst of discovering that it was possible to be as normal as everyone else.

Getting on our shuttle and boarding the Carnival ship Jubilee was also a bit tense since we were unfamiliar with the process, but we kept on putting one foot in front of the other.

We made our way to our cabins. We had reserved one for us and one for Kyle and Casey. We knew they would not be thrilled with being cooped up with us for four days and wanted them to have some time together. We had been warned by others who had been on cruises that the cabins were extremely small, but they exceeded our expectations.

As the ship pulled out from shore, we stood on deck and watched the buildings on land shrink smaller and smaller. I knew I would soon be where I never expected to be—surrounded by water with no land in sight. For some reason, by this time I wasn't dreading it but was excited about the adventure that lay ahead.

After we docked in Nassau, Flynn and I decided to stay on or near the ship, but Kyle and Casey wanted to take a taxi into the downtown area. I had concerns about the kind of trouble they might encounter, but trust had to begin somewhere. It was heart-warming watching them walk away talking and laughing and then climbing into the taxi together. It was a sight I could only dream about for the previous five years.

I could never get my equipment to work properly when we went snorkeling at Paradise Island, but I enjoyed sitting on the beach watching Flynn, Kyle and Casey searching for shells and other ocean treasures and bringing them up to show me.

The other excursion we chose was a trip in a glass-bottomed boat. I had hoped to see a lot of colorful sea life, but mostly all we saw was a lot of the same species of grey-colored fish. It was fantastic just being together as a family, though, posing for pictures together and watching Kyle snap photos during the boat ride.

My Favorite Sunset

One night of the trip we all donned our dress clothes and made our way to the formal dining room. We were seated right in front of the huge outside window. As we dined on delectable food and sipped our tea from wine glasses, the sun begin its descent into the water. As we watched the huge orange glow fade into the horizon, for that moment I couldn't help but surmise, "This is about as good as it gets on this earth."

Kyle returned back to live at Shelley's dad's house and obtained a job stuffing pillows and delivering mattresses for a local manufacturing plant. He totally avoided interactions with his old drug-using friends. I had prayed for people to come into his life and influence him into getting back in church. Shelley's grandmother was instrumental in doing so.

Kyle had been baptized at age 15 but dropped out of church soon afterward and continued in his rebellious behavior. He admitted that his only reason for being baptized was to gain more trust.

One Sunday afternoon, he came by after church and told me he had almost responded to the invitation song after the sermon in order to be baptized for the right reason. He knew how much his dad and I wanted to be there, so he was waiting until the evening service.

As he was immersed into the water that night, I couldn't hold back the tears. Kyle had been freed from his physical prison, and now through the grace of Jesus Christ, he received spiritual freedom.

Flynn, Casey, Brad and his family and I all stood at the front of the building with church members holding hands and praying as Kyle came out of the water as a new creation in Christ.

Shortly after this he told us he wanted to marry Shelley, whom by that time he'd been dating for two years.

Though Kyle was 21, we felt we were dealing with a case of "arrested development" due to his heavy drug use during developmental years. Flynn and I did not think he was mature enough for marriage, and we explained our misgivings.

Kyle assured us that he was old enough to make that decision. The only choice I had in the matter was to choose whether to love and support him or fall back into the trap of trying to be in control of someone else's life. I was aware of the heights people could rise to if they fixed their eyes on Jesus.

Greater Communication

Though our marriage is not perfect (but whose marriage is?), Flynn and I have read more of the Bible and other helpful books, and prayed more together in the past two or three years than in the previous 40. It is a joy to be able to delight together with our grandchildren as our golden years approach.

We read a book together titled *The Five Love Languages*. It became clear we had been speaking a foreign language to one another in our ways of expressing love. This book was quite helpful in helping us understand the mistakes of our past. The author, Gary Chapman, makes this observation, which certainly applies to us:

> Most of us have more potential than we will ever develop. What holds us back is often courage. A loving spouse can supply that all-important catalyst. Of course, encouraging words may be difficult for you to speak. It may not be your primary love language. It may take great effort for you to learn this second language. That will be especially true if you have a pattern of critical and condemning words, but I can assure you that it will be worth the effort.[1]

I have tried to discard that which was not working in my marriage in favor of praise, affection, using "I" statements and ignoring annoyances as much as possible rather than speaking out or nagging.

I try to keep this scripture on the tip of my tongue. "Let no unwholesome word proceed from your mouth, but only such a *word* as is good for edification according to the need *of the moment*, so that it will give grace to those who hear" (Ephesians 4:29, pp. 268-269).

While I haven't perfected this, I'm at least aware that it will produce the best end result.

I had often accused Flynn of being a perfectionist in his work but have realized that label also fits me. I have finally accepted the fact that we live in a world corrupted by sin, and made up of seriously flawed human beings, including myself. I've had to learn to become content with progress not perfection (which is unattainable anyway).

I am grateful now for the circumstances that led me down this path. Suffering may serve a purpose for this Christian. Had it not been for the traumatic period of my life involving Kyle's addiction, I may have never sought a spiritual solution to my problems.

The Apostle Paul proclaimed, "...but we also exult in our tribulations, knowing that tribulation brings about perseverance; and perseverance, proven character; and proven character, hope; and hope does not disappoint, because the love of God has been poured out within our hearts through the Holy Spirit who was given to us." (Romans 5:3-5, p. 220).

Kyle also admits that the discipline, rehabilitation counseling, anger management classes, church services and even defensive driving courses into which he was forced have proven to be valuable and taught him about living life on life's terms.

He and Shelley have had their share of marital problems but thus far have refused to give up. They have given us three precious grandchildren.

I am so proud of the devoted father he has become. He was just promoted from a meter reader to a ground man for the local utility company and also runs a lawn-care business. While riding his mower, he sometimes listens to sermons on his headphones, quite an improvement from the rap music we so often argued about.

He attends church regularly and he and his 11-year-old daughter are active in the benevolent work there. He also participates in an addiction-recovery class at church.

Kyle has admitted to relapsing with both drugs and alcohol a few times in the past. Though I still have concern at times when he is under stress, I know it is beyond my ability to control so I try to let him manage his addiction. I try to focus on my own issues because there is always an area where I can use improvement.

My Life Now

There were many years when I prayed that Kyle and I could just sit down and have a meal together. He now works close to our home and often comes by for lunch. We spend a lot of time discussing spiritual matters and family issues. As we talk, it is apparent he is growing spiritually. I am extremely proud of his progress and grateful we have this chance to make up for lost time.

I have worked part-time the last several years as a caregiver for elderly people. This job allows me some time for multi-tasking. While my patient is resting, I often have time to work on my writing, Bible lessons, or cards and letters of encouragement to church members and prisoners. Otherwise, the majority of my time is spent caring for some of my eight grandchildren who live nearby.

As I look to the past, I realize I did the best I could with what I knew at the time. I can now understand that other people can only make decisions based on their physical and spiritual maturity at that particular moment.

I am much less critical about my sons' relationships with their spouses and the raising of their children than I would have been otherwise. Some decisions they have made that I was convinced were wrong either turned out okay or else they learned a valuable lesson.

I have to continue to remind myself that I don't possess the knowledge to determine what is right for everyone else in every situation.

I wish I could paint the picture of us having a model family but that would be far from the truth. I mentioned in the beginning that I suspected another son would be harmed the most from the family dysfunction and that intuition has proved correct. Brian has distanced himself from us spiritually, emotionally and even physically by hundreds of miles. I try to keep the line of communication open and continue to pray daily for him. Brian has tremendous potential, and I trust God will do phenomenal things through him in His timing.

As situations change, worry still drops in for a visit, but I have learned not to let it move in to stay.

Flynn is recovering from hip replacement surgery and is possibly facing two more surgeries in the next few months. My oldest daughter-in-law was recently diagnosed with breast cancer and is facing chemotherapy and a double mastectomy which will likely mean more responsibility for me with my granddaughter and mentally challenged grandson.

It seems when life gets the most overwhelming, I find it easier to turn it over to God and focus on one day at a time. I've learned to turn my worry into prayer. I've accepted that life is tough, relationships are complicated and it will never be smooth sailing until we reach Heaven—which I now know is attainable! It's amazing how well I sleep at times when I could find plenty to worry and be anxious about.

In the words of the Apostle Paul, "…I do not regard myself as having laid hold of *it* yet; but one thing *I do*: forgetting what *lies* behind and reaching forward to what *lies* ahead, I press on toward the goal for the prize of the upward call of God in Christ Jesus" (Philippians 3:13-14, p. 273).

End Note

1. Gary Chapman, *"The Five Love Languages,"* Northfield Publishing, Chicago, 1995, 45.